Many critics have seen the writing of Henry James as resistant to questions of power, history, and ethics. The Jamesian mode of writing, it has been claimed, actively works against an understanding of the way truth and history circulate in his texts. In this collection of essays, leading scholars of James analyse the strategies he used to address these crucial issues. *Enacting history in Henry James* proposes a new performative paradigm for reading James's work. It claims that because the reader can never know the truth in any verifiable sense, the type of knowledge available in his fiction is never of a cognitive kind. Rather, the Jamesian text promises an experiential type of knowledge, one that is attained by participating in the power games and moral dramas that unfold within the text. This collection argues that to read James is to enact the history that is staged by the narrative, so that, ultimately, James's texts require not just an emotional responsiveness, but also an ethical assumption of responsibility for the act of reading. By placing James's work in a fresh theoretical context, this book throws new light on this most enigmatic of writers.

ENACTING HISTORY IN HENRY JAMES

ENACTING HISTORY IN HENRY JAMES

Narrative, power, and ethics

EDITED BY
GERT BUELENS
University of Ghent

PUBLISHED BY THE PRESS SYNDICATE OF THE UNIVERSITY OF CAMBRIDGE
The Pitt Building, Trumpington Street, Cambridge CB2 1RP, United Kingdom

CAMBRIDGE UNIVERSITY PRESS
The Edinburgh Building, Cambridge CB2 2RU, United Kingdom
40 West 20th Street, New York, NY 10011–4211, USA
10 Stamford Road, Oakleigh, Melbourne 3166, Australia

© Cambridge University Press 1997

This book is in copyright. Subject to statutory exception and to provisions of relevant collective licensing agreements, no reproduction of any part may take place without the written permission of Cambridge University Press.

First published 1997

Printed in the United Kingdom at the University Press, Cambridge

Typeset in Baskerville 10/12½ pt. [CE]

A catalogue record for this book is available from the British Library

Library of Congress cataloging in publication data
Enacting history in Henry James: narrative, power, and ethics /.
edited by Gert Buelens.
p. cm.
Includes index.
ISBN 0 521 57089 1 (hardback)
1. James, Henry, 1843–1916 – Knowledge – History.
2. Literature and history – United States – History.
3. Power (Social sciences) in literature. 4. James, Henry, 1843–1916 – Technique.
5. Reader-response criticism. 6. Ethics in literature. 7. Narration (Rhetoric).
8. Fiction – Technique.
I. Buelens, Gert.
PS2127.H5B84 1997
813'.4–dc21   96-54615   CIP

ISBN 0 521 57089 1 hardback

Voor mama en papa

Contents

Notes on contributors xi
Acknowledgments xiii
List of abbreviations xiv

    Introduction 1
    Gert Buelens

1 Power relations in the novels of James: the 'liberal' and the 'radical' version 16
   Winfried Fluck

2 Multiple germs, metaphorical systems, and moral fluctuation in *The Ambassadors* 40
   Richard A. Hocks

3 James and the ethics of control: aspiring architects and their floating creatures 61
   Sarah B. Daugherty

4 James and the shadow of the Roman Empire: manners and the consenting victim 75
   Adrian Poole

5 *What Maisie Knew*: Henry James's Bildungsroman of the artist as queer moralist 93
   Alfred Habegger

6 The double narrative of "The Beast in the Jungle": ethical plot, ironical plot, and the play of power 109
   Michiel W. Heyns

7 Homoeroticism, identity, and agency in James's late tales   126
   Hugh Stevens

8 'A provision full of responsibilities': senses of the past in
   Henry James's fourth phase   148
   David McWhirter

9 Possessing the American scene: race and vulgarity,
   seduction and judgment   166
   Gert Buelens

10 History, narrative, and responsibility: speech acts in 'The
   Aspern Papers'   193
   J. Hillis Miller

Index   211

Notes on contributors

GERT BUELENS is a Postdoctoral Fellow of the National Fund for Scientific Research (Belgium), attached to Ghent University. He has co-edited *Deferring a Dream: Literary Sub-Versions of the American Columbiad* (1994), and is the author of *Henry James: Style, Ethics and History: A Bibliographical Essay* (1996). In 1996-7 he is a Visiting Scholar at Harvard.

SARAH B. DAUGHERTY is Professor of English at Wichita State University. She is the author of *The Literary Criticism of Henry James* (1981) and of the chapter on this subject in the *Companion to Henry James Studies*. Her current work is on the criticism of Howells and his problematic relationship with Twain.

WINFRIED FLUCK is Professor and Chair of American Culture at the Freie Universität, Berlin. He has written *Populäre Kultur* (1979), *Theorien amerikanischer Literatur* (1987), and *Declarations of Dependence: Revising Our View of American Realism* (1993).

ALFRED HABEGGER is an independent biographer and scholar living in Oregon. He has edited *The Bostonians* (1976) and written *Gender, Fantasy, and Realism in American Literature* (1982), *Henry James and the 'Woman Business'* (1989), as well as *The Father: A Life of Henry James, Sr* (1994).

MICHIEL HEYNS was educated at Trinity College, Cambridge, and at the University of Stellenbosch, South Africa, where he is at present Professor of English. His *Expulsion and the Nineteenth-Century Novel: The Scapegoat in English Realist Fiction* appeared in 1994.

RICHARD HOCKS is Professor of English at the University of Missouri. Among his publications are *Henry James and Pragmatistic Thought* (1974), *Henry James: A Study of the Short Fiction* (1990), and *The*

Wings of the Dove: A Norton Critical Edition (with J. Donald Crowley) (1978). He was President of the Henry James Society in 1993, and has written James chapters for *American Literary Scholarship*.

DAVID MCWHIRTER, the 1995 President of the Henry James Society, is Associate Professor of English at Texas A&M University at College Station. He has written *Desire and Love in Henry James: A Study of the Late Novels* (1989), and edited *Henry James's New York Edition: The Construction of Authorship* (1995). His work in progress is on tragicomic modes in literary modernism.

J. HILLIS MILLER is Distinguished Professor of English and Comparative Literature at the University of California at Irvine. Before coming to the University of California, he taught at The Johns Hopkins University and Yale University. His most recent books include *Versions of Pygmalion*, *Theory Now and Then*, *Ariadne's Thread*, *Illustration* and *Topographies*. He is at work on a book on 'Speech Acts in Henry James'.

ADRIAN POOLE is Reader in English and Comparative Literature and a Fellow of Trinity College, Cambridge. His publications include books on Henry James, George Gissing, and Greek tragedy, and articles on George Eliot, Hardy, James, and Kipling. He is also the co-editor of *The Oxford Book of Classical Verse in Translation* (1995).

HUGH STEVENS is a lecturer in the Department of English and Related Literature, University of York. He received his PhD from Cambridge in 1994, with a thesis on 'Sexuality and Desire in the Writing of Henry James', and is currently working on a study of constructions of masculinity in modernism.

Acknowledgments

The editor would like to acknowledge the advice, help, and support received at various stages of this project from Ian F. A. Bell, William Boelhower, Lieve Bracke, Nicola Bradbury, Ortwin de Graef, Bart Eeckhout, Evelyne Ender, Alfred Habegger, Richard A. Hocks, David McWhirter, Christelle Méplon, Adrian Poole, John Carlos Rowe, Werner Sollors, Tony Tanner, and Kristiaan Versluys, as well as from the anonymous readers appointed by Cambridge University Press. At the Press itself, Josie Dixon, Ray Ryan, and Kevin Taylor played an invaluable part.

Quotation from unpublished letters in Alfred Habegger's essay is by the kind permission of the Houghton Library, Harvard University. An earlier version of J. Hillis Miller's essay was delivered as the Routledge lecture and first appeared in *Textual Practice*, 9 (1995), 243–67 (© J. Hillis Miller).

Abbreviations

AB	*The Ambassadors*, New York Edition, 24 vols. (New York: Scribner's, 1907–9), vols. XXI, XXII.
AD	*The Altar of the Dead, The Beast in the Jungle, The Birthplace, and Other Tales*, New York Edition, 24 vols. (New York: Scribner's, 1907–9), vol. XVII.
AM	*The American*, New York Edition, 24 vols. (New York: Scribner's, 1907–9), vol. II.
AN	*The Art of the Novel: Critical Prefaces*, ed. Richard P. Blackmur (New York: Scribner's, 1934).
AP	*The Aspern Papers, The Turn of the Screw, The Liar, The Two Faces*, New York Edition, 24 vols. (New York: Scribner's, 1907–9), vol. XXII.
AU	*Henry James, Autobiography*, ed. Frederick W. Dupee (Princeton University Press, 1983).
CN	*The Complete Notebooks of Henry James*, ed. Leon Edel and Lyall H. Powers (New York: Oxford University Press, 1987).
CT	*The Complete Tales of Henry James*, ed. Leon Edel, 12 vols. (Philadelphia: Lippincott; London: Hart-Davis, 1962–4).
CTW-I	*Collected Travel Writings: Great Britain and America*, ed. Richard Howard (New York: Library of America, 1993).
CTW-II	*Collected Travel Writings: The Continent*, ed. Richard Howard (New York: Library of America, 1993).
DM	*Daisy Miller, Pandora, The Patagonia, and Other Tales*, New York Edition, 24 vols. (New York: Scribner's, 1907–9), vol. XVIII.
GB	*The Golden Bowl*, New York Edition, 24 vols. (New York: Scribner's, 1907–9), vols. XXIII, XXIV.
HJL	*Henry James Letters*, ed. Leon Edel, 4 vols. (Cambridge, Mass.: Belknap-Harvard University Press, 1974–84).

LC-I	*Literary Criticism: Essays on Literature, American Writers, English Writers*, ed. Leon Edel with the assistance of Mark Wilson (New York: Library of America, 1984).
LC-II	*Literary Criticism: French Writers, Other European Writers, the Prefaces to the New York Edition*, ed. Leon Edel with the assistance of Mark Wilson (New York: Library of America, 1984).
MTD	'Mr. Tennyson's Drama', *Galaxy*, 20 (1875), 393–402.
NS	*Notes of a Son and Brother* (New York: Scribner's, 1914).
PL	*The Portrait of a Lady*, New York Edition, 24 vols. (New York: Scribner's, 1907–9), vols. III, IV.
RH	*Roderick Hudson*, New York Edition, 24 vols. (New York: Scribner's, 1907–9), vol. I.
SB	*A Small Boy and Others* (New York: Scribner's, 1913).
T	*The Tales of Henry James*, ed. Maqbool Aziz, 3 vols. (Oxford: Clarendon, 1973–84).
WD	*The Wings of the Dove*, New York Edition, 24 vols. (New York: Scribner's, 1907–9), vols. XIX, XX.
WWS	*William Wetmore Story and His Friends: From Letters, Diaries and Recollections*, 2 vols. (Edinburgh: Blackwood, 1903).

Introduction
Gert Buelens

On 26 July 1909, Henry James writes to Frederick Macmillan to enlist his publisher-friend's help in a delicate matter. James indicates his wish to direct the then sizeable sum of £100 discreetly to his 'accomplished and greatly valued friend of many years Morton Fullerton', explaining that he 'know[s] something – a good deal, of his personal and family situation, and especially of the financially depleting effect on him, lately aggravated, of the condition of his father, ill and helpless these many years in the US, and to whom he has had constantly to render assistance' (*HJL*, IV, 529). Since Fullerton, the head of the Paris bureau of the (London) *Times*, has just been invited by the firm of Macmillan to write a book on the French capital, it strikes James 'as not unlikely that he may have to write and ask for some advance on the money he is to receive from you, for getting more clear and free for work at his book'. James wonders whether Macmillan would at that point 'be willing to send [the £100] to him, as a favour to me, *as* from yourselves (independently of anything you may yourselves send him?) and with no mention whatever, naturally, of my name in the matter?'

At first sight, James's letter offers touching testimony to a magnanimous impulse. Here, we might say, is the sixty-six-year-old James applying, in duly circumspect fashion, such pecuniary and social clout as he has by now attained to the altruistic cause of enabling a younger friend to devote himself to his writing. Or, to put it more programmatically in terms of the present volume's title, here is James briefly emerging from the ivory tower of his art, and using his power to enact an ethical role in history.

Another letter of 26 July 1909 is addressed to Edith Wharton (*HJL*, IV, 527–8). This letter hints at a narrative that is rather different. For one thing, the offer of £100 appears to originate from the munificent Mrs Wharton and not from 'poor impecunious and helpless me' (*HJL*, IV, 530), for another, the immediate purpose they are to serve is to enable her lover, Fullerton, to retrieve compromising letters from a former mistress of his. James remains discreet about the less than straightforward reasons he gave Macmillan for his friend's neediness ('I named them a little', he tells Wharton). A missive to Macmillan of 3 August 1909 suggests further complications. It reveals that James's apparent benevolence has caused the publisher to make a generous gesture of his own, inviting James merely to 'become surety' for a publisher's advance of £100 on top of the one that had already been offered to Fullerton, to be paid out at the latter's request only (*HJL*, IV, 531).[1] James's reply, gratefully agreeing to Macmillan's arrangement, also shows that the publisher's letter carried an invitation to the Macmillans' summer home at Cromer, a privilege James had not heretofore enjoyed.[2]

Taking into account the clues now available, one is led to adopt a diminished view of Henry James's moral stature.[3] Not only does he intentionally misrepresent facts to aid a questionable cause (helping a friend give in to blackmail), the effect of his actions is to deceive another friend so successfully as to prompt the latter to show a generosity both to the protégé (offering to advance an extra £100 himself) and to the petitioner (inviting him to Cromer) that seems misplaced under the circumstances. The protagonist of *this* narrative has used his power – a power that resides in the social and ethical reputation he enjoys with his friends as well as in his superior command of narrative (his effective representation of Fullerton's case) – to ends that are ethically dubious, to say the least.

The trajectory through James's biography that we have been following is the classically hermeneutical one of a search for clues, with a generous admixture of moral appraisal on the basis of the biographical evidence unearthed. It is a trajectory much facilitated in the case of James's life by the availability of a large amount of evidence. Not only is there the five-volume biography (1953–72) by Leon Edel that one can turn to, but also the latter's four-volume collection of James's letters (1974–84), just to mention the bulkiest tomes. The reader may thus be excused for entertaining the hope that definitive answers will be forthcoming, that James's life can be fully known.

What, then, could have motivated James to undertake such crooked actions? What was the extent of James's feelings for either Wharton or Fullerton that he did not turn a hair at going to such length for them? The friendship between Wharton and James is well documented. In Edel's estimate, Wharton perceived a greater intimacy in the relationship than did James: 'His affection was genuine; his reservations were strong.'[4] It is not likely that James would have felt called upon to render services of the type outlined for Wharton, if his interest in the other party concerned had not been vivid. Edel is less outspoken in his account of James's feelings for Fullerton, this 'priapean New Englander' who 'had flirted with homosexual love' (*HJL*, IV, xxv, xxiii). James, we learn, 'was from the first much intrigued by him' (*HJL*, IV, xxv), or 'James had always been fond of him.'[5] But, reading between the lines of Edel's discussion of the blackmail affair, one may discover that James's 'fondness' went deeper and must have been the driving force behind his later epistolary interventions. Responding to Fullerton's revelations, James writes: 'I think of the whole long mistaken perversity of your averted *reality* so to speak, as a miserable *personal* waste, (that of something – ah, so tender! – in *me* that was only quite yearningly ready for you, and something all possible, and all deeply and admirably appealing in yourself, of which I never got the benefit'; this 'clearing of the air . . . removes such a falsity (of defeated relation) between us'.[6]

More explicit than Edel, Fred Kaplan's recent biography finds the relationship to have been charged with 'homoerotic intensity', at least on James's side.[7] He quotes liberally from the sequence of truly love-lorn letters James addressed to Morton Fullerton around the turn of the century, letters that were drawn on sparingly in Edel's major epistolary collection (*HJL*) and biography, where he characterized them as simply 'affectionate'.[8] 'Can't you now, oh *can't* you, make your presence here for a fortnight a solid, secure fact?', James beseeches Fullerton in the spring of 1899.[9] A year later, James complains half jocularly, towards the end of an otherwise brisk and optimistic letter, that his 'life is arranged – if arranged it can be called – on the lines of constantly missing you'.[10] 'Don't exaggerate or morbidise the *difficulty* of being with me for a few days', he adjures his friend in September, 'I am intensely, absurdly convenient . . . You shall be surrounded here with . . . rest & consideration. You talk of the *real thing*. But that is the real thing. *I* am the real thing. I send you a photograph . . . What talk with you I want! I embrace you meanwhile with great tenderness.'[11] 'I'm alone', he sighs in a next missive, 'I'm alone & I think of you. I can't say fairer . . . I'd meet you at Dover – I'd do anything for you.'[12] And a few days later: 'I want in fact more of you. You are dazzling . . . you are beautiful; you are more than tactful, you are tenderly, magically *tactile*. But you're not kind. There it is. You *are* not kind.'[13]

With the discovery of these clues, we would appear to have solved the riddle. Here at last is our explanation for James's 'queer' behaviour – an oddity that turns out to be rooted in homosexual desire. Against some odds, we have discovered that he was hopelessly in love with Fullerton and would truly 'do anything for [him]', even to lie and to collude. Put in more speculative terms, we have managed 'to force that knowledge to *reveal itself*, to reveal itself, indeed, both as cognition and as pleasure'.

Those are the words Shoshana Felman uses to characterize the activity indulged in by James's governess in *The Turn of the Screw*.[14] The parallel between our own situation and the governess's is worth exploring further. When, at the end of James's novella, Miles 'surrender[s]' the name of the ghost that has been allegedly possessing him, 'this ultimate triumph of reading', for Felman, 'remains . . . highly ambiguous[:] the very act of naming, which the governess takes to be the decisive answer to her questions, is in the child's mouth, in reality, itself a question'.[15] Miles does pronounce the name of 'Peter Quint', yet is unable to locate the apparition and asks his governess for help. His final word, before dying in her arms, is '*Where?*' As Felman comments, 'If the act of naming does indeed name the final truth, that truth is given not as an answer to the question about meaning, but as itself a *question* about its *location* . . . The final meaning, therefore, is not an answer, but is itself a question, which also questions its own pursuit. In considering that question as an answer, the governess in effect stifles its nonetheless ongoing questioning power.'[16]

Reconsidering the 'answer' that we seemed to have hit upon at the end of our biographical investigation, it appears that that answer too was, in fact, a question. Indeed, each of the letters to Fullerton takes the form of a question, whether explicit or implicit, which could be formulated at its most direct level as 'when will you visit me?', at a deeper level as 'why don't you love me?'. However, to most modern sensibilities, the latter question implies a desire for sexual responsiveness that James's eroticism, in fact, steered clear of. Kaplan has persuasively demonstrated that if James, from the 1890s, is driven by a strong interest in the sexual in general, and his own homoeroticism in particular, his desire is enacted on a symbolical level; James always maintains the screen of language in between himself and carnal, erotic experience. Yet Kaplan's excellent biography too readily, and too conventionally, assumes that James's 'emphasis on friendship, not on physical consummation' can be adequately ascribed to 'conventional inhibitions', which caused sex to remain 'as dangerous, as threatening, as morally and culturally difficult for him as it had always been'.[17] Eroticism, friendship, passionate letters are, for Kaplan, no more than poor substitutes for 'the real thing' shunned by the fearful puritan, Henry James.

A better account of the relationship between 'real thing' and symbolic approximation in James is implicit in Shoshana Felman's gloss on one of the most intriguing sentences in *The Turn of the Screw*: Douglas's pronunciamento that 'the story *won't* tell . . . not in any literal vulgar way'. 'The literal', Felman writes, 'is "vulgar" because it *stops* the *movement* constitutive of meaning, because it blocks and interrupts the endless process of metaphorical substitution. The vulgar, therefore, is anything which misses, or falls short of, the dimension of the symbolic, anything which rules out, or excludes, meaning as a loss and as a flight.'[18] Sexuality, in the full sense of the word, can only be meaningful if it exceeds the 'literal sexual act',[19] if it, too, participates in the inevitable processes of substitution, loss and flight that constitute any language. As Hillis Miller argues elsewhere in the present volume, the sex act is paradigmatic of a kind of bodily, experiential knowledge (as in 'Adam knew Eve') that cannot, in itself, be narrated but only performed, enacted (Felman's knowledge as 'pleasure').[20] In a love relationship, the other may thus be 'known' in a material sense by means of a sex act that is describable in a technical respect, yet whose intimate brand of knowledge cannot be narrated, communicated, or transmitted through language; it can only be striven for anew in a repetition of the act itself. But this performative knowledge, which could be termed 'empty of meaning' from a cognitive, narratable point of view, is only one object of the lovers' desire, is only one aspect of sexuality – though arguably its core. Another is the craving for cognitive knowledge of the other (as in 'tell me all about yourself'). This type of knowledge (Felman's knowledge as 'cognition') is open to narration, yet, as such, becomes subject to the substitutions and ambiguities of language. Sense, meaning, can be communicated here, yet will remain elusive because of the metaphorical nature of rhetoric. There is thus always a gap between the conscious (knowing and feeling) subject and an object that can only be known either performatively, by means of a direct and full presence that is itself non-narratable, non-communicable, or cognitively, by means of the indirect and incomplete approximation that can be achieved in language.[21]

The distinction between narratable and non-narratable modes of knowing might seem to imply that literature can only provide access to one of the two. Yet, invoking Felman once more, it is surely true that one of the major distinguishing marks of literature as opposed to, say, scientific uses of language, is 'its reserve of silence',[22] its capacity, in other words, to suggest that which cannot be narrated, to appeal to emotion and not just cognition. James's ability to achieve this literary effect was singled out for particular praise by Virginia Woolf: 'Perhaps it is the silence that first impresses us [in *The Turn of the Screw*] . . . Some unutterable obscenity has come to the surface . . . Can it be that we are afraid? But it is not a man with red hair and a white face whom we fear. We are afraid of something unnamed, of something, perhaps, in ourselves . . . still we must own that something remains unaccounted for.'[23] At their most successful, James's narratives enable the reader to experience an 'unutterable', 'unnamed' something that remains 'unaccounted for', cognitively separated from the reader by an unbridgeable gap.[24]

It is this gap which the usual, hermeneutical paradigm for reading Henry James has sought to fill, attempting to fix meaning, to unearth the truth at the centre of his narratives, in ways that have been insensitive to the *seeking in vain* that is so strongly James's experience (whether as a result of culturally determined inhibitions or because of something more akin to existential perception) and that his fiction invites the reader to repeat. The desire to 'know the truth' will always be frustrated in reading Henry James, because the heart of James's interest – in his fiction as in the biographical narrative we began by unfolding – is formed by a quantity that is unknowable in any observable, verifiable sense. Regarded from the author's perspective, James's fiction may be said to rehearse in fictional form events that, at least at the time of writing, only existed *in potentia*. Edel has thus noted that it seems as if James 'had foretold' the affair between Fullerton and Wharton in *The Wings of the Dove* (whose Merton Densher is simply based on Morton Fullerton but whose Kate Croy was created prior to James's acquaintance with

Wharton), and as if James had invented in *Roderick Hudson* the sculptor Hendrik Andersen, whom he would meet and love only much later (*HJL*, IV, xxiii).[25] Rather than dismiss such convergences between fiction and biography as 'coincidences' (ibid.), we could consider them as parallel instances of James's desire for experiential knowledge of the other. In fiction, he rehearses such knowledge vicariously; in 'real' life he seeks out and sometimes couples those persons on whom (or on whose type) his imagination dwells most insistently. The reader of the Jamesian text can never get at any ultimate cognitive truth; what he or she can do is to imaginatively relive – 'like a creature responsive & responsible' – such unknowable historical events, such experiential truth, as the narrative itself performatively rehearses.[26]

The phrase just quoted from James, 'responsive & responsible', reactivates the ethical dimension that we had considered at the outset. The moral sense that James seems to mobilize here implies a commitment to a course of action whose effect on reality, whose historical impact, is unknown and unknowable at the time when it is embarked upon. If such a subsequent history could be charted, foretold, narrated at the outset, then the act (if it would still merit that name) would belong to the domain of narration or logic – of knowing; not to that of performance or ethics – of doing. This is why the assumption of a true responsibility involves such a heavy burden: it requires a willingness to be held accountable, at a later time, for actions whose effect will only then be measurable, whose knowability, narratability, will only emerge *post factum*.

We can, at this point, make a renewed attempt to invoke the terms of the volume's title. The history that Henry James's narratives may be said to enact is that history-as-events that is itself inaccessible to narration or cognition but open to *rehearsal* and *reiteration* at a performative level. The reader's hermeneutical impulse to gain unmediated access to the events that constitute this history will remain frustrated inasmuch as it is a desire to grasp an object that is essentially elusive. The reader may, for one part, attempt to make such events cognitively accessible by transforming them into history-as-a-narrative, into a knowable and explicable past. Such an attempt, however, may also amount to an escape from the burden of responsibility, in that it tries to substitute cognition for performance. Its success is moreover jeopardized by the fact that turning history into narrative also involves subjecting it to the unstable realm of linguistic meaning. For another part, the silences within the Jamesian text invite the reader to enact their ungraspable history, that is to say, to make it one's own by repeating it imaginatively. As such, Jamesian narrative demands of the reader not just an emotional responsiveness, but also an ethical assumption of responsibility for the history that is enacted, for the event that takes place in the process. Here we may recall Virginia Woolf's comment on the power of *The Turn of the Screw* to make us feel morally responsible for the 'unutterable obscenity' that its narrative adumbrates, which we end up by looking for 'in ourselves'. A similar experience was registered by a contemporaneous review in *The Independent*: 'The feeling after perusal of the horrible story is that one has been assisting in an outrage . . . and helping to debauch – at least by helplessly standing by – the pure and trusting nature of children.'[27]

All of the essays collected in this volume address such questions of knowability, performance, responsibility and narrative empowerment or disempowerment as have here been raised. Winfried Fluck's opening chapter, 'Power relations in the novels of James: the "liberal" and the "radical" version', situates the issues against the background of James criticism, focusing on the output of the past decade and in particular on the controversial issue of James's authorial assumption of 'power'. Fluck exposes the limitations of the two main readings of James: the 'liberal' one, in which James defends universal humanist values, and the 'radical' one, in which he is implicated in oppressive ideologies of gender, power, and representation. He argues instead that both have been blind to the way James himself foregrounds questions of power in language, social and sexual relations, and artistic representation. Of all nineteenth-century authors, James strikes Fluck as probably the most sensitive to aspects of dominance, dependence, and manipulation in linguistic and social relations; at the same time, James is not only unwilling to regard these effects as 'systemic', but also considers the 'work of art', its power to enact history by empowering the reader, as the best antidote to the irresponsibility implicit in the 'systemic' view.

Richard Hocks's chapter, 'Multiple germs, metaphorical systems, and moral fluctuation in *The Ambassadors*', further pursues James's negotiation of the tension between freedom and determinism, between ethical responsibility and systemic constraint. Hocks argues that the performative rhetoric of James's late novel – its poetics of metaphor and motif – allows him to adopt a philosophical stance between the traditional competing arguments. Examining the genesis of *The Ambassadors* – its multiple versions from the 'germ' recorded in his notebooks (Howells's imperative to Sturges: 'Live all you can!', itself a cognitively 'unknowable' statement, which derives its meaning only from the performative force it achieves if acted upon) to the commentary of the New York Edition Preface – Hocks finds that, while James has retained the germ speech as a repository for the book's central philosophical question (whether or not we act as free agents, whether or not we can choose to 'be right'), the novel itself enacts an intricately mediating reply to this question.

For Sarah Daugherty, James's fiction is born from the creative tension between the cognitive drive for knowledge and its performative counterpart. Analysing James's literary criticism in her chapter, 'James and the ethics of control: aspiring architects and their floating creatures', Daugherty shows how, on the one hand, James was attracted to, yet suspicious of, the performative force of romantic fabulation, and, on the other, credited realist writers with an architectural strength derived from their cognitive grasp on reality but criticized them for the cruelly excessive control they exerted over their characters. Daugherty traces James's attempts in his own fiction to balance the often conflicting demands of his own critical precepts. The concluding pages of *The Portrait of a Lady* and the second volume of *The Golden Bowl* demonstrate that James sometimes could only deal with the corners he had painted himself into by leaving the reader to seek a way out, forced as the latter is to speculate on scenes that take place outside the text. Yet, this apparent weakness may also be regarded as a strength, when one recognizes and comes to share James's ultimate acceptance of the reserve of silence at the heart of literary representation – that which leaves room for the reader's enactment of history.

Adrian Poole's chapter, 'James and the shadow of the Roman Empire: manners and the consenting victim', articulates the problematical relationship between James's protagonists (particularly those of the major-phase novels) and the idea of empire. Poole shows how James interrogates power, questioning the manipulative operations his protagonists engage in; yet James is also keenly aware of the latter's need to act in history, to assume a role in a reality where power is an inescapable force. 'Rome' here serves as a figure for the grounding of cognition in questions of power and empowerment. If the protagonists of James's late novels are not allowed to choose between the illusory alternatives of the assumption of power and submission to it, but have to try and achieve impossible resolutions of contradictions, so, for the reader, the choice cannot be the simple one between submission to the potency of his writing or defiance of it, between entering James's empire of words or staying outside. Rather, the responsibility thrust upon the reader is to reiterate the power moves of James's narrative.

In '*What Maisie Knew*: Henry James's Bildungsroman of the artist as queer moralist', Alfred Habegger examines the way in which *Maisie* enacts James's private history no less than does *A Small Boy and Others*. What we get in both the novel and the autobiography is a hero who triumphs by learning the trick of transforming painful subjection into a highly responsive and responsible kind of living (Maisie) or of art (James). Yet, as Habegger argues, because the kind of moral act that writing *Maisie* amounts to is one that recapitulates the writer's own formative ordeal, it turns out to be an exceedingly *specialized* moral act, as evasive as it is constructive. It makes a special case for a certain kind of survivor-mentality, and it goes in for smothered raptures and supreme, inward victories. As a moral narrative, it testifies to a sense of history as that which must be read; as a (more ironical) speech act, it bears witness to the fact that history cannot be read or narrated, but only repeated. It is because so much of James's writing leads up to these kinds of fraught moral acts, he concludes, that it is a mistake to regard him as a sound moral guide.

Like Habegger, Michiel Heyns addresses the uneasy relation between the moral sense of Jamesian narrative and its ironical dimension. His chapter, 'The double narrative of "The Beast in the Jungle": ethical plot, ironical plot, and the play of power', shows up the poverty of hermeneutical readings of 'The Beast in the Jungle'. These focus on the narrative's ethical plot, which confronts Marcher with the nullity of his own history and highlights his inability to recognize the romantic feelings May Bartram cherishes for him. A recent variation on this interpretation is Eve Kosofsky Sedgwick's, which posits a repressed homosexual desire as the cause of Marcher's failure. Heyns complicates this hermeneutical picture by devoting sustained attention to the ironical and performative power enjoyed by the apparent victim, May Bartram. In withholding information from Marcher, May effectively punishes him for his obtuseness during her life. The longer it takes him to gain cognitive insight, the greater her performative power, and, therefore, that of the beast, becomes, culminating finally in the springing of the beast by the side of her grave.

If interpreting 'The Beast in the Jungle' depends in part on how we read the hero's (homo)sexual identity, for Hugh Stevens, James's performative force is apparent from the way he never defines homosexual identity or characterizes it directly. Stevens's chapter, 'Homoeroticism, identity, and agency in James's late tales', examines 'Mora Montravers', 'The Jolly Corner', and 'The Altar of the Dead'. It should not be assumed, Stevens maintains, that these veiled references are merely the product of historical, systemic constraint, James being forced to refrain from explicitness; rather, his late fiction may be seen to question such definitional mechanisms as would pinpoint any particular sexual identity, and to empower instead a specific enactment of sexual drives that are in principle 'unknowable'. For many of James's 'poor sensitive gentlemen', homosexual identity is a difficulty, even an impossibility. However, for these poor gentlemen, an 'identity' foreclosing the homoerotic is equally difficult, equally problematic. Thus arise the messy triangles of these late tales, in which desire and identification are apparently hopelessly confused. It is through plots that perform a resolution at the level of fantasy and camp that James is finally able to address the contradictory demands that face his gentlemen – the restrictive ethical demands of a late-Victorian social structure that homosexual bonds be denied, and the psychic demands that such bonds be acknowledged.

If Hugh Stevens demonstrates James's unwillingness to define sexual identity, David McWhirter's chapter '"A provision full of responsibilities": senses of the past in Henry James's fourth phase', similarly argues that the late James's interest in the past (in such works as the *Autobiography*, *The American Scene*, and the New York Edition) does not spring from any desire to define the past, but from a need to determine anew who he is in the present. Drawing on Ricoeur, McWhirter shows how James understands identity not so much as a commitment to an unchanging core of personality but as a discontinuous, ever unique, realization of selfhood. In order to achieve such selfhood, the subject must assume responsibility for each performance of that self – a performance that is now no longer protected by the weight of past habits and customs. In the fourth phase, McWhirter finds, what we see is James exploring his *own* cultural, authorial, and personal identity under the sign of a revisionary model of selfhood that is articulated in the always proliferating *senses* of the past, the never final, always provisional quest for new circuits of connection and continuity with a past that remains *other*.

My own chapter, 'Possessing the American scene: race and vulgarity, seduction and judgment', explores in greater detail one of the works also discussed by David McWhirter. In particular, I challenge the critical basis of some readings of *The American Scene* which have charged James with a failure to denounce the racism he encountered in the South. Arguing that such criticism is rooted in ambiguously moral objections rather than in the straightforwardly political ones professed, I claim for James's engagement with the intertwined problematics of race and vulgarity the status of an alternative, non-violent political practice that can stand the test of comparison to the contestatory model propounded by James's critics. In *The American Scene*, I further contend, James values ghostly modes of possessing the scene and reliving the past over vulgarly material appropriation and violent assertion. Functioning as symbolic substitutes for vulgar literality, language and manners accordingly become crucial elements in James's enacting of history (where enacting implies both agency and staging; history both events and narratives-of-events).

The final chapter offers a speculative endpiece to the collection. In 'History, narrative, and responsibility: speech acts in "The Aspern Papers"', J. Hillis Miller investigates how James's novella complicates the continuity that is generally supposed to exist between history and its narration by the admixture of an ethical component: responsibility. The narrator of 'The Aspern Papers', a literary scholar in active, manipulative pursuit of the biographical truth about his subject (the papers in the possession of Aspern's erstwhile mistress Juliana), is placed in an impossible double bind – becomes powerless to act – when Tina Bordereau, Juliana's niece, offers him her hand. He cannot have the author's papers if he remains an outsider, so cannot publish them. He can have them if he becomes an insider, but then cannot publish them because he will have incurred the responsibility of a husband to keep his wife's family secrets. This is the same kind of responsibility Juliana incurred toward Aspern by becoming his mistress. Hence, marriage to Tina would be a performative act that repeats the historical event the narrator is trying to gain knowledge of. The knowledge he would have as Tina's husband would re-enact the knowledge Aspern had, but it would not bring the kind of knowledge that can or should be narrated in a cognizable historical text. Thus James shows up a breach between history and narrative that cannot be crossed: a historical event cannot be narrated but only performatively repeated. For that repetition, the doer (including the reader of a tale such as this one) must take responsibility.

NOTES

1 Hardly any letters *to* James survived (since he made sure to burn them), so that in most cases we have only his side of any correspondence. *Pace* Edel, it is unclear whether Fullerton ever requested the extra £100 (*Henry James: The Master, 1901–1916*, vol. v of *The Life of Henry James* (London: Hart-Davis, 1972), 426–7). The blackmail affair may have been resolved prior to this exchange, but compare Fred Kaplan's claim that '[t]he money was to be used to purchase back the stolen letters, a process that dragged on for almost two years' (*Henry James: The Imagination of Genius: A Biography* (New York: Morrow, 1992; edn cited: London: Sceptre-Hodder, 1993), 512). In any case, Fullerton's book was never written, yet, according to Kaplan, James's surety never exacted.
2 Relations between Frederick Macmillan and James had been friendly for more than three decades, and James had regularly visited at the Macmillans' London residence (Kaplan, *Henry James, passim*).
3 None of the contributors to the present volume pretend to distinguish systematically between the terms ethics, morals, morality, or their respective adjectives; neither do we believe James's writing to have drawn on any such putative distinction.
4 *Life*, v, 211.
5 Ibid., 421.
6 Ibid., 425.
7 Kaplan, *Henry James*, 409.
8 *Life*, IV, 349.
9 Henry James, Letter to Morton Fullerton, 11 May 1899, Houghton Library; quoted Kaplan, *Henry James*, 408.
10 Henry James, Letter to Morton Fullerton, 22 March 1900, Houghton Library; quoted ibid., 408; reprinted in *HJL*, IV, 137.
11 Henry James, Letter to Morton Fullerton, 16 September 1899, Houghton Library; quoted ibid., 408. The letter is also quoted by Edel (*Life*, IV, 349), but attributed to the year 1900, which seems plausible in view of the other material; instead of 'surrounded here with . . . rest &

consi*der*ation' Edel quotes 'surrounded here with every circumstance of tranquillity and comfort, of rest and cons*ecr*ation' (emphasis added).
12 Henry James, Letter to Morton Fullerton, 21 September 1900, Houghton Library; quoted Kaplan, *Henry James*, 409; reprinted in *Henry James: Selected Letters*, ed. Leon Edel (Cambridge, Mass.: Belknap-Harvard University Press, 1987).
13 Henry James, Letter to Morton Fullerton, 26 September 1900, Houghton Library; quoted Kaplan, *Henry James*, 409; reprinted in *Henry James: Selected Letters*, ed. Leon Edel.
14 'Turning the Screw of Interpretation', *Yale French Studies*, 55-6 (1977); reprinted in *Literature and Psychoanalysis: The Question of Reading: Otherwise*, ed. Shoshana Felman (Baltimore: Johns Hopkins University Press, 1982), 160.
15 Ibid., 161.
16 Ibid.
17 *Henry James*, 402.
18 'Turning the Screw', 107.
19 Ibid., 110.
20 See p. 203.
21 It is possible to speculate further about what Kaplan has called James's 'taste for playing the role of facilitator-voyeur' with regard to Fullerton's sexual relationships with Wharton (*Henry James*, 513) and other people (ibid., 407). If, for Kaplan, this can be explained as James's 'way of furthering his own intimacy with his young friend' (ibid.), could we not, more boldly, see James's attempts to arrange sexual relationships for his loved ones as a means of ensuring the very elusiveness and frustration on which his desire could feed? Could it not be that, attuned to the fundamentally insatiable nature of desire and the cognitive emptiness at the heart of meaning, James accepts and actively *works* the unbridgeable gap between himself as conscious subject and others as unknowable objects?
22 'Turning the Screw', 193.
23 *The Turn of the Screw: Norton Critical Edition*, ed. Robert Kimbrough (New York: Norton, 1966), 179-80.
24 There may be a suggestion of this kind of gap in the description of Miles's death in *The Turn of the Screw*, which is said to be accompanied by 'the cry of a creature hurled over an abyss' (ibid., 88).
25 One might also add here another intimate friend, Jonathan Sturges, first met in 1889, but later described in terms highly reminiscent of Hyacinth Robinson, created in 1885: compare 'His bones were small, his chest was narrow . . . his whole figure almost childishly slight . . . he had a very delicate hand – the hand . . . of a gentleman. . . . his eyes . . . had . . . a kind of witty candour . . . He looked both ingenuous and slightly wasted' (*The Princess Casamassima, Henry James: Novels 1886–1890*, ed. Daniel Mark Fogel (New York: Library of America, 1989), 55-6)

and 'a very nice little chap – ingenious, straightforward – a gentleman
... his poor little blighted physique' (Henry James, Letter to Henrietta
Reubell, 19 October 1893, Houghton Library; quoted by Kaplan, *Henry
James*, 404).
26 Henry James, Letter to Morton Fullerton, 2 October 1895, Houghton
Library; quoted Kaplan, *Henry James*, 408.
27 *Norton Critical Edition*, 175.

CHAPTER 1

Power relations in the novels of James: the 'liberal' and the 'radical' version

Winfried Fluck

In James-criticism, 'demystifying the master' seems to have become the main agenda.[1] In spite of the fact that the work of James, as that of other major representatives of the established canon, has by now been repeatedly unmasked as being 'compromised to the core',[2] revisionist critics keep coming back to James. The reason is not hard to find. Because James continues to be one of the culture heroes of liberal modernism, the authority and dominance of that cultural system can best be undermined by revealing James's limitations of awareness and his unwitting complicity with a social system which his work claims to distance or even transcend by art. If it can be shown that the master was not so masterful after all, but in the grasp of hidden anxieties about his lack of success in the market-place, his masculinity, or his class status, that he was, in other words, not in control, but himself 'controlled' by desire or certain discursive practices beyond his own comprehension, then the modernist myth of aesthetic transcendence could be exploded most effectively.[3] The charge of an unwitting complicity with the system (of consumer capitalism, patriarchy, or society's disciplinary practices) – in an extreme form, even the claim of a 'criminal continuity' between cultural practice and social regimes[4] – has become one of the main strategic moves of the new revisionism because it is ideally suited to undermining the liberal claim for a supreme oppositional potential of art.[5] Where the charge of complicity is considered too strong, on the other hand, another route of revision is taken, namely to point to covert, submerged aspects and operations of his texts which reveal James to be really a poststructuralist *avant la lettre*, a reluctant feminist, or even a latent Marxist.[6] In this way, all schools of contemporary theory have come to claim James as one of their own.[7]

No matter, however, whether the new revisionism takes the form of 'complicity-criticism' or 'theoretical kinship-criticism', what unites these otherwise different approaches is that they constitute themselves in the critique of a liberal myth of James as master craftsman and supreme practitioner of a liberal theory of art and society. In their critique, they draw attention to the way in which the James we have come to know was created by a post-war liberalism as it re-emerged in the US after the collapse of Marxist thought. In American literary criticism, this rediscovery and reappreciation of James played an essential role in repositioning the liberal tradition itself. Important examples are provided by Lionel Trilling's seminal essays 'Reality in America' and 'Manners, Morals, and the Novel'.[8]

Throughout Trilling's essays his revolt against a left liberalism compromised by its uncritical fellow-travellership with Stalinism is coded in the contrast between Dreiser and James, the one regarded as bad writer, but good realist by left liberalism, the other habitually dismissed as escapist and failed realist: 'Dreiser and James: with that juxtaposition we are immediately at the dark and bloody crossroads where literature and politics meet.'[9] In this contrast, the work of James becomes the focal point for redefining the social responsibilities of the writer. James, 'the moral mind with its awareness of tragedy, irony, and multitudinous distinctions'[10] is heralded as exponent of a moral realism designed to serve as protection against 'the dangers which lie in our most generous wishes' and grandiose moral passions:

Perhaps at no other time has the enterprise of moral realism ever been so much needed, for at no other time have so many people committed themselves to moral righteousness ... Some paradox of our natures leads us, when once we have made our fellow men the objects of our enlightened interest, to go on to make them the objects of our pity, then of our wisdom, ultimately of our coercion. It is to prevent this corruption, the most ironic and tragic that man knows, that we stand in need of the moral realism which is the product of the free play of the moral imagination.[11]

Ultimately, the function and social use of James's moral realism lies in its ability to complicate our view of reality, and thereby also to prevent our 'moral fervour' from becoming dogmatic by acknowledging difficulty and social difference, disagreement and cultural conflict as an inherent part of social reality.

For Trilling, one criterion of a successful complication of our perception of reality lies in the aesthetic dimension. For him, it seems, the aesthetic emerges when the mind meets difficulties.

Literary form is thus not a mere clothing of thought; it is in itself a characteristic and instructive way of appropriating reality. Dreiser's lack of art (and the tacit liberal indulgence of that lack) is a scandal, not because Trilling is an aesthete or a formalist, but because the artistic quality of a work is a measure of how 'deeply' the artist was willing to penetrate reality.[12] Art and the social function of literature are thus inextricably intertwined, and the novel is the literary genre best suited to bring the two together. In a time of dangerous ideological simplifications, this is the reason why Trilling put his hopes on the novel as 'the most effective agent of the moral imagination' within the last two hundred years.[13]

Because of his own almost exclusive interest in the 'political' novels of the middle period, Trilling remained too narrowly focused to occupy a place at the centre of James-criticism. However, the case he makes for the importance of James is not only exemplary in its clarity, it is also representative of the liberal defence of James, including its reconceptualization of art as an eminently social activity.[14] This, I take it, and not a vaguely defined formalism, lies at the basis of the liberal rediscovery and 'reinvention' of James after World War II. Formalism in itself is not an intellectual framework, it is the (rather broad and unspecific) designation for a certain approach to, or method of, interpreting cultural objects. Without a broader context of ideas about reality and the function of art within social life, it must remain meaningless. This broader context was the immense usefulness of James for a redefinition of the relation between art and life, aesthetics and social meaning in which art would gain renewed importance, even priority – not, however, at the expense of disregarding questions of moral and social commitment, but in the attempt to complicate them. For an international group of scholars, James became a major figure, not because his work suggested a separation of art and life, aesthetics and society, or because it seemed to support an ontological claim for the autonomy of the work of art, but because it allowed critics to focus on the problem which had become crucial for the liberal redefinition of art and its function after World War II: the question of what difference art makes in the creation of social meaning. Should James's complication of moral issues be finally revealed to stand in the service of a flight from commitment, then the hope invested in the saving powers of art would collapse and another turn towards a more forceful and explicit social commentary would be in order. If it could be characterized as successful, on the other hand, the authority of the master could serve to bolster the case for a heuristic separation of the aesthetic and the social in order to prevent them from becoming identical and thus easily interchanged. What stands at the centre of the current debate between liberal and radical versions of American literary history is, in other words, not a disagreement between one position that denies social meaning and function to art and another one that reaffirms it, but a struggle between two different versions of that relation, and, linked with it, a fundamental disagreement about the potential and function of literature.

In terms of intellectual history, this struggle can be described as a conflict between a liberal consensus emerging after World War II and a new cultural radicalism that begins to constitute itself in the critique of that liberal consensus in the sixties. This new form of radicalism manifests itself in a wide and, at first sight, seemingly irreconcilable variety of different approaches, ranging from poststructuralism to such explicitly political approaches as cultural materialism, the new historicism, and recent forms of race, class, and gender studies. Different as these approaches may be in their views of language, reality, and the text, they are strikingly similar in their theories of society, power, and the role of culture (hence the frequent use of the umbrella term 'critical theory' to characterize them collectively). By the term cultural radicalism, I thus want to designate all those forms of literary study after the linguistic turn which have replaced earlier forms of 'left-wing' or political radicalism. While political radicalism placed its hope of radical change in a Marxist political theory and analysis of capitalist society, subsequent disappointment over the lack of acceptance by the 'masses' pushed radicalism towards the analysis of 'systemic effects' of the social order. The various forms of cultural radicalism, in one way or another, all emphasize fundamental systemic features (such as the state apparatus, the symbolic order, a discursive formation, logocentrism, or 'Western' thought) which pervade all acts of sense-making and thus also determine political attitudes because they constitute the very concepts and modes of experience through which the social order is understood. This is true to such an extent that even oppositional gestures must be considered mere effects of the system and the promise of reform its shrewdest strategy of containment. In this situation, experience loses its power as a source of knowledge. Only (critical) theory can reveal the 'absent cause' of that which organizes the system. Art can only do so where it can be shown to possess a 'theoretical dimension', that is, where it can be interpreted allegorically as unwitting re-enactment of contemporary theory. From this point of view, all positions that argue for social change within a framework of political pluralism, based on the idea of a citizen who is able to 'know' his or her own interests, become part of a liberal tradition (whether 'left' or 'conservative', like Trilling's version, no longer matters) for which art holds the (illusory) promise of individual development and an increase in self-awareness.

The redefinition of power as structural effect (*strukturelle Gewalt*) is the founding assumption of the new cultural radicalism. As long as political power is equated with force and actual repression, arguments about the repressive nature of liberal democracies are not terribly convincing. Cultural radicalism severs political power from its equation with force and broadens it as a concept to include all forms of coercion by language, symbolic systems, and discursive practices.[15] Power does not rule from the outside, but is embedded in language and discursive practices. In this way, culture becomes the actual source of domination and supreme disciplinary regime within the system. It is this redefinition of power as discursive practice which informs Mark Seltzer's provocative study of James, for example. Again, following a pattern of 'complicity-criticism' established by Carolyn Porter and, above all, Walter Benn Michaels, the starting assumption is that of a deep-seated, hidden complicity:

> Questioning the traditional assumption that James is essentially a nonpolitical novelist, I explore the ways in which James represents social movements of appropriation, supervision, and regulation, and examine how both the content and the techniques of representation in James's works express a complicity and rigorous continuity with the larger social regimes of mastery and control that traverse these works. I want to suggest that art and power are not opposed in the Jamesian text but radically entangled . . . Put as simply as possible, the art of the novel is an art of power.[16]

The Jamesian text, critics like Seltzer have argued, 'resists the imposition of power in the name of a radical (literary) freedom'. Instead, Seltzer wants 'to suggest that James's art of representation always also involves a politics of representation, and one reason for suspecting this link between art and power is that James works so carefully to deny it'. It is this 'criminal continuity between art and power and the ways in which the novelist and critic – through an aesthetic and theoretical rewriting of power – have worked to disown it that I want to examine'.[17]

One of the most striking applications of this revised perspective in reading James is Seltzer's interpretation of *The Golden Bowl*, where he sees 'a power of *normalization*' at work, 'a disciplinary method that induces conformity and regulation not by levying violence, but through an immanent array of norms and compulsions ... an immanent policing so thoroughly inscribed in the most ordinary social practices that it is finally indistinguishable from manners, cooperation, and care' (61). This 'policing' through thoroughly internalized forms of behaviour explains the basic paradox of the 'well-policed character' of the novel: '*The Golden Bowl* is a novel about power – conjugal, commercial, and imperial – but throughout the novel power is represented in terms of "mildness," "harmony," and "calm." More precisely, the name that James gives to the exercising of power in *The Golden Bowl* is love' (62).[18] Supervisory functions have thus been 'comprehensively taken over by other less obtrusive, less "shameful" networks of surveillance' (63). Traditionally, in James-criticism the two terms love and power have been kept apart: 'But I have begun to suggest that *The Golden Bowl* displays precisely a criminal continuity between these terms. Far from being opposed, love and power in *The Golden Bowl* are two ways of saying the same thing' (66).

James's skilful 'dispersion of the political into the most ordinary and everyday relations' affects other aspects of human relations as well (67). It seems, in fact, to affect all aspects of human relations, including sympathy, empathy, caring, schooling, learning, and, also, the creation of aesthetic structures: what 'appears on the level of social and vital organization as a power of normalization reappears on the aesthetic as the rule of organic form' (87). Thus, at 'one extreme, *The Golden Bowl* articulates its dismissal of the punitive and policing apparatus; but at another, the novel traces a widening of the orbit of this apparatus to include the most positive administrations of care' (75–6). Seltzer's extension of the meaning of the term power – including its unmistakably melodramatic connotation 'policing' (which largely contradicts an emphasis on the enabling dimension of power which he dutifully, but somewhat inconsequentially mentions at another point of his argument) – is so all-embracing that it must ultimately include all forms of intimacy, of inner-directedness and psychic self-regulation, and, in the final analysis, all forms of social relation. The exertion of power is so thoroughly inscribed in the most ordinary and everyday relations that it becomes finally indistinguishable from social interaction, because social interaction must always contain a certain degree of 'appropriation, supervision, and regulation', must always imply a certain demand for co-operation and consensus, and is usually based on a desire for love and on expectations of social support.

Seltzer's reading is not a 'productive' interpretation of James's work in the sense of a concrete and detailed explanation of the text and its strategies. In accordance with the 'revised' role literature plays in 'critical theory', its basic mode of interpretation is allegorical, drawing its inspiration and main arguments almost exclusively from Michel Foucault's *Discipline and Punish* without ever acknowledging the particular and problematic position of this book in the development of Foucault's thought. Still, in its redefinition of power through the concept of social network, Seltzer's argument has the merit of carrying the radical approach to James to a logical extreme and thus revealing a good deal of its underlying premises. In the final analysis, in the new cultural radicalism the concepts of power and domination comprise all forms of inequality and 'asymmetry' in social relations, so that power is redefined as any kind of social or symbolic coercion. Coercion manifests itself in all forms of dependence, in all claims on the self by others, including those valued most highly by liberalism, like love, care, familial and marital bonds. This radicalization of the concept of power has as its own tacit norm a utopian egalitarianism based on the promise of a complete dehierarchization in social relations (or, where absolutely unavoidable, asking for only temporary and short-lived hierarchies). And the same principles apply to the level of literary form and textualization: wherever meaning is created and skilfully represented, there is also already an element of coercion at work. This point, in fact, is one of the genuine insights of the new radicalism. It introduces a heightened sensitivity to the presence of constant power plays in language as well as in social relations; to the tyranny one person can exert over another by inserting and trapping him or her in certain roles; to the way in which spectatorship, including that of the narrator, is never innocent, but is always a mode of intruding into another person's life; and, finally, to the way in which sympathy and care can also function as impositions, forms of possession, and modes of disciplining through intimacy.[19] What it does not acknowledge is that this is also one of the major insights and experiences in the work of James.

Of all nineteenth-century writers, James is probably the one who is most aware of the permanent presence of manipulation and the constant re-emergence of social asymmetries in relations. Deceiving and exploiting others is the major crime in his fictional world, and it is part of his historically remarkable achievement that, in contrast to the unmistakably melodramatic roots of his work, these instances no longer manifest themselves in overtly melodramatic fashion, but are traced to often almost unnoticeable nuances of the most 'civilized' forms of social interaction. Asymmetries in relations – whether between representatives of Old World and New World, or in class and gender relations, between family members or members of the same social group, or between self and other – form the dramatic nucleus (or, to use his favourite term, 'germ') of his fiction. For James, social interaction is thus always potentially also a form of manipulation. His fiction offers a virtual inventory of the various forms such asymmetries and manipulations can take, as well as the complications resulting from them.[20] In fact, it seems that without them there simply would be no Jamesian fiction. James's fiction abounds in constellations of dominance and dependence, deception and duplicity, only to set such constellations in motion and test the possibilities of awareness and response they provoke. Moreover, by dramatizing the fact that seeing, the imagination, and the synthesizing activities of consciousness all play their own part in constituting experience, James links these various 'creative' faculties to the power plays which he considers social interaction and manipulation to be. Altogether, his fiction relentlessly investigates the fortunes and fates of social relations in all their possible states of imposition and coercion ranging from victimization to triumphant counter-manipulation.

Despite claims to the contrary, the work of James thus offers the most comprehensive study of social relations of any American writer of the nineteenth century (if not the twentieth century as well).[21] This heightened social awareness, which greatly surpasses that of his contemporaries and fellow realists, Howells and Twain, is tied, I think, to James's particular version of what could, in a wide sense of the word, be called the realist project. Such a link can, in turn, help to clarify the notoriously difficult status of James's 'realism'. Clearly, there is a tendency to narrow his realism down to a literary programme derived from, above all, French and Russian models of the period. In this limited sense, James became a (tentative and short-term) realist when he set out to imitate French models of realism, based, above all, on the 'reality effect' of verisimilitude.[22] After his 'realist' novels *The Bostonians* and *The Princess Casamassima* turned out to be failures, he gave up realism and returned to new experiments in the art of fiction which ultimately led to the modernist breakthrough. There is a broader, more comprehensive possibility, however, of defining the term realism, namely as an epistemological claim in which the perception of reality and the acquisition of knowledge are put on a new epistemological basis (and, as a consequence, linked with new literary strategies). What unites otherwise different writers of the realist period in American writing, such as Stoddard, Twain, Howells, and James, or the female local colour writers of the Northeast, is obviously not a common literary programme based on 'objectivity', 'representativeness', or 'verisimilitude', but a new epistemology in which experience replaces metaphysical speculation as the primary source of knowledge. In order to provide valid knowledge, however, this experience has to be socially shared and shareable. As long as individuals draw conclusions from their own experiences alone, they will always be in danger of falling prey to their imagination and thus remain 'transcendentalists'. It is social experience, then, which provides a 'test' of individual perceptions, as well as a need to give coherent shape to one's own impressions so that they can be communicated and compared.

One interesting point in tracing the history of American realism is to see how realist writers defined this element of social experience quite differently. For writers like Stoddard or the female local colourists, the social encounter is a source of 'unnameable' suggestions that initiate self-knowledge and self-development. For Twain, only the spontaneous, humorously charged social encounter provides knowledge, because the social is the site of the conventional, and hence needs to be 'defamiliarized' by humorous discrepancy or a collision of different worlds. Confrontational encounters therefore stand at the centre of his work; where the discrepancy in knowledge becomes too great, however, the result is an ultimately self-destructive solipsism. For Howells, knowledge emerges out of a carefully worked out system of conversations in which an event can be retrospectively discussed and assessed in its meaning.[23] What James shares with Howells – his close friend and fellow representative of the 'new American school' – is a reliance on the idea of social interaction as an act in which knowledge is not only exchanged, but literally created in the process of communication; what separates him from Howells, is his much greater awareness of the elements of domination and manipulation that are at work in these 'endless conversations' of social life. If social experience is pervaded by strategies of domination and coercion, however, then knowledge is constantly threatened. This, I think, is the reason why James so persistently screens social relations in search of elements of deception, coercion, exploitation, and victimization, and why he organizes his novels and tales around a whole phenomenology of social manipulation, ranging from breach of contract to the 'acquisition' of another person as part of one's own collection of precious objects.

So extensive is the connection between knowledge and social manipulation in James, in fact, that one eventually has to place him at the opposite end of Howells. For Howells, genuine knowledge emerges where social interaction is successful, so that, as Heinz Ickstadt has pointed out, the success of a social event such as a dinner conversation, or, more generally, the failure or success of courtship and marriage, can become his basic criterion for the possibility of communication – and thus of a consensus about social change – in America.[24] Where such communication fails, one result is a radicalization of Howells's views and of his work. For James, on the other hand, 'asymmetries' in social relations do not endanger knowledge, but become a driving force in the pursuit of knowledge and, in the process, a crucial source for the development of imaginary activities, the emergence of social awareness, and, through the refinement of consciousness, of the aesthetic sense. Although painful, experiences of manipulation can function, in other words, as an impetus of creative imaginative work and are, in this sense, 'productive' in unexpected ways. This is also the reason, I think, why James's stories are never mere melodramas. As a rule, they draw much of their gratification from a gradual rehierarchization of balances and symmetries in social relations. But the final triumph is not, as in traditional melodrama, the result of a transcendent law of moral retribution. It is 'earned' by the initially victimized individual in a painful process of growing awareness and expanding consciousness: because it is thus literally a triumph of a creativity provoked by social manipulation, this triumph – much to the chagrin and irritation of many, and especially of the younger readers of James who respond to the story of melodramatic victimization according to its emotional logic – has to remain 'mental' and cerebral in order to emphasize the elements of creativity over those of vengeance and retribution. Thus, Isabel can return to Osmond because the act of returning can signal the highest form of triumph over her melodramatic impulses.

Many of James's most interesting novels are centred in a recurring pattern in which the point of departure is that of a national or social asymmetry, in which the possibilities of deception and manipulation emerging from this constellation drive the narrative, and in which a promise of rehierarchization provides its conclusion. The starting-point is a character constellation James inherited from the genre which stands at the beginning of his career as a novelist, the domestic novel. One of its main elements consists of a male figure who acts as appointed or self-appointed guardian of a young and innocent (i.e. inexperienced) woman. In this recurring scenario, James's first novel *Watch and Ward* already establishes a pattern to which he returned time and again, although with interesting variations in plot and character relations. In each case, the courtship-and-marriage motif provides the basic narrative frame, not because James failed to liberate himself from outworn conventions, as an influential segment of criticism on American realism has it, but because, for James (as well as Howells), courtship and marriage illustrate the formation of a new, yet nascent social unit and dramatize the ensuing problems of choice, adequate perception, and the possibility of deception and dependence most forcefully. In *Watch and Ward*, for example, the young heroine, Nora, has to choose between two representative suitors, a virile, but morally crude Westerner, and an effete and dishonest Easterner. She reveals a lack of adequate knowledge of reality by failing to realize that her devoted, though unspectacular guardian, Roger Lawrence, is the only man in the universe 'who has a heart' and therefore the only fitting companion for her. Roger, however, although clearly in possession of superior moral insight, cannot further his own course, because this would constitute an act of manipulation. The heroine has to go through her own experiences, and she is left to do so because 'adequate perception of reality' in a domestic novel like *Watch and Ward* can only mean recovering one's own innate moral sense after a temporary flirt with passion. 'Experience' thus leads to a reaffirmation of the superior moral authority of the guardian-figure.

What makes *Watch and Ward* still an interesting novel, in spite of its thorough conventionality, is an early acknowledgment of self-interest and desire even in the representative of moral authority. When the frequently frustrated suitor, Roger Lawrence, adopts the orphan, Nora, he soon decides to raise her so that she can become his own bride when she comes of age. In the world of domestic fiction, this fantasy of possession can only be realized, however, if this 'selfish' wish is hidden behind a complete and unfailing show of unselfishness, which, as a consequence, becomes the domestic novel's privileged, because morally legitimized, mode of social manipulation. Already in *The American*, this possessive urge is acknowledged more openly, however, in the suitor and collector, Christopher Newman, who is attracted to Mme. de Cintré as the 'real' embodiment of culture in contrast to all the bad copies sold to him. Still, Newman's boisterous, good-natured pride of possession pales in comparison with the manipulative power and evil selfishness of the Bellegardes, so that this confident would-be guardian becomes the victim of a power encoded in social forms which he can hardly grasp. *Watch and Ward* and *The American* thus offer early versions of a narrative to which James returned again and again, above all in *The Portrait of a Lady* and his late novels *The Wings of the Dove* and *The Golden Bowl*. In *The Portrait of a Lady*, it is again the courtship pattern which serves as a testing ground for the possibilities of acquiring knowledge through experience. Experience in itself, however, is not enough. It only becomes productive when Isabel begins to process her observations by means of her imagination in her famous midnight vigil in chapter 42 of the novel. This is the moment when she begins to develop from a passive, incompetent reader of reality to a reader of heightened awareness – a gain which, in turn, is the basis for liberating herself from the manipulation to which she has been subject, so that, in the end, she can try to become the author of her own life.

There is a fourth figure in *The Portrait* who is already present in *Watch and Ward*, but has now changed her function completely. In place of an unselfish elder confidante, Mme. Merle has been transformed into a social competitor and the supreme manipulator of the novel. With this transformation, James has the character constellation for his late novels in place. From the point of view of the development of the guardian-figure, some of his well-known novels of the middle period offer fascinating experiments in rearranging the relations between guardian and ward. While in *The

Bostonians, both of the potential guardians of Verena turn out to be equally possessive and 'overpowering', *The Turn of the Screw* presents an ambiguous conflation of guardian-figure and developing subject in the person of the governess who, depending on the reading of the tale, is either an intruding, possessive guardian or a developing subject cut off from social experience and thus victim of her own overheated imagination. It is in the late novels, and especially in *The Golden Bowl*, however, that all the elements of social interaction with which James experimented throughout his career, are finally brought together. In this return to a basic theme and concern of his work, *The Wings of the Dove* establishes a basic shift in emphasis. The benevolent guardian becomes a remote, shadowy figure, while the scheming Old World couple gains in prominence so that the novel, in large parts, becomes the story of their manipulative skill, but also of their trials and tribulations. This does not take anything away from the innocent American, however, who not only reaches a 'breakthrough' in the awareness of the manipulation to which she has been exposed, but also acts on that knowledge in a way that, for the first time, constitutes a subtle imposition in reverse. By turning the tables on Densher and Kate Croy, Millie Theale reasserts the power of her own imagination and entraps them in an exceedingly clever and 'creative' scheme of her own.

These new elements in the 'spiritualized' melodrama of power relations in James are brought into a new symmetry in *The Golden Bowl*, where the benevolent guardian and father figure, Adam Verver, is moved back to the circle of actors; Kate Croy and Merton Densher have extremely skilful successors in Charlotte Stant and the Prince, and the American heroine finds a new life in a Maggie Verver who, for the first time in the history of that recurring character in the work of James, not only elevates renunciation to a high art, but lives up to Old World standards of social manipulation without losing her superior moral status. This, in fact, is the actual drama (and 'art') of *The Golden Bowl*: There are no longer any 'innocent' characters who are forced by experience to renounce their own part in the world. Instead, there is a circulation of social energies, set in motion by the assertion of social power through manipulation, which may 'corrupt' the innocent but, through their response, also provides a kind of moral regeneration to the manipulators. As a consequence, binary oppositions of good and evil, corruption and innocence, possession and freedom lose their explanatory power.[25] Instead, James unfolds an ongoing process of social interaction in which such moral oppositions remain open to semantic transformation by the constant possibility of a change of positions in the endless power game between the main characters of the novel.

This new reciprocity and exchange of semantic qualities has become possible because the main characters are no longer primarily moral representatives, but defined by social relations. As moral representative, a character may be part of a social network and be exposed to an ongoing series of social experiences; since the 'given' of these social encounters is an idea of the moral self that 'responds' to society, however, the awareness of being manipulated by others can only either result in acts of revenge or retreat, or lead to a melodramatic scenario of the corruption and 'fall' of the moral self. Where the self constitutes itself in, and through, interaction, on the other hand, the term 'manipulation' must lose its moral force and melodramatic connotation, and become part of the act of social interaction itself. Inevitably, to interact also means to manipulate. Seltzer is right: a radical redefinition of social interaction as, in the final analysis, inevitably manipulative and inherently possessive can thus also include expressions of love and caring. But, ironically enough, Seltzer is not as radical as James, because he retains a latent moralism in his tacit, unacknowledged equation of true knowledge with radical theory. Thus, in Seltzer's version of the social network as a disciplinary regime, the concept of the disciplinary carries unmistakable connotations of moral condemnation and implies the necessity of radical liberation; in fact, the clever claim that James and other major writers were unable to achieve such liberation is the whole point of the new historicist endeavour. For James, on the other hand, forms of imposition and coercion unfortunately, but inevitably, exist even in the most benevolent forms of social relations and are part of a network of exchange that literally 'creates' society. For Seltzer, theoretical awareness of the 'absent cause' might have liberated James from his apparent reproduction of the disciplinary practices of nineteenth-century realism; for James, Seltzer's book and his use of theory could only present the highly fascinating and hence admirably 'dramatic' spectacle of yet another 'power game', this time by means of 'critical theory' and Seltzer's constant appeal to a theoretical 'guardian-figure' named Foucault.

The long-established, endlessly repeated accusation of James's flight from moral and social commitment into the aestheticism of the late period stands at the beginning of Seltzer's challenge to James. The Jamesian redefinition of power relations in terms of 'moves', 'strategies', and 'power games' comes dangerously close, in Seltzer's view, to a reconceptualization of power relations in terms of performance, and thus, to an aestheticizing of social relations. For Seltzer, the aesthetic is not a separate realm distinct from the political, but only another, cleverly 'disguised' mode of it. Again, I think, however, that James is much more radical and aware of the problem than Seltzer is willing to acknowledge (because he wants to claim superior oppositional insights). One of the consequences of the sweeping redefinition of power in terms of subtly coercive and manipulative forms of social interaction must be that the aesthetic and the 'political' (in the sense of any exertion of social power) become inextricably intertwined. For, if social interaction is 'always already' potential manipulation, then it must be distinguished by the various forms and modes this manipulation takes, by how it is executed through form, in short, by the 'art' of manipulation (or, to use Seltzer's title, by the 'art of power'). James is very much aware of this 'contamination', so that *The Wings of the Dove*, but especially *The Golden Bowl*, are also, to a large extent, books about the 'art' of manipulation that, in the hands of Kate Croy, Charlotte Stant, but also Millie Theale and Maggie Verver, almost reach the level of a cultural accomplishment.

However, although James clearly sees (and repeatedly emphasizes) the close proximity of the aesthetic and the political, he never conflates them. Whereas Seltzer assumes a hidden identity, James insists on a difference, not because he wants to make a case for the 'autonomy of art', but because he does not want to give up the idea of the creative potential of interaction and, thus, of exchange. For the new cultural radicalism, art is the allegory of an 'absent cause', or systemic effect;[26] for James, it can also be an exemplary source of awareness that holds the promise of a liberation from victimization. It is this link with the possibility of awareness and, hence, with the possibility of a defence against coercion (and not a vague 'formalism') that explains James's increasing focus on the aesthetic dimension in fiction and makes his work one long, increasingly subtle meditation on the forms that would be best suited to fulfil the promise and function of the aesthetic.

As I have tried to show in a different context, in this ongoing reflection the relation between guardian and developing subject not only serves as a model of social relation, but also as a *mise en abyme* of the function of fiction, and, linked with it in James, of the aesthetic.[27] As long as the guardian-figure is defined as a moral authority exerting social control through 'ostentatious unselfishness', the implications for the novel must be to act as a guardian of the reader by giving plenty of room to a whole range of 'guilty pleasures' only to harness them the more effectively through a melodramatic sequence of imaginary indulgence, the threat of a loss of moral identity, and a final salvation by moral revelation. Where 'experience' becomes the main source of knowledge, on the other hand, as it does in *The Portrait of a Lady*, the novel must take back its own guidance and manipulation of the reader and expose him or her to a series of hypotheses that are then tentatively addressed by the novel, only to raise new questions and hypotheses and so on and so forth, so that the experience of 'reality' becomes, in tendency, that of being exposed to an open, ongoing process of interpretation. In order for this process to produce knowledge, however, the various sense impressions and individual observations have to add up to a coherent structure which convinces the observer of its representative nature and truth value by the 'rightness' of its shape and ordering power, that is, in the final analysis, by its aesthetic quality.[28] Paradoxically enough, James's 'demelodramatization' of reality and his opening up of the concept of reality through the idea of its processual character must thus also result in an increased importance of the idea of aesthetic structure as a criterion of knowledge. This transformation of the concept of reality from an initially moral definition to an ultimately performative one also explains why seeing and knowing are closely related in the work of James.

The increased importance of the aesthetic in James thus does not signify a growing retreat from life to the ivory tower. Quite the contrary, it is logically tied to the relentless self-investigation at work in his novels and tales which led him to first transform the domestic novel into the realist novel, as demonstrated in the transition from *Watch and Ward* to *The Portrait of a Lady*, and then, not in a break with the realist project but in a rigorous radicalization of its basic premises, to broaden the realist novel into the proto-modernist complexity of his major novels of the late period. This development has its own consistency: where, in contrast to domestic fiction, moral knowledge can no longer be secured through the moral authority of a guardian figure, it must be authorized by experience; experience, however, must be social experience, in order to provide a common ground of knowledge; social experience, in turn, must be processed by consciousness in order to make sense; finally, the *gestalt* in which this ordering takes shape must become a criterion of the adequateness of perception, so that knowledge acquires an increasingly performative, aesthetic dimension. This 'aestheticization', however, always remains in the service of the search for an adequate perception of reality. It does not present, in other words, a flight from the complexity of reality, but provides a new chance of intensifying one's awareness of it. And the same applies to questions of power: 'aesthetic transcendence' in James does not at all mean that one can avoid manipulation or asymmetry in relations by retreating to the ivory tower of artistry, but that the development of an 'aesthetic sense', that is, an expanded consciousness capable of linking isolated observations, is the only mode of perception 'creative' enough to realize the full extent of this manipulation. Hence, it is also the only form to provide the basis for a defence against it.

The fact that the 'aesthetic' thus becomes an essential criterion of knowledge for James does not mean that the aesthetic stands outside of power or transcends it. The aesthetic is not only an inevitable part of the ongoing power plays in social interaction, but also is especially useful for them. If the 'aesthetic sense' provides a version of reality that convinces by its *gestalt* quality and promise of an equilibrium, then such impressions can, in turn, be manipulated. In *The Golden Bowl*, 'symmetry' is a pattern that is repeatedly used by the characters to position the social actors within roles they have not sought for themselves and would rather escape. The 'beautiful symmetry' of the initial arrangement is a trap, a clever construction designed to deceive. Although they are indispensable for making social life possible, social and aesthetic forms are thus also potential forms of imposition. As many critics have shown, the novel is filled with intimations about affinities between economic practices and the aesthetic sense. But, in contrast to the new historicism, James also retains a sense of the aesthetic as 'intense creativity' in social life that redeems its manipulative potential, because it can also serve as a model of creative and productive self-assertion. When the symmetry of the original arrangement is reinstalled at the end of *The Golden Bowl*, its participants have been transformed as a result of an ongoing process of imaginary anticipation, creative response, and social rearrangement. 'Arrangement', as a word in which social and aesthetic goals coalesce, no longer refers to a static design, but suggests possibilities of reshaping and creative transformation.

The difference between these two possible functions lies in the definition of what constitutes the aesthetic for James: as long as the aesthetic is identified with a particular form or structure, such as symmetry, or a certain type of pattern, so that it can be recognized and used as a ready-made criterion of differentiation and hierarchization, it is reduced to taste and thus to a collector's definition of the aesthetic. This reduction of the aesthetic to taste is part of a system of dominance, illustrated in the figure of the collector Osmond and continuing to shape social relations at the beginning of *The Golden Bowl*, where the Ververs 'buy' Amerigo as precious addition to their Old-World collection. The 'aesthetic' way in which this entrapment is overcome and transformed, on the other hand, does not have a particular appearance or pattern to which it can appeal for authority. Rather, it is a mode of processing reality, and thus an activity within the social realm, not a beautiful object or structure standing apart from it. In its characteristic mode and indulgence of 'interminable elaboration', *The Golden Bowl* therefore acts out its own resistance to the manipulative potential of form.[29]

In this sense, the 'liberal' interpretation does more justice to James than the radical revision of recent years, which has effectively obscured his awareness of the close link between art and power in order to be able to put up a claim for superior oppositional insights. The difference between the Jamesian view and that of cultural radicalism does not lie in the denial of a relation between art and power, but in the different definitions of this relation and in the conclusions to be drawn from it. In order to define this difference as one between 'formalism' and a new historicism, cultural radicalism must trivialize James's aesthetics. It has suppressed any acknowledgment that the aesthetic in James is not tied to one particular form and function, but constitutes a creative social activity whose changing manifestations are dependent on the situation to which they respond. Interdependence, however, is not identity. In the binary logic of the new cultural radicalism, which can only admit an all-pervasive power, on the one side, and illusory counter-worlds such as love, desire, or art, on the other, the aesthetic is automatically trapped in the position of that which pretends to be non-power, so that it becomes an ideal object for unmasking invisible power effects.

Such a reconceptualization of art as power effect is a response to a certain kind of liberal appropriation of James, which has tried to legitimize the aesthetic by turning it into a superior source of moral philosophy centred around redemptive values such as 'depth', 'complexity', 'tragedy', 'love', 'the promise of life', 'mature self-awareness', and the 'fusion of form and idea'.[30] It is in the demystification and problematization of the liberal rewriting of James in terms of such naïve, essentially metaphysical concepts as humanity, universality, or love, that the radical revision has its strong point. In this sense, both approaches to James are complimentary. However, such an analysis of the liberal and the radical version of James in terms of potential reciprocity would point not to the need for another demystification of James, but to the full recovery of his insights.

NOTES

1 Ruth Bernard Yeazell, 'Demystifying the Master', *American Literary History*, 5 (1993), 314–25.
2 The formula 'compromised to the core' is taken from Frank Lentricchia's review of Carolyn Porter's *Seeing and Being: The Plight of the Participant Observer in Emerson, James, Adams, and Faulkner* (Middletown, Conn.: Wesleyan University Press, 1981), which was one of the first books to signal a new revisionist approach to the major American writers: 'Porter's interpretation reveals this wholly absorbing drama: major American authors earn their titles by writing penetrating radical critiques of our society even as those very same critiques show distressing signs of being compromised to the core by the society which they would alter. In other words, the force of Porter's book is political' (*American Literature*, 54 (1982), 445). This type of 'complicity-criticism' became the basic mode of procedure for almost all interpretations of the new revisionism in American literary history.
3 What Yeazell says about studies of James by Freedman and Posnock can be applied to the new revisionism as a whole: 'Both writers strenuously resist any attempt to understand the artist as somehow transcending the forces of his culture, a mystifying move that they identify with the triumph of high modernism' ('Demystifying the Master', 315).
4 Mark Seltzer, *Henry James and the Art of Power* (Ithaca: Cornell University Press, 1984), 24.
5 Initially, such studies focused, with varying degrees of acrimony, on James's ambivalent relation to the literary market and the newly emerging consumer capitalism. See, for example, Henry Nash Smith, *Democracy and the Novel: Popular Resistance to Classic American Writers* (New York: Oxford University Press, 1978); Marcia Jacobson, *Henry James and*

the Mass Market (Tuscaloosa: University of Alabama Press, 1983); Jean Christophe Agnew, 'The Consuming Vision of Henry James', in *The Culture of Consumption: Critical Essays in American History 1880–1980*, ed. Richard Wightman Fox and T. J. Jackson Lears (New York: Pantheon, 1983), 67–100; Michael Anesko, *'Friction with the Market': Henry James and the Profession of Authorship* (Oxford and New York: Oxford University Press, 1986); Daniel Borus, *Writing Realism: Howells, James, and Norris in the Mass Market* (Chapel Hill: University of North Carolina Press, 1989); Jonathan Freedman, *Professions of Taste: Henry James, British Aestheticism and Commodity Culture* (Stanford University Press, 1990). These studies bent on 'rehistoricizing' James were quickly out-radicalized, however, by readings inspired by the new historicism, which had their first and most radical manifestation in Mark Seltzer's study. See also Richard Godden, *Fictions of Capital: The American Novel From James to Mailer* (Cambridge University Press, 1990); Susan M. Griffin, *The Historical Eye: The Texture of the Visual in Late James* (Boston: Northeastern University Press, 1991): 'Because he sees historically, James participates, despite himself, in the very commodification of America that he condemns' (22); and Kenneth Warren, *Black and White Strangers: Race and American Literary Realism* (University of Chicago Press, 1993). In a review of some of the current studies of James, Lynn Wardley summarizes the recent development: 'James's essays and fiction were resituated within the context of politics of early twentieth-century race relations, commodity fetishism, and class interaction' in an attempt 'to gain distance from the critical phenomenon of "the Master"'. In this revision, 'one project being launched is to look again at familiar topics in James criticism . . . through the critical lenses provided by gay studies, feminism, and the new historicism . . . This is to say that recent work departs from a model of Henry James as the worldly intellectual on whom nothing is lost to construct a Henry James whose consciousness, and that of his protagonists, is structured by the cognitive rules and suppositions of an historically specific discourse' ('Henry James in the Nineties', *New England Quarterly*, 67 (1994), 142).

6 See John Carlos Rowe, *The Theoretical Dimensions of Henry James* (Madison: University of Wisconsin Press, 1984). For recent feminist readings, cf. Elizabeth Allen, *A Woman's Place in the Novels of Henry James* (New York: St. Martin's Press, 1984), Lynda S. Boren, *Eurydice Reclaimed: Language, Gender, and Voice in Henry James* (Ann Arbor: UMI Research Press, 1989), Peggy McCormack, *The Rule of Money: Gender, Class, and Exchange Economics in the Fiction of Henry James* (Ann Arbor: UMI Research Press, 1990), and Priscilla L. Walton, *The Disruption of the Feminine in Henry James* (University of Toronto Press, 1992). As a rule, these readings see James consciously and subconsciously subverting patriarchal values, whereas Alfred Habegger finds James's work infused with anti-feminism and patriarchal ideology and tied to an 'elusive male

authoritarianism' (*Henry James and the Woman Business* (Cambridge University Press, 1989), 7, 26). For Ross Posnock, James pursues a politics of non-identity by dissolving the stable oppositions that define selfhood as a discrete and intelligible entity (*The Trial of Curiosity: Henry James, William James, and the Challenge of Modernity* (New York: Oxford University Press, 1991), 103). Generally, one may say with Dietmar Schloss: 'The works of Henry James provided a feast for the critical avant-garde of the seventies and eighties' (*Culture and Criticism in Henry James* (Tübingen: Narr, 1992), 1).

7 Schloss, *Culture and Criticism*, 1.
8 Both essays can be found in Trilling's collection *The Liberal Imagination: Essays on Literature and Society* (Garden City, N.Y.: Doubleday, 1953), 1–19, 199–215. Within American intellectual history, these essays were crucial in the attempt to dissociate liberal thought from the authority of V. L. Parrington and the left liberalism exemplified by his monumental *Main Currents in American Thought*. For an interesting discussion of personal and social reasons for the importance of James for Trilling, see Jonathan Freedman, 'Trilling, James, and the Uses of Cultural Criticism', *Henry James Review*, 14 (1993), 141–50.
9 Trilling, 'Reality in America', in *The Liberal Imagination*, 8.
10 Ibid., 9.
11 Trilling, 'Manners, Morals, and the Novel', in *The Liberal Imagination*, 213, 215.
12 Metaphors of a 'depth' that contains a hidden truth are thus shared by liberalism and the recent forms of radicalism. The difference lies in what the two positions want to find in that subterranean fundament of reality: while the liberal post-war vision looks for 'tragic' manifestations of humanity, the new radicalism looks for an 'absent cause' that generates structures of power. For the one, art is the privileged mode of access to that depth, for the other, critical theory.
13 Trilling, 'Manners, Morals, and the Novel', in *The Liberal Imagination*, 215.
14 Similar arguments can be found in readings of James by other well-known exponents of American liberalism of the time, such as Philip Rahv or, later, Irving Howe. See Philip Rahv, 'Attitudes to Henry James', *New Republic*, 15 February 1943, 220–4; Irving Howe, *Politics and the Novel* (New York: Horizon, 1957), 139–56, 182–200. In a less politically minded way, focusing more on the affirmation of universal human values, Blackmur and Matthiessen contribute to the same liberal argument. See R. B. Blackmur, 'Henry James', in *The Literary History of the United States*, ed. Robert Spiller *et al.* (New York: Macmillan, 1948), 1039–64; F. O. Matthiessen, *Henry James: The Major Phase* (New York: Oxford University Press, 1944).
15 In doing so, it takes its cue from Herbert Marcuse's concept of repressive tolerance, which had re-emerged in Sacvan Bercovitch's

argument about the shrewd containment effected by a liberal rhetoric of consensus (*The Rites of Assent: Transformations in the Symbolic Construction of America* (New York: Routledge, 1993)).

16 Mark Seltzer, *Henry James and the Art of Power*, 13–14.
17 Ibid., 15, 16, 24. All further references to Seltzer are given parenthetically in the text.
18 The Jamesian may note here a reference to two classical liberal interpretations of James. As early as 1957, Frederick C. Crews had written of *The Golden Bowl*: 'The subject of the novel, in my opinion, is power' (*The Tragedy of Manners: Moral Drama in the Later Novels of Henry James* (New Haven: Yale University Press, 1958), 85). In typical liberal fashion, Crews, however, had looked for the 'true motivation' of the characters' power games in a detailed discussion of their different social conditions. 'Love', on the other hand, evokes Dorothea Krook's reading of *The Golden Bowl* as 'a great fable – one of the greatest in modern European literature – of the redemption of man by the transforming power of human love' (*The Ordeal of Consciousness in Henry James* (Cambridge University Press, 1962), 240).
19 On this point, see Richard Brodhead's analysis of the domestic novel as a disciplinary strategy (*Cultures of Letters: Scenes of Reading and Writing in Nineteenth-Century America* (University of Chicago Press, 1993), 13–47).
20 For an excellent discussion of social relations in James see Paul B. Armstrong's chapter on *The Golden Bowl* (*The Phenomenology of Henry James* (Chapel Hill: University of North Carolina Press, 1983), 136–86).
21 This may look like a bold claim in view of the fact that James usually focuses on a narrow, exclusive social circle and hardly deals with the working classes. Indeed, James starts out at a much more elementary social level, the moment when society emerges out of the need of the individual to establish social relations – which is also the moment of potential manipulation, deception, and subtle coercion. In the description of this process of 'socialization', James offers something like a comprehensive phenomenology of social relations. Thus, 'what James calls "the fundamental fewness" of his characters acts more as a help than a hindrance for exploring the relation between Self and Other, because this very economy emphasizes the variety of problems and possibilities inherent in that relation' (Armstrong, *Phenomenology of Henry James*, 136). In comparison, novels dealing with the working classes are narrowly focussed in their descriptions of social relations, because they usually restrict themselves to two types: class oppression and class solidarity. From a Jamesian point of view, however, social groups created by ideas such as solidarity are as endangered by processes of deception and manipulation as are groups engaged in other relations. If socialist intellectuals had not suppressed this knowledge, they might have saved themselves from the fate of becoming unwitting accomplices of such practices.

22 Cf., for example, Richard Brodhead's 'James, Realism, and the Politics of Style' in his otherwise excellent book *The School of Hawthorne* (New York: Oxford University Press, 1986), 140–65.

23 I am referring to the description of the Howellsian novel by Heinz Ickstadt:

> It seems therefore possible to rephrase Howells' theory of realism in terms of a theory of communication. To be sure, it was the business of the novelist to make people 'understand the real world through its faithful effigy of it' but also 'to arrange a perspective . . . with everything in its proper relation and proportion to everything else'. To represent reality (i.e. 'life as one has *seen* and *known* and *felt* it') was to reveal in the experience of it an innate 'perfect principle' – a principle that Howells variously identified as shared tradition, as shared ideal of conduct, or as belief in human nature 'that . . . is the same under all masks and disguises that modern conditions have put upon it.' The very experience of reality is thus based on common faith and confirmed by consensus. It is a consensus established *in* the novel through conversation and debate, and *by* the novel in the act of reading which was to help people know themselves and one another better, so that they might all be 'humbled and strengthened with a sense of their fraternity'

('Concepts of Society and the Practice of Fiction: Symbolic Responses to the Experience of Change in Late Nineteenth Century America', in *Impressions of a Gilded Age: The American Fin de Siècle*, ed. Marc Chénetier and Rob Kroes (Amsterdam: Universiteit Amsterdam, 1983), 85).

24 Cf. Ickstadt's lucid characterization: 'The inner space of communication, for Howells, always has ideal implications. Where it works democracy is experienced in the free exchange of opinions, right conduct affirmed or redefined in rational discourse, experience reflected in dialogue. When conversation deteriorates or collapses, a deeper crisis is always indicated – many of his novels are centred in such catastrophes of communication' ('Concepts of Society', 86).

25 The more Maggie triumphs, the more complicated our attitude towards her becomes: 'In the second half, as she increasingly becomes the most knowledgeable character in the drama, our feelings for her undergo a strange transformation. We both respect her more (because she's intelligent) and pity her more (because she perceives she's been betrayed); but, as she begins to use this knowledge to alter her situation, we also begin to draw back from – what to call it? – her exercise of power, her manipulation, her emotional tyranny' (Wendy Lesser, *His Other Half: Men Looking At Women Through Art* (Cambridge, Mass.: Harvard University Press, 1991), 102–3).

26 On the crucial role of the idea of an 'absent cause' in the new cultural radicalism, see the excellent analysis by Wolfram Schmidgen, 'The Principle of Negative Identity and the Crisis of Relationality in Contemporary Literary Criticism', *REAL: Yearbook of Research in English and American Literature*, 11 (1995), 371–403.

27 See my essay 'Declarations of Dependence: Revising Our View of

American Realism', in *Victorianism in the United States: Its Era and Legacy*, ed. Steve Ickringill and Stephen Mills (Amsterdam: VU University Press, 1992), 19–34.

28 Cf. Sergio Perosa's characterization of James's view of the potential of the novel: 'If art is for him essentially form, construction, architecture, and composition, it aims at something other than the mimetic and, ultimately, at the non-representative. It does not reflect or represent life but transforms it, fixes it into something different. Art involves the coherence of parts, life fluidity' ('James, Tolstoy and the Novel', *Revue de Littérature Comparée*, 57 (1983), 364–5).

29 Significantly, in the case of *The Golden Bowl*, Seltzer must base his new historicist argument that power and literature resemble and reinforce each other as cultural practices through a homology of form on the vague concept of 'organic form'.

30 For a helpful survey of the critical reception see R. B. J. Wilson, *Henry James's Ultimate Narrative: The Golden Bowl* (London: University of Queensland Press, 1981), 13–39.

CHAPTER 2

Multiple germs, metaphorical systems, and moral fluctuation in 'The Ambassadors'
Richard A. Hocks

A remarkable feature of Henry James's great novel, *The Ambassadors*, is that its genesis and composition bespeak his unprecedented 'ease' and sense of assurance regarding its artistic merit, yet the novel's central 'register' of consciousness, Lambert Strether, the figure who carries all the weight of James's easeful composition and comprises the medium for James's artistic unity, is a character in opposition to those very elements suggested by his creation: burdened with regrets and ambiguity, 'groping' for interpretation, bewildered by his experiences, Strether morally fluctuates in his need 'to be right'. An analogous contradiction is that Strether's ambassadorial power, delegated by Mrs Newsome, is systematically frittered away so that other ambassadors arrive to replace him, whereas James himself rejoices at his successful delegation of artistic consciousness to Strether, a favourite among his fictional 'deputies'. To see whether this general feature of *The Ambassadors* evokes any sense of difficulty or is merely an erroneous confusion between subject-matter and craftsmanship, it may help to re-enact the essential history of the book's composition and gradually inquire into Strether's predicament.

I. MULTIPLE GERMS

One of the better-known cases in American literature of a single generative incident which gave rise to a major novel is the famous 'germ' of *The Ambassadors*, when William Dean Howells stood in a Parisian garden owned by James McNeill Whistler sometime in 1894 and declared to his young thirty-year-old *confrère*, Jonathan Sturges, 'Live. Live all you can: it's a mistake not to.' Rarely has a single genetic source so successfully initiated and eventually pervaded a hefty novel, playing itself out in multiple directions and culminating in what James later called 'frankly, quite the best, "all round", of all my productions' (*LC*-II, 1306).¹ Besides its being James's last novel published serially, *The Ambassadors* is also the only James novel with a surviving prose Scenario, sent to Harper's in 1900 and entitled 'Project of Novel', a document the novelist himself in a letter to H.G. Wells two years later wrongly believed was destroyed.²

It may surprise even readers familiar with this book and some of its vast scholarship to realize that there are probably more than half a dozen extant versions of the 'germ', some before the novel, one within it, and some after it. To be sure, the actual number of versions depends, as such things generally do, on how you count. The *very* first version of the 'germ' speech is, of course, not preserved, because it was related to James by Sturges. But whatever Howells actually said to Sturges in McNeill Whistler's garden was less than what James said in his first entry in his *Notebooks* 18 months later, 31 October 1895: '"Oh, you are young, you are young – be glad of it: be glad of it and *live*. Live all you can: it's a mistake not to. It doesn't so much matter what you do – but live. This place makes it all come over me. I see it now. I haven't done so – and now I'm old. It's too late. It has gone past me – I've lost it. You have time. You are young. Live!"' (*CN*, 141). James immediately adds, 'I amplify and improve a little – but that was the tone. It touches me – I can see him – I can hear him.' Henry James, I dare say, not only 'hears' Howells, he already begins to reinvent Howells's outburst on the spot; he responds with more than Wordsworthian 'wise passiveness' to the impulse transmitted by Sturges's account the previous evening. By the end of his productive 'self-talk', James has come a surprisingly long way into his 'Howellsian' character and situation, all in the space of roughly 1,400 words; the man is a widower, coming out to retrieve the son of a widow to whom he is engaged to be married; he is fifty-five; he undergoes a total 'volte-face' of his mission; he feels the 'dumb passion of desire' even though 'it's too late, too late *now*, for HIM to live'; he is 'literary almost . . . The Editor of a Magazine . . . not at all of a newspaper.' James even thinks in terms of the tale's burgeoning genre, of his 'deepen[ing] the irony, the tragedy' (*CN*, 141–2).

James initially conceives the ambience of his character's situation to be one of sorrow, of tragedy, and irony. Later he will add more consciously the element of comedy to the novel. To this day, however, all readers and critics alike of *The Ambassadors* have to deal with its beautifully mixed tonal mode. Like *Don Quixote*, which elicits

its 'hard' and 'soft' readings, each of which may go in and out of fashion, *The Ambassadors* can modulate from a sort of Freudian 'Mourning and Melancholia' text to a sharp comedy of manners tethered to curiosity, bewilderment, miscalculation, and misinterpretation – somewhat like Molière. James preserves this mixed mode right to the very last lines of the novel itself, when we read that Maria Gostrey 'sighed it at last, all comically, all tragically, away' (*AB*, II, 327; bk. 12, ch. 5). Her 'sigh', we might well say, started all the way back with his, the man in the garden's, in the earliest versions of the germ. Et in Arcadia Ego.

The third germ comes from James's remarkable 'Project of Novel', the 20,000-word Scenario sent in the autumn of 1900 to Harper & Brothers after his agent, James B. Pinker, had first seen it. Partly because of its length and amplitude, James's 'Project of Novel' is an extraordinary piece of writing, at times resembling one of his own nouvelles, at other moments reminding the reader, almost with a jolt, that this 'text' is actually an extended statement to his publisher, yet one which also resembles the procreative self-talk found in the *Notebooks*. Indeed, Martha Banta's observation ten years ago about James's notebooks generally, that they reveal his 'access to the writer's workplace' and the 'principle of rank organicism let loose upon the world', is exemplified to a high degree in the 'Project of Novel'.[3] Our responding to it as a creative work is salutary, I think, if only to turn our minds away momentarily from the sort of issue we usually attend to, such as Waymarsh's name being 'Waymark' or Little Bilham's being 'Burbage', or such matters as Strether's young son having died in a swimming accident, or that the 'vulgar article of domestic use' produced by Mr Newsome in Hartford or Worcester (not yet Woollett) is 'to be duly specified' – which of course it never was (*CN*, 547). These issues, I say, are momentarily put aside if we attend instead just to the way James conceives and moulds his main character, allows Strether's consciousness to unfold, then punctuates the Scenario with clusters of dialogue between Strether and Gostrey, Strether and Chad, Strether and Marie, simulating in advance and in miniature the picture/scene modulation which is a hallmark of *The Ambassadors* itself. If one has ever spent much time studying James's tales, his 'Project of Novel', I would argue, really 'wants to' act like a tale and either cannot quite do it, or else all but does it, depending on your emphasis. James divides the Scenario into a formal prologue followed by three numbered untitled sections of symmetrical length, each corresponding to successive stages in Strether's experience and burdensome discoveries. Such structuring and numbering, together with its spider-like descent into the web of Strether's mind, is what makes the Scenario reminiscent of a Jamesian tale. The one major ingredient missing, however, is his rich imagery, the highly metaphorical language of James in 1900, the same year, for example, that he penned 'The Great Good Place', with its abstract language in tandem with highly charged metaphors and conceits. This lack of such imagery – there is hardly any in the Scenario – is mainly what prevents me from suggesting that 'Project of Novel' is to *The Ambassadors* what the Rembrandt sketch, let us say, is to the major oil canvas. What makes one think of the analogy, however, is the obvious parallel of a major artist doing in effect something like a preliminary sketch.

In this Scenario we actually get two statements of the germ, thus constituting versions three and four in my count. The first and richer of the two comprises the entire prologue, which suggests that, structurally speaking, the prologue stands in relation to the three numbered untitled sections that follow pretty much as does the Scenario itself to the composed novel. In any case, James now formally identifies the episode as 'my starting-point' and 'the germ of my subject'. The incident now is far more delineated than in 1895. First of all, he carefully evokes the Sunday afternoon garden party and meticulously explains the geography and architecture of the 'old houses of the Faubourg St.-Germain', identifying the residence and garden both of McNeill Whistler (here called simply 'a friend of mine') and also a very similar house 'contiguous' with it in which James himself had spent considerable time. This careful preliminary description soon gives rise to a cascade of personal associations and memories analogous to the nostalgic mood and ambience out of which the 'anecdote' of the older 'distinguished and mature' man's lament to the younger man bursts forth. James reads into the Howells figure the pith and precision of his character's emotion, calling it at one point a sense of seductive European charm that – for an American – 'was practically as new, as up-to-that-time-unrevealed (as one may say) as it was picturesque and agreeable' (*CN*, 541–2). Gradually he approaches the speech by writing:

Well, this is what the whole thing, as with a slow rush the sense of it came over him, made him say: 'Oh, *you're* young, you're blessedly young – be glad of it; be glad of it and *live*. Live all you can: it's a mistake not to. It doesn't so much matter what you do – but live. This place and these impressions . . . that I've been receiving and that have had their abundant message, make it all come over me. I see it now. I haven't done so enough before – and now I'm old; I'm, at any rate, too old for what I see. Oh, I *do* see, at least – I see a lot. It's too late. It has gone past me. I've lost it. It couldn't, no doubt, have been different for me – for one's life takes a form and holds one: one lives as one can. But the point is that *you* have time. That's the great thing. You're, as I say, damn you, so luckily, so happily, so hatefully young . . . Don't, at any rate, make *my* mistake. Live!' (*CN*, 542–3).[4]

James immediately comments, 'I amplify and improve a little, but that was the essence and the tone.' These words, of course, are the identical ones he spoke to himself five years earlier, prompted by Sturges' anecdote. Clearly, each time he 'amplifies and improves a little' his inch turns into a more extended ell and he guesses still more of the unseen from the seen. In any case, he summarizes the germ-episode and concludes his prologue by referring to the foregoing as the 'dropped seed' from which 'the real magic of the *right* things' was 'to spring' (*CN*, 543). This seems to be a Jamesian template for genesis, composition, and nascent interpretation all together.

There is also a briefer second version of the germ in the Scenario – my number four (or your number three if you wish to designate the actual Sturges conversation with Howells the 'ur-text'). It occurs in Scenario section II, its placement co-ordinating with its mid-point stage in the plot. James refers to the 'very special note . . . alluded to in my few preliminary pages' – i.e. earlier in the prologue (*CN*, 556). He alludes again, too, to ' "do"[ing] the occasion and the picture', 'evok[ing] the place and influences', and he also speaks of Strether as our 'fermenting friend', and of the moment charged with 'wonderful intensity . . . a real date' (*CN*, 557).

A number of intriguing issues engage the James critic when he or she puts down this Scenario and thinks about the novel. None of them is really independent of the originating germ because of its extraordinary interconnection with all that occurs in the book it brought forth. Yet one can, surely, distinguish between certain ideas that are more or less emphasized in the Scenario and the novel respectively. For example, James makes a great point of saying he must, and will, 'do' Mrs Newsome in the novel, though she never directly appears; and all readers agree that is just what he did. On the other hand, he does a superb job of summarizing and specifying all the advantages that Strether stands to lose if he sides with Chad and Marie away from Mrs Newsome and Sarah Pocock, whereas in the novel itself the particularity of that sacrifice has to be mostly inferred by the reader, except for one episode on Chad's balcony, in which the young man, apparently testing the waters for any cupidity in Strether (and finding none), alludes suggestively to all that Strether will have to renounce. Chad is suggestive, yes, but not comprehensive nor with James's own solidity of specification found in the Scenario. The key here was James's committed point of view: that is, Strether's character as 'deputy' throughout the story virtually disallows such specific massing together of his own advantages-in-jeopardy, because Strether has no more fundamental drive for worldly goods than has, say, Merton Densher in *The Wings of the Dove*.

Another important feature for one who comes to the Scenario with both the novel and the 1895 notebook entry in mind is that James is marrying a comedy of manners to the book's melancholia. That is, he continues to speak of Strether as 'rueful', and the proposed work as '[t]he whole comedy, or tragedy, the drama, whatever we call it' (*CN*, 564). The plot-directed reversals begin to cascade, the second wave of ambassadors arrives, 'Waymark' finally gets his second wind with Sarah, Jim Pocock is ready to live all *he* can – these and many other similar elements achieve that Quixote-like suspension referred to earlier, as the comic personality of the book competes with its originating meditative theme of 'too late', found back in James's February 1895 Notebook. Such competing moods, however, do not change James's hope, at the end of the Scenario, that this work would possess the structure and, one assumes, the beauty of 'a rounded medallion, in a series of a dozen hung, with its effect of high relief, on a wall' (*CN*, 575–6). Considering his eventual judgment of the work and its effective twelve-book structure, one must assume James believed he had indeed crafted some such medallion-like series – despite, for instance, the continuing scholarly dispute about the alleged reversal of chapters 28 and 29 in the first American and New York Editions, a debate most recently joined by Jerome McGann. Since the dispute inevitably involves the question of temporal sequence, perhaps its lesson is to remind us that, in late James, much of the 'main' action occurs retrospectively, is recollected in the mind at a sometimes unspecified 'future' moment. Right or wrong, McGann's hypothesis makes us appreciate the non-linear element within James's late narrative method.[5]

II. METAPHORICAL SYSTEMS

The fifth version of the germ is, of course, the fully realized episode in the second chapter of Book Fifth of *The Ambassadors*. When a reader examines this powerful moment in the novel itself on the heels of studying the October 1895 notebook entry and then the prologue to the 1900 Scenario, he or she perforce is struck by the evolving progression of all three versions. First, the preliminary ambience of the occasion stressed by James in the Scenario is now extended and distributed over the first chapter of Book Fifth and half-way into the second; Strether is given ample time to imbibe the seductive charm of the visual scene in Gloriani's garden, of letting the 'rather grey interior' of his mind 'drink in for once the sun of a clime not marked in his old geography' (*AB*, 1, 196–7; bk. 5, ch. 1). James follows this with the impact of Strether's introduction to Madame de Vionnet, who impresses him as has no one since his arrival from America except, quite arguably, the transformed Chad himself, who immediately whisks her away after Strether receives the full measure of her charming presence, leaving him alone once more with Little Bilham and thus ready to deliver the germ speech.

The speech in *The Ambassadors*, far more than in the Scenario, has the character of a full soliloquy, except that Little Bilham's presence, of course, disqualifies it technically as soliloquy. James, as the poet says, loads his rift with ore, principally by interlacing the rhetorical stages of the speech with figurative language presumably welling out from Strether because of the emotion and intensity of the moment.

It's not too late for *you*, on any side, and you don't strike me as in danger of missing the train; besides which people can be in general pretty well trusted, of course – with the clock of their freedom ticking as loud as it seems to do here – to keep an eye on the fleeting hour. All the same don't forget that you're young – blessedly young; be glad of it on the contrary and live up to it. Live all you can; it's a mistake not to. It doesn't so much matter what you do in particular, so long as you have your life. If you haven't had that what *have* you had? . . . I see it now. I haven't done so enough before – and now I'm old; too old at any rate for what I see. Oh I *do* see, at least; and more than you'd believe or I can express. It's too late. And it's as if the train had fairly waited at the station for me without my having had the gumption to know it was there. Now I hear its faint receding whistle miles and miles down the line. What one loses one loses; make no mistake about that. The affair – I mean the affair of life – couldn't, no doubt, have been different for me; for it's at the best a tin mould, either fluted and embossed, with ornamental excrescences, or else smooth and dreadfully plain, into which, a helpless jelly, one's consciousness is poured – so that one 'takes' the form, as the great cook says, and is more or less compactly held by it: one lives in fine as one can. Still, one has the illusion of freedom; therefore don't be, like me, without the memory of that illusion . . . Do what you like so long as you don't make *my* mistake. For it was a mistake. Live! (*AB*, I, 217–18; bk. 5, ch. 2)[6]

Apart from the pacing of this speech (James says, 'with full pauses and straight dashes, Strether had so delivered himself' (*AB*, I, 218; bk. 5, ch. 2)) and the iterative use of the word 'mistake' somewhat like incremental repetition in poetry, it is the striking insertion of the metaphors which seem to bind this moment to the novel as a whole, thus collaborating James's view that the germ stretches out from one end of the book to the other. For example, the train that Strether laments to have missed, even though it awaited him past departure time, so to speak, is finally 'caught' by him later in Book Eleventh ('selected almost at random', says the text (*AB*, II, 245; bk. 11, ch. 3)) when he rides it to the French countryside and eventually chances upon Chad and Madame de Vionnet in an attitude inferring their sexual intimacy, thereby collapsing his own elevated interpretation of what Little Bilham has called their 'virtuous attachment'. In other words, the train metaphor points directly across the canvas of the novel to its great recognition/meditation scene, which, reminiscent of Isabel Archer's all-night vigil in *The Portrait of a Lady*, might likewise be described with James's language from the later Preface to *The Portrait* as, 'obviously the best thing in the book, but . . . only a supreme illustration of the general plan' (*LC*-II, 1084). Next, the metaphor of the 'great cook' and his 'tin mould' for ornamental jellied dishes, although its immediate function is surely to represent the limitations of free agency, is another image that extends across the entire book in both directions, establishing connection with Strether's series of meals that act as benchmarks of his European apprenticeship. First there is his recollection of dining out back home with Mrs Newsome during the excitement of his very different evening dinner in Book Second at his London hotel with Maria Gostrey, whose dress is '"cut down"', as he believed the term to be, in respect to shoulders and bosom, in a manner quite other than

Mrs. Newsome's' (*AB*, I, 50; bk. 2, ch. 1). Then there is the soft sensual meal later on the left bank with Madame de Vionnet in Book Seventh after he runs into her by accident at Notre Dame Cathedral, a meal that marks still greater initiation away from the Puritan tone of his evenings out with Mrs Newsome and also, to Strether's own surprise, distancing him even from his London outing with Maria Gostrey. Still later, there is the meal set for him by the hostess at the Cheval Blanc in the rustic village Strether wanders into in Book Eleventh. He is 'hungry', has worked up an 'appetite', and is told by the hostess that 'she had in fact just laid the cloth for two persons who, unlike Monsieur, had arrived by the river – in a boat of their own'. Strether is even offered 'a "bitter" before his repast' (*AB*, II, 254; bk. 11, ch. 3). It culminates in the awkward meal he shares with Chad and Marie de Vionnet after he accidentally espies them, 'too prodigious, a chance in a million', in the boat together, after which all three must sit down to eat (*AB*, II, 257; bk. 11, ch. 4). His 'bitter' thus becomes his 'repast', so to speak, and the three eventually continue the charade, though thinly, by riding back to the city on the train. No wonder Strether later that evening in meditation thinks of Chad and Marie's make-believe as 'disagree[ing] with his spiritual stomach' (*AB*, II, 265; bk. 11, ch. 4).

The tin-mould metaphor functions also, however, as the principal signifier of consciousness and freedom, or more properly, as both the limitations and felt experiences of human freedom. James chooses the germ speech itself as the repository within the novel to embed the book's central philosophical question, whether or not we act as free agents. Strether is, of course, a character, not the author, and yet a certain number of readers tend to read this book as in part a kind of spiritual autobiography. Even if one does not identify Strether all that closely with James, one does sense that at least these particular statements about the nature of consciousness and freedom are, for James, unusually authorial. But, then again, when Strether goes on to say, 'don't be, like me, without the memory of that illusion', we feel we *are* back with the character, with the 'mature and distinguished man' who originated, distantly, in Howells. The concept of there being varying degrees of fixed sensibility and consciousness, from plain to ornamental, in tandem with the concept of freedom as illusion, is an intricately mediating philosophical stance between the traditional competing arguments of freedom and determinism; and it answers remarkably to the nuanced position taken by Henry

James's brother William James in his philosophical doctrines.[7] What should be stressed in this regard is that Henry James's philosophical 'indeterminism', to appropriate William James's term, is given credence not only by the sheer variety of consciousnesses and the positive side of freedom as an actual, functioning illusion, but also by the emphatically 'chance' encounters that transpire in the novel, such as Strether's encounter with Marie at Notre Dame or with the couple in the boat at Cheval Blanc at the end of a train 'selected almost at random'. With its metaphorical systems, *The Ambassadors* seems composed like a web in which, when you 'touch' in one place, the entire design vibrates.

What James has done with the germ speech in the novel, then, is to take the all-too-human moment and weave his philosophical, thematic, and psychological values onto it through a poetics of metaphor and motif, a process suggesting those linked 'medallions' he hoped for in his Scenario to Harper's. Even the metaphor of the clock, whose loud ticking Strether associates with freedom, is implicitly a complex image consistent with these ideas above: for while the clock is rhetorically associated with the free European life, as opposed to New England constriction, the self-same image is psychologically associated with the speaker's feeling that for him it is 'too late', which is precisely why the clock ticks so loud. The sense that Strether cannot ultimately transcend his own temperament – which is also the sense in which 'the illusion of freedom' sounds its negative side – is captured at the end of the novel in Book Twelfth, when Strether humorously compares himself and his adventure to one of the figures on the clock in Berne, Switzerland, who came out on one side, 'jigged along their little course in the public eye, and went in on the other side' (*AB*, II, 322; bk. 12, ch. 5). Like the actual train rides compared to the metaphorical trains, the Berne clock diminishes the expectations of free autonomy proposed by the ticking metaphorical clock. Despite his sense of new personal freedom after he disembarks from America, despite his fermenting declaration to live, despite his cultivating European appetite, Strether cannot transcend his own temperament, even though his, fortunately, is one greatly embossed and not at all dreadfully plain. No wonder Emerson in his great bittersweet essay 'Experience' denominated 'temperament' as one of the 'lords of life' that will not brook transcendence.

The sixth and seventh versions of the germ reside briefly in two letters to Howells, written exactly a year apart in 1900 and 1901. He speaks of the work as 'lovely – human, dramatic, international, exquisitely "pure", exquisitely everything; only absolutely condemned, from the germ up, to be workable in not less than 100,000 words' (*HJL*, IV, 160). 'From the germ up' insinuates the same sense of ease and frictionless composition found again and again with *The Ambassadors*. The second letter to Howells comes after James has completed the novel and sent it off to Harper's. This statement – my number seven – is also the one in which he finally declares to Howells that he himself was the germ-source.

James now expounds in his own way a curious paradox about his creative process: that Howells is at once deeply disconnected from the novel while, in another sense, and only after the fact, very much connected with it. '[M]y point', he says, 'is that it had long before – it had in the very act of striking me as a germ – got away from *you* or from anything like you! had become impersonal and independent. Nevertheless', James continues, 'your initials figure in my little note; and if you hadn't said the five words to Jonathan [Sturges] he wouldn't have had them (most sympathetically and interestingly) to relate, and I shouldn't have had them to work in my imagination. The moral is that you are responsible for the whole business' (*HJL*, IV, 199). Both sides of this alchemic equation are rather compelling. That is, Howells had turned into the 'distinguished and mature' literary man almost immediately in James's gestation process. At the same time, James's half-humorous insistence that Howells is 'responsible' for it all reaffirms the deep and mysterious sense of life's interconnectedness. Philosophically speaking, it is William James's definition of unity as residing in conjunction, contiguity, and ambulation through every intervening part of experience rather than transcendence; dramatically, it is one with Strether's lament and defense to Sarah Pocock's accusations that '[e]verything has come as a sort of indistinguishable part of everything else' (*AB*, II, 200–1; bk. 10, ch. 3); genetically, it is the recognition that the initials 'W. D. H.' in his 1895 notebook entry signal an initiating germ whose metamorphosis extended all the way through to the completion of the novel.[8]

The eighth and final version of the germ is found in James's New York Preface to *The Ambassadors*, written in 1909. This last version is, in one sense, the most exuberant commentary, primarily because James, in rereading the novel, was struck afresh by the sheer extent to which the initiating germ permeates the book from one end to the other. In no other Preface does he speak like this: '[n]othing is more easy than to state the subject of "The Ambassadors"', or '[n]othing can exceed the closeness with which the whole fits again into its germ', or '[n]ever can a composition of this sort have sprung straighter from a dropped grain of suggestion', or 'never can that grain, developed, overgrown and smothered, have yet lurked more in the mass as an independent particle' (*LC*-II, 1304–5). And so he takes us yet again to Strether's 'irrepressible outburst' to Little Bilham in Gloriani's garden on Sunday afternoon, this time rendering the germ speech from bits and combinations of language found in the 1895 Notebook, the prologue to the Scenario, and from the novel itself, although much reduced and hence considerably diminished in size from the novel's extended 'soliloquy'. James reiterates the point that he can remember 'no occasion on which, so confronted [with a germ], I had found it of a livelier interest to take stock, in this fashion, of suggested wealth'. For this reason he concludes that '[f]ortunately thus I am able to estimate this as, frankly, quite the best, "all round", of all my productions' (*LC*-II, 1305–6). The word '[f]ortunately' is the key word here, in part because the germ itself was such a fortunate one, but, more importantly, because James sensed that, given such a quintessentially ideal 'seed', had the book composed from it *not* been successful, that fact might have invalidated his conception of his own creative process. The note of compositional ease suffuses this entire Preface: at one point he compares the writing process to 'the monotony of fine weather', at another point he says that the steps and stages of his 'fable' placed themselves with such promptness that he himself huffed and puffed 'from a good way behind, to catch up with them, breathless and a little flurried, as [I] best could' (*LC*-II, 1306, 1311).

This Preface, of course, addresses a number of other items, mostly technical ones, which have long since been the province of James scholarship and criticism. The most familiar include the necessity to restrict the point of view to Strether as a third-person 'register' (together with the comparative drawbacks of first-person narration); the more complicated function of a *ficelle* figure like Maria Gostrey transcending her role; the successful 'alternations' of picture and scene; the successful presence, throughout, of the 'grace of intensity'. And yet, beyond these technical considerations, James obviously feels the deep presence of his hero, whose germ speech is now called 'melancholy eloquence', whose opportunity allows James to 'bite into' the 'promise of a hero so mature', and whose fundamental character allows him the 'immeasurable' chance to ' "do" a man of imagination' (*LC*-II, 1306–7). Upon rereading the novel, James sees that the power of this germ's habitat in the depths of Strether's psyche is what enables the novel both successfully to have ' "led up" to' the melancholy outburst in the garden and, just as important, to have followed through with '[Strether's] very gropings' to the end (*LC*-II, 1309, 1313). One of James's most perspicacious remarks in this respect is that Strether's irrepressible outburst to Bilham is likewise 'the voice of the false position' (*LC*-II, 1309). Such an assessment may open up the novel for a critique of Strether by a certain kind of critic so predisposed, yet it equally permits an empathetic approach to him by a very differently minded critic, since a 'false position', for the latter, is still the human one; and besides, it resides more or less half-way through Strether's adventure and does not necessarily mean to characterize the ending – where the first critic, so to speak, already awaits and says it does. These opposing critical positions, each responding to Strether's declination of Maria Gostrey's proffered love and his decision to leave for home, have solid enough Jamesian justification: the first has the continuity of Strether's deepest unyielding 'temperament', the Emersonian lord of life; the second has James's commitment to a dynamic central character, one who can have a *Bildungsroman* experience in middle age, and who lives in a William Jamesian world where things are never static but always 'in the making'.

III. MORAL FLUCTUATION

'She keeps *him* up – she keeps the whole thing up . . . She has simply given [Chad] an immense moral lift, and what that can explain is prodigious' (*AB*, I, 283–4; bk. 6, ch. 3). So speaks Lambert Strether to Little Bilham in the flush of his new allegiance to Chad and Marie de Vionnet. But here also is Strether later in the novel after the Cheval Blanc episode: '[Marie] had but made Chad what he was – so why could she think she had made him infinite? She had made him better, she had made him best, she had made him anything one would; but it came to our friend with supreme queerness that he was none the less only Chad' (*AB*, II, 284; bk. 12, ch. 2).

These passages are in no wise special to the novel, but they do typify the continual fluctuation of Strether's moral assessment, not only of the younger couple, but also of his entire experience of Paris, Europe, and the ambassadorial mission. Strether's ongoing dialectic of faith and suspicion does not arise because his moral rigour is lax or even intermittent – quite the opposite – but because James situates him deep within an interpretive field of reality-as-flux, so that his own consciousness must enter into and complete whatever he seeks to know. When he attributes to Chad's 'moral lift' the capacity for 'prodigious explanations', he gives away the secret to, and reveals the problem of, James's own narrative invention: that ethics are never separable from the ceaseless process of knowing; and that process, within William James's pluralistic universe, is both never ending and less what one might observe than how one understands. When James sends Strether to Chad's apartment for the very last time on Madame de Vionnet's behalf, and he has to climb up four flights 'without a lift', the reason is only superficially that 'the lift, at that hour, [had] ceased to work' (*AB*, II, 306, 305; bk. 12, ch. 4); the deeper narrative reason is that Strether no longer believes in the Chad of the 'moral lift'. Even the physical world of the novel reshapes and re-presents itself in answer to the interpretive world through James's metaphorical system; the same principle is at work as Strether now sees from the Boulevard below the 'more solid shape' of Chad on the balcony in sharp contrast to the early substitute-shape of Little Bilham the first time he arrived at that address (*AB*, II, 305; bk. 12, ch. 4). Chad's 'solidity' answers to Strether's now less luminous interpretation of him; his 'shape', moreover, replaces that of the 'amiable' Bilham, author of the heretofore soothing phrase, 'virtuous attachment'.

Paul Armstrong affirms rightly that, by 'focusing on Strether's "groping" efforts to understand, James transforms the composing powers of consciousness into the central action of his narrative'.[9] This feature opens up the novel and makes it a 'hymn' to William James's 'ambulatory rather than saltatory relations, in which the "intervening parts of experience" – i.e. Strether's "process of vision" – supersede every other consideration'.[10] And yet, this very feature means that explanations, however 'prodigious', do not bequeath assurance or agreement from others. When Strether first encounters the 'transformed' Chad, for instance, his 'burden of conscience' compels him to 'communicat[e] quickly with Woollett'; however, 'his heart always sank when the clouds of explanation gathered'. For '[w]hether or no he had a grand idea of the lucid, he held that nothing ever was in fact – for any one else – explained. One went through the vain motions, but it was mostly a waste of life' (*AB*, I, 141; bk. 3, ch. 2). This judgment certainly proves true with Mrs Newsome, whose reaction to Strether's copious 'explanations' in his letters is an abrupt silence followed by her decision to launch a second ambassadorial delegation headed by her daughter Sarah.

But the problem of explanations for others, Strether learns, can prove no more severe than it does for oneself. When he lunches on the quay with Marie de Vionnet after their chance encounter at Notre Dame, he recollects that his dinner with Maria Gostrey in London 'had struck him as requiring so many explanations. He had at that time gathered them in, the explanations – he had stored them up; but it was at present as if he had either soared above or sunk below them – he couldn't tell which; he could somehow think of none that didn't seem to leave the appearance of collapse and cynicism easier for him than lucidity' (*AB*, II, 13; bk. 7, ch. 1). The supreme irony, therefore, is that, in a novel where reality-in-the-making dictates how one understands rather than what one sees, the status of explanations – whether for another or even for oneself – is dubious.

And yet, were we to 'step back' momentarily to the realm of simple perception, so-called, the situation would be more of the same than one might think. Susan Griffin demonstrates convincingly that Strether's visual perception throughout *The Ambassadors* illustrates the functionalist psychology associated with William James: hence 'the active, interested, attentive nature of functional perception means that in the act of seeing, Strether shapes his world and his past'.[11] Griffin agrees that his 'self-interested activity' of perception is never solipsistic but is limited by certain 'outside determinations of his environment';[12] so that Strether's 'interaction between arranged environment and attentive eye' bespeaks the functionalist system enunciated in William's *Principles* rather than the associationist schools he opposed.[13] What all this suggests is that, much as William's earlier psychology adumbrates his later pragmatistic philosophy, so Strether's interested and attentive selectivity at the very nexus of perception adumbrates what Armstrong eloquently defines as his 'bridge over the darkness [through] the ceaseless meaning-making of consciousness' at the higher levels of reality and interpretation.[14] In short, not only does James's distinctive narratology emphasize understanding over observation, as noted earlier, but observation itself in late James, by virtue of its functionalist mode, repeats – or does it initiate? – the shaping agency distinctive to Jamesian consciousness. So if all 'explanations' are eventually problematic, they come by it honestly having emerged from the level of 'simple' perception.

James's narrative epistemology, as I have just defined it, results in Strether's inevitable moral fluctuation. If only he were monistic, if only prescriptive and a priori like Sarah and her mother, he could escape the dialectic of faith and suspicion. But he would not then be the medium of consciousness in the late James. As it is, he illustrates instead William James's insistence that pragmatism, unlike rationalism, disallows 'moral holidays', because one can never rest on the laurels of the transcendent absolute if one inhabits a universe both plural and in constant flux, where ideas, even the most profound and useful ones, are 'transitional'. In *The Ambassadors*, 'virtuous attachment' is just such an idea; it undergoes as many modifications of meaning in the hands of James and his protagonist as does Walter Besant's dictum that one should write from experience at the hands of James the critic, in 'The Art of Fiction'. Just as Strether generally 'reconstructs' Chad after meeting him anew in Paris, then 're-reconstructs' him after critical episodes culminating in Cheval Blanc, so too does he fluctuate from Chad as pagan to gentleman, as smooth to brute, as knowing how to live to, potentially, 'a criminal of the deepest dye' should he desert Marie (*AB*, II, 311; bk. 12, ch. 4).

Such profound interdependence of ethical imperatives and interpretive attitudes is epitomized by the great boat scene at Cheval Blanc. Armstrong insightfully proposes that

> even when Strether confronts reality, James is more interested in how his hero understands than in what he sees. Strether learns the truth about Chad and Madame de Vionnet not by facing unmediated facts but by following out the implications of various clues. Never given direct evidence of their intimacy, Strether must ponder a series of small, subtle signs requiring skilful reading.[15]

This formulation of Strether's discovery evokes Michael Polanyi's theory of 'tacit' and 'focal' knowledge expounded in works like *Knowing and Being* and *Personal Knowledge*, and it does so not only because of the linear descent of *Gestalt* thought from William James, but also because Henry James, like both William and Polanyi, seems bent on capturing the human processes of construal along the lines of a humanistic science.[16] A comparable formulation of the same episode is this: 'Strether actively and radically meets the discovery; he enters into a reciprocal relation with it, grafting meaning while receiving in kind; he empties every possible insight about himself, his previous assumptions, the thoughts of the two lovers in having to deal with *him*, and even the imagined responses of those back at Paris, into it.'[17] In stressing the active shaping of Strether's consciousness in the face of life's fluidity, both formulations suggest why Strether's 'gropings' make him vulnerable to deception: he is a believer, and, within his dialectic, suspicion, though inevitable, is never sought, whereas faith is always welcomed. Strether's moral stance in this regard seems that of William James's in 'The Will to Believe', especially his theme that '[d]upery for dupery, what proof is there that dupery through hope is so much worse than dupery through fear?'[18]

And yet, Strether's moral fluctuation, though seasoned with good humour in William's spirit up through the final breakfast scene with Maria Gostrey, also resonates with that undertone of melancholia James first detected in the germ and continued to convey in all his subsequent versions of it, as when denominating Strether 'rueful' or addressing the novel's mixed tragedy/irony mode, as discussed earlier. The problem for 'poor Strether', as he is so often called, is, in his own words to Maria, that he truly needs '[t]o be right' (*AB*, II, 326; bk. 12, ch. 5) in the face of all the bewilderment and fluctuation he has experienced. Yet how does one do that in a world that can only begin with 'Strether's first question', and only end with 'Then there we are!' – in other words, an indeterminate world going everywhere horizontally but nowhere vertically? As usual, Armstrong provides the best answer one can find: 'The most we can hope for, James seems to suggest, is a sense of integrity – a sense that our lives have composed themselves into a whole that we can accept as our own . . . By espousing the value of integrity, James asserts that we can live a moral life; but *The Ambassadors* also shows that integrity, as an ethical goal, is infinitely variable and open to interpretation'.[19] The norm Strether invokes is ultimately existential, grounded on the structure of experience and belief in 'the illusion of freedom' with both its positive and negative poles, and answering to William's iterative claim of pragmatistic thought as both 'tender and tough-minded'. But in late James these norms are intrinsic rather than extrinsic values, derived neither from society nor a priori imperatives. While problematizing the issue of representation in a way that stamps his modernity, James, like Strether, must somehow steer a middle course between reality and interpretation, thereby evoking William's 'mediating philosophy', on one side, and the hermeneutical circularity of phenomenology he anticipates, on the other. The phenomenological James is one with William's concept of the never-ending confluence of experience-as-apparent, wherein one must not distinguish where one cannot experientially divide. On this account, Strether is most 'phenomenological' in his anxiety-based defense to Sarah's attack in the same speech that begins, 'Everything has come as a sort of indistinguishable part of everything else.'[20]

For Strether, there has been something exhilarating in the ambiguity of a woman who 'had taken all his categories by surprise' (*AB*, I, 271; bk. 6, ch. 3) and who spoke 'now as if her art were all an innocence, and then again as if her innocence were all an art' (*AB*, I, 116; bk. 9, ch. 1). But even pragmatistic novelty can turn rueful as when Strether later ponders 'the general spectacle of his art and his innocence, almost an added link and certainly a common priceless ground for them to meet upon' (*AB*, II, 278; bk. 12, ch. 1). Regarding this irony, a reader may swing back and forth between its grimness and its good humour. But, either way, William James, in 'The Moral Philosopher and the Moral Life', rings true for Strether when he insists: 'Neither moral relations nor the moral law can swing *in vacuo*. Their only habitat can be a mind which feels them; and no world composed of merely physical facts can be a world to which ethical propositions apply.'[21] Nevertheless, Joyce Rowe represents a certain type of reader when she claims that, like Huck or Ishmael, Strether 'ends a spiritual orphan' whose 'finale forces us to reconsider once again the cost of American moral idealism'.[22] If this position goes too far and ignores the book's comedic side, it does do justice – more than justice – to the 'rueful' melancholia intrinsic in James's germ. Once again, William James seems to address the issue when he writes that 'there is always a *pinch* between the ideal and the actual which can only be got through by leaving part of the ideal behind . . . Every end of desire that presents itself appears exclusive of some other end of desire . . . Some part of the ideal must be butchered and [the moral philosopher] needs to know which part.'[23]

Although 'to butcher' sounds much too coarse for Strether (who is called by Waymarsh a 'fine-tooth comb' not fit 'to groom a horse' (*AB*, I, 109; bk. 3, ch. 1)), he does, ultimately, cut away parts of his ideal. He severs himself from Mrs Newsome, like the Hegelian slave who comes to a new consciousness of her as under the gaze and censure of the master. He severs himself from Marie de Vionnet, even though he also tries valiantly to persuade Chad not to desert her. And he severs himself from Maria Gostrey, whose companionship he has cherished and who offers him her love. As a quondam ambassador, he has known power for a time and then squandered it, as I suggested at the beginning of this chapter. In regard to such power, he resembles his predecessor, Fleda Vetch, in *The Spoils of Poynton*, and his successor, Merton Densher, in *The Wings of the Dove*, both of whom renounce their possibilities for control on behalf of a more compelling need for personal integrity – a comparable need, if you will, 'to be right'. In this respect he is unlike Maggie Verver in *The Golden Bowl*, who combines the shaping burden of consciousness with the gradual acquisition of power other than the composing 'powers' of consciousness *per se*, although such momentous power makes it impossible, finally, for Maggie to feel very sanguine about, and thus certain of, her being right. Perhaps one overlooked clue to Strether's lack of ultimate power acquisition is that his character is a reconceived, rewritten draft of Christopher Newman in *The American*: for, whereas Newman sought in a woman 'the best article in the market' (*AM*, 49) but still came up empty, Strether insists '[n]ot, out of the whole affair, to have got anything for myself' (*AB*, II, 326; bk. 12, ch. 5); and, whereas Newman spoke of wash tubs and leather as his business ventures, Strether never names the Woollett 'article'. Perhaps still another connection, albeit a less direct one, is to *The Turn of the Screw*, wherein a person in possession of delegated power misuses it and thereby loses Jamesian integrity in her obsession 'to be right'.

Nevertheless, neither these nor other analogues can account for Strether. His predicament, like his ethic, remains intrinsic to him, and also to the remarkable germ that brought him forth. His power *does* remain that of consciousness, and there is no reason to disbelieve him when he tells Maria of his returning home that 'I shall see what I can make of it' (*AB*, II, 325; bk. 12, ch. 5). At the same time – indeed, perhaps for the same reason – a reader senses that at least some part of Strether refuses Maria Gostrey because, unlike Marie de Vionnet, she never *has* taken all his categories by surprise – the very surprise that can trigger 'melancholy eloquence'.

NOTES

1 This assessment is, of course, from James's Preface to the New York Edition. For a possible 'subconscious' connection between Strether's 'Live' speech and James's early character of Louis Leverett in 'A Bundle of Letters' (1879), see Oscar Cargill, *The Novels of Henry James* (New York: Macmillan, 1961), 304.
2 Cf. J. Donald Crowley and Richard A. Hocks, eds., *The Wings of the Dove: Norton Critical Edition* (New York: Norton, 1978), 454–5.
3 Martha Banta, '"There's Surely a Story In It": James's Notebooks and the Working Artist', *Henry James Review*, 9 (1988), 155–7.
4 James's reiteration of the 'too late' theme in all major versions of the germ speech is likewise anticipated in an earlier notebook entry, 5 February 1895, which begins, 'What is there in the idea of *Too late*' (*CN*, 112).
5 The dispute about the chapters, that is, has taken an entirely new 'reversal' by McGann's essay, in which he argues that it was the first English Edition – which James did *not* use for his Scribner's revision – that has the chapters in the wrong order; whereas the first American Edition – which James did revise from – had the chapter sequence right all along (the original magazine text in *The North American Review* had omitted chapter 28 altogether). Hence, for McGann, all the editions we used to believe had it 'wrong' have been right, and the ones we now think have 'corrected' it have it wrong! (Jerome McGann, 'Revision, Rewriting, Rereading; or An Error [Not] in *The Ambassadors*', *American Literature*, 64 (1992), 95–110.) See S. P. Rosenbaum, ed., *The Ambassadors: Norton Critical Edition*, 2nd edn. (New York: Norton, 1994), 360–1, for a cogent refutation of this view.
6 It is noteworthy that this central speech was not substantially revised from either the first American or first English editions, aside from the removal of a few commas in keeping with James's general style in the New York Edition (cf. Henry James, *The Ambassadors* (New York: Harper, 1903), 149–50); furthermore, it is just possible that the metaphorical train's receding 'whistle' may be James's punning 'signature' for the originating germ-location at the home of James McNeill Whistler.
7 For a fuller interpretation along these lines see Richard A. Hocks, *Henry James and Pragmatistic Thought: A Study in the Relationship between the Philosophy of William James and the Literary Art of Henry James* (Chapel Hill: University of North Carolina Press, 1974), 152–87, as well as section III of this chapter.
8 A year later, in 1902, one still finds this 'germ-like' sentiment in James's letter to Edith Wharton, wherein he expresses his 'desire earnestly, tenderly, intelligently to admonish you while you are young, free, expert, exposed (to illumination) . . . admonish you, I say, in favour of the *American Subject*. There it is round you. Don't pass it by – the

immediate, the real, the ours, the yours, the novelist's that it waits for. Take hold of it and keep hold, and let it pull you where it will' (*HJL*, IV, 235–6).
9 Paul B. Armstrong, *The Challenge of Bewilderment: Understanding and Representation in James, Conrad, and Ford* (Ithaca: Cornell University Press, 1987), 63.
10 Hocks, *Henry James and Pragmatistic Thought*, 158.
11 Susan M. Griffin, *The Historical Eye: The Texture of the Visual in Late James* (Boston: Northeastern University Press, 1991), 33.
12 Hocks, *Henry James and Pragmatistic Thought*, 177.
13 Griffin, *Historical Eye*, 51.
14 Armstrong, *Challenge of Bewilderment*, 105.
15 Ibid., 92.
16 Michael Polanyi, *Knowing and Being* (University of Chicago Press, 1969); *Personal Knowledge: Towards a Post-Critical Philosophy* (University of Chicago Press, 1958).
17 Hocks, *Henry James and Pragmatistic Thought*, 63.
18 William James, *Essays on Faith and Morals* (Cleveland: World, 1962), 58.
19 Armstrong, *Challenge of Bewilderment*, 102.
20 By far the best discussion of James and post-William Jamesian phenomenology remains Paul B. Armstrong, *The Phenomenology of Henry James* (Chapel Hill: University of North Carolina Press, 1983); Merle A. Williams, *Henry James and the Philosophical Novel: Being and Seeing* (Cambridge University Press, 1993), however, combines Merleau-Ponty, Husserl, and Derrida in her approach to James.
21 William James, *Essays*, 190.
22 Joyce A. Rowe, *Equivocal Endings in American Literature* (New York: Cambridge University Press, 1988), 98.
23 William James, *Essays*, 202–3.

CHAPTER 3

James and the ethics of control: aspiring architects and their floating creatures

Sarah B. Daugherty

In the Preface to *The Portrait of a Lady*, James explores a dialectic that shaped his paradoxical conception of his authorial role. Using a familiar trope, he likens the novel to 'a structure reared with an "architectural" competence' and calls attention to his powers as a master builder: 'I would build large – in fine embossed vaults and painted arches, as who should say, and yet never let it appear that the chequered pavement, the ground under the reader's feet, fails to stretch at every point to the base of the walls' (*LC*-II, 1080). But his characters, he suggests, enjoy a measure of independence: they 'floated into [his] ken' as if 'by an impulse of their own' and still resist the builder's efforts to contain them, even if his bricks are 'scrupulously fitted together and packed-in' (*LC*-II, 1081, 1083). Hence James's remark on the 'latent extravagance' of the novel as a genre, and hence his caveat that 'I would rather, I think, have too little architecture than too much – when there's danger of its interfering with my measure of the truth' (*LC*-II, 1075, 1072).

Turning to James's notebooks, we can see that his efforts to reconcile form and freedom depend on the art of strategic omission. His entry on *The Portrait of a Lady* anticipates the Preface he wrote more than two decades later:

> The obvious criticism of course will be that it is not finished – that I have not seen the heroine through to the end of her situation – that I have left her *en l'air*. – This is both true and false. The *whole* of anything is never told; you can only take what groups together. What I have done has that unity – it groups together. It is complete in itself – and the rest may be taken up or not, later. (*CN*, 15)

Notice that James offers a dual defense of his experimental ending. On the one hand, it creates the illusion that Isabel's life extends beyond the text; and on the other, it contributes to the novel's formal unity. Thus James sought to improve on the design of the Victorian novel, which might have figured for him as a sprawling prison like Millbank in *The Princess Casamassima*. But he could not easily synthesize the values that are still contested by theorists. The instability of his metaphors presages the interpretive battles between formalist defenders of 'architecture' and postmodern champions of 'extravagance'. Moreover, to the extent that James satisfies critics in both camps, his achievement results in large measure from what he leaves out, notwithstanding his portrayal of himself as a votary of 'doing' with an excess of zeal for treating his subjects (*LC*-II, 1084). I shall argue, indeed, that James could resolve his aesthetic dilemma only by evading the task of representation, and that such ethical philosophers as Martha Nussbaum have overvalued his accomplishments. The house with an open plan contains more structural flaws than James or his admirers have been willing to recognize. But James's formal experiments deserve to be understood as responses to texts by other nineteenth-century writers, whose limitations he perceived more clearly than his own.

His sense of his characters' freedom was derived from his reading of the Romantics, who figure prominently in his reviews and essays of the 1860s and 70s. These discussions underscore the difference between fluid art, imaged in metaphors of water and air, and the earthbound process of construction. Sir Walter Scott, he wrote, 'pours out a stream of wondrous improvisation', while Victor Hugo's manner 'is as diffuse as that of the young woman in the fairy tale who talked diamonds and pearls would alone have a right to be' (*LC*-I, 1203; *LC*-II, 455). The supreme writer of fluid, feminine fiction was George Sand, whom he likened to Shelley's skylark: 'No writer has produced such great effects with an equal absence of premeditation' (*LC*-II, 712). For James, this lack of artifice enhanced the writer's ability to create the illusion of life without undue reliance on actual models: 'a hint – a mere starting point – was enough for [Sand]' (*LC*-II, 719). James subsequently developed his metaphor of the germ, counselling aspiring authors to be receptive to 'every air-borne particle' and to convert 'the very pulses of the air into revelations' (*LC*-I, 52).

But such a Romantic conception of genius was ultimately too passive and undisciplined to satisfy the analytical critic. Repeatedly he suggested that his enjoyment of romance was a guilty pleasure, more suitable for credulous children than for adults (*LC*-I, 1203-4; *LC*-II, 730-1). The narratives of Sand, in particular, were 'too limpid, too fluent, too liquid' to be susceptible to the kind of formalist criticism James advocated. 'Does any work of representation, of imitation, live long that is predominantly loose?' he asked, answering his own question in the negative (*LC*-II, 700, 759). These critiques had an ethical dimension as well as an aesthetic one, because James suspected that pure fabulation might simply be frivolous. Scott, he said, was a writer of 'the novel irresponsible' that 'proposed simply to amuse the reader' (*LC*-I, 1202). Sand, he concluded after some debate with himself, 'was a very high order of sentimentalist, but she was not a moralist' (*LC*-II, 733). As Naomi Schor has noted, James's masculine bias shaped his image of Sand, who in turn influenced his view of the romance as a genre unworthy of serious readers: '[Her imagination] is indefatigable, inexhaustible; but it is restless, nervous, and capricious; it is, in short, the imagination of a woman' (*LC*-II, 699).[1] Sand's intellectual heirs, the French feminists, might have met with James's amusement or disdain, but never with his approval.

James adhered to his stereotypes of gender in regarding the pursuit of form as an essentially male occupation. 'To work successfully beneath a few grave, rigid laws', he wrote in one review, 'is always a strong man's highest ideal of success' (*MTD*, 398). We can see the justice of Donadio's comparison of James with Nietzsche, for both of whom 'the activity of art' became 'a means for the continual reassertion of personality and the mastery of experience'.[2] This will to power was an important motive behind James's experiments with drama, which, he maintained, was the genre most in need of 'a masterly structure' (*MTD*, 398). In the realm of fiction, the exemplary figures for James were the French realists. Among his earliest tributes to 'architecture' is his 1866 review of Alexandre Dumas's *Affaire Clémençeau*, a novel which became a source of his own *Roderick Hudson*. 'From beginning to end there is not a word which is accidental, not a sentence which leaves the author's pen without his perfect assent and sympathy . . . Such writing is reading for men' (*LC*-II, 280). During the 1870s, his acquaintance with Flaubert's circle increased his impatience not only with female sentimentalists, but also with Anglo-Saxon amateurs of both sexes. 'Nothing is more striking in a clever French novel, as a general thing, than its superiority in artistic neatness and shapeliness to a clever English one' (*LC*-I, 41).

Yet James also believed that excessive control destroyed the life of a novelist's characters. Flaubert's *Madame Bovary*, he conceded, 'remains a living creature' in spite of – not because of – 'the elaborate system of portraiture to which she is subjected'; but he called *L'Education sentimentale* a '*dead*' book, the product of a fatal 'want of spontaneity' (*LC*-II, 172, 176). The writing of Flaubert's disciples, Edmond and Jules de Goncourt, was characterized by its 'perfection of manner'; none the less, said James, it 'gives me the impression of something I can find no other name for than cruelty' (*LC*-II, 182). As for Emile Zola, his *Nana* reinforced James's belief that the Anglo-Saxons had 'a deeper, more delicate perception of the play of character and the state of the soul' (*LC*-II, 870). All in all, the writers of the new school ignored 'the charm that intense reality may have when it is reached by divination, by the winged fancy, rather than by a system more or less ingenious' (*LC*-II, 182). Donadio therefore overstates his case when he says that James, along with Nietzsche, yearned for 'the experience of ordering the world like God'.[3] Rather, James sought to achieve a balance between the irresponsibility of mere wordplay and the cruelty resulting from misguided attempts at linguistic domination.

His critical writing, however, is less notable for its syntheses than for its oscillations. 'The Art of Fiction' (1884) is a confusing manifesto because it begins as a defence of French formalism, but concludes as 'a plea for liberty'.[4] The division of James's sympathies is also apparent in the subjects he chose for his late essays, when the pressures of reviewing were behind him. His enduring fascination with Romantic genius can be seen in his memorials to Sand (1897, 1902, 1914) as well as in his 1907 paean to Shakespeare – the 'divine musician who, alone in his room, preludes or improvises at close of day' (*LC*-I, 1210). But he also elevated Flaubert to the status of literary hero, awarding him the title of 'the novelist's novelist' (*LC*-I, 346). Indeed, James's focus on individual authors is a mark of his resistance to theory. During his later years, he made no attempt to write prescriptive general essays or to present his own 'case' as the sole measure of others.

He did, however, learn a common lesson from his various masters: the perils of excessive representation, which jeopardized both form and freedom. Two of his literary forebears, George Eliot and Honoré de Balzac, were especially vulnerable to charges of 'overtreatment'. Although James admired Eliot's humanity, he complained that her lengthy novels failed to gratify readers 'with a sense of design and construction'; even *Middlemarch* he labelled 'a treasure-house of details, but . . . an indifferent whole' (*LC*-I, 958). Still worse, in his view, was Eliot's 'absence of spontaneity' (*LC*-I, 100), observable in her tendencies to philosophize and to tie up the loose ends of her plots. A superior novelist, he said, would have made the end of *Adam Bede* 'the logical consequence of Adam's final state of mind', instead of depicting his marriage to the pious heroine. If 'the art of storytelling' were perfected, the protagonist would appear to have a life beyond the text, in the imagination of 'the sympathetic reader' (*LC*-I, 922). The massive works of Balzac reinforced James's belief in the modernist dictum that less is more. While applauding the magnitude of the novelist's attempt, James argued that his fiction lacks 'that slight but needful thing – charm' because of his tendency 'to squeeze things into a formula that mutilates them' (*LC*-II, 68, 41). And Balzac, too, neglected composition 'in handing over his *data* to his twin-brother the impassioned economist and surveyor' (*LC*-II, 96).

Ivan Turgenev, in contrast, provided a model of artistic restraint. This 'delightful, mild, masculine figure' (*LC*-II, 1015), with his androgynous qualities, showed James how to escape from the prison-house of nineteenth-century fiction. Though he treated individual characters as the 'centres' of his stories and brief novels, Turgenev avoided the excess of architecture that made Flaubert 'ungenerous in his genius' (*LC*-II, 1022, 1024). Unlike Eliot and the Victorians, he limited the omniscience of his narrators: 'the drama is quite uncommented; the poet never plays chorus; situations speak for themselves' (*LC*-II, 983). And, unlike Balzac, he presented his characters with an air of 'charmed expectancy' (*LC*-II, 979), allowing readers to speculate on their lives as on those of actual persons. An example cited by James is the conclusion of *A Nest of Noblemen*, in which Lavretsky, unable to marry the pious Lisa after discovering that his unfaithful wife is still alive, catches a glimpse of his beloved in the chapel of her remote convent. ' "What must they both have thought, have felt?" . . . "Who can know? who can say? There are moments in life, there are feelings, on which we can only cast a glance without stopping" ' (*LC*-II, 981). Thus Turgenev fostered James's sense of the sacred – of abysses of feeling unrepresentable in language.

Nonetheless, James advanced an important argument against Turgenev's philosophy, which he believed to be unduly pessimistic:

Life *is*, in fact, a battle. On this point optimists and pessimists agree. Evil is insolent and strong; beauty enchanting but rare; goodness very apt to be weak; folly very apt to be defiant; wickedness to carry the day; imbeciles to be in great places, people of sense in small, and mankind generally, unhappy. But the world as it stands is no illusion, no phantasm, no evil dream of a night; we wake up to it again for ever and ever; we can neither forget it nor deny it nor dispense with it. We can welcome experience as it comes, and give it what it demands, in exchange for something which it is idle to pause to call much or little so long as it contributes to swell the volume of consciousness. In this there is mingled pain and delight, but over the mysterious mixture there hovers a visible rule, that bids us learn to will and seek to understand. (*LC*-II, 998)

This passage indeed marks the divergence between James's view of experience and Turgenev's. *A Nest of Noblemen*, among other novels by the Russian, demonstrates that consciousness itself is a tragic burden: Lisa, troubled by her love for Lavretsky, can only escape from the world, while Lavretsky is tortured both by Lisa's uncomprehending innocence and by the cynicism of those who reunite him with his adulterous wife. But in much of James's fiction (certainly in *The Portrait of a Lady* and arguably in *The Golden Bowl*), the growth of the protagonist's awareness mitigates the tragedy.

We therefore come to a major source of the interpretive problems that have confronted James's critics: his partial adoption of Turgenev's techniques to develop his own more positive themes. Renunciation may be conveyed through silence and absence, but the swelling of consciousness demands representation. Readers may be baffled, then, by the sudden ascent of characters into the void; or, conversely, they may feel trapped in the maze of metaphors that James uses to capture the life of the mind. Sceptics may also take issue with Jamesian optimism, especially when consciousness fails to result in action. Following Turgenev's lead, he promoted character at the expense of '"plot", nefarious name' (*LC*-II, 1071); but generations of doubters have questioned the logic of Isabel's return to Osmond.

Further complications arise from James's ambition to 'build large'. Although he admired Turgenev's lyrical short fiction, his greatest desire was to construct monumental novels in the manner of his literary father, Balzac. This process entailed the creation of secondary figures who, as James recognized, could disrupt the design of his novels by asserting their independence from the original 'centre'. Thanks to the Romantic side of his heritage, he often relinquished formal control, allowing even minor characters the space they seemed to demand. But such plenitude draws attention to his omissions, some of which deserve to be called evasions. If we look closely at *The Portrait of a Lady* and *The Golden Bowl* – two novels centrally concerned with the dialectic of form and freedom – we can appreciate their peculiar amalgam of boldness and conventionality.

The Portrait of a Lady illustrates the close connection between James's critical writing and his fiction. Indeed, it can easily be interpreted as an allegory of Jamesian reading. Isabel, who 'regard[s] the world as a place of brightness, of free expansion', at first has a sense of being 'floated' by her own romantic spirit and by 'the current of . . . repaid curiosity' (*PL*, I, 68, 60, 72). Naturally she resists the Lord of Lockleigh, Warburton, who conceives 'the design of drawing her into [his] system', and the unyielding Caspar Goodwood, who shows 'his appetites and designs too simply and artlessly' (*PL*, I, 144, 165). She remains vulnerable, however, to more subtle artists. Madame Merle, with her talents for music and embroidery, appears to be a romantic improviser, but her Balzacian speech on houses identifies her as a votary of architecture (*PL*, I, 287–8). Poor Ralph Touchett encourages Isabel to spread her wings without realizing, as Henrietta warns, that her inheritance will 'shut [her] up more and more [with] a few selfish and heartless people' (*PL*, I, 319, 310).

Eventually Isabel is seduced by her own enthusiasm for Italian architecture, seen first in her attraction to Mrs Touchett's Florentine villa (*PL*, I, 354–5). Unfortunately she fails to observe that Osmond's house is an emblem of masculine control: 'There was something grave and strong in the place; it looked somehow as if, once you were in, you would need an act of energy to get out' (*PL*, I, 364). Ominously, too, she fails to note the significant divergence between her reaction to St Peter's and that of Osmond. She perceives the cathedral as 'very large and very bright' and calls it 'the greatest of human temples', while he complains, 'It's too large; it makes one feel like an atom' (*PL*, I, 427). But, in other respects, her downfall results less from her blindness than from her inevitable enclosure in the structure of the novel. As she explains to Ralph, 'You talk about one's soaring and sailing, but if one marries at all one touches the earth' (*PL*, II, 74).

The second volume of *The Portrait of a Lady*, however, dramatizes Isabel's resistance to entrapment. She refuses to promote a match between Pansy and Warburton – a union that would threaten her own freedom as well as the young girl's. ('To see you under my roof', says Warburton, '. . . would be a great satisfaction' (*PL*, II, 271).) She escapes from Osmond's 'house of suffocation' to visit the dying Ralph (*PL*, II, 196). And, of course, she flees from Goodwood's final embrace, presented as an 'act of possession' (*PL*, II, 436). Further, as numerous critics have noted, the novel's open ending signals James's relinquishment of authorial control. Originally he had planned to give Henrietta 'the last word – . . . a characteristic characterization of Isabel' (*CN*, 16); but he wisely avoided a formulaic summary. Not surprisingly, then, the novel has been praised both for its careful design and for its 'critique of a culture and civilization that have come to prize formalism over life'.[5]

But sceptics have in turn resisted this Jamesian reading. Sandra Fischer, among others, sees Isabel as 'a repressed and rather mundane person' who actually prefers enclosure to liberty.[6] One problem is that Osmond's cruelty is presented with greater dramatic force than James himself may have recognized, to the point that readers seeking evidence of Isabel's desire for freedom are likely to expect a more direct view of her resistance. When Henrietta questions her at Gardencourt, Isabel explains that Osmond objected to her visiting Ralph but did not create 'what you'd call a scene' (*PL*, II, 397). In fact, however, the final scene between her and Osmond (chapter 51), when she is still ignorant of his relationship with Madame Merle, is sufficiently powerful to make Isabel 'afraid' (*PL*, II, 361). In the absence of a companion scene – one that would show her confronting Osmond with her new knowledge – she may well be regarded as a woman defeated by her own anxieties.

Moreover, Isabel's consciousness of Osmond's evil nature is presented much more fully than her motives for returning to him. While chapter 42 deserves the acclaim it has received, its success highlights the vagueness of Isabel's later reflections, as during her journey to Gardencourt: 'The past and the future came and went at their will, but she saw them only in fitful images, which rose and fell by a logic of their own' (*PL*, II, 390). And there is no denying the comparative banality of her thoughts on marriage: '[Osmond] was not one of the best husbands, but that didn't alter the case. Certain obligations were involved in the very fact of marriage, and were quite independent of the quantity of enjoyment extracted from it' (*PL*, II, 421). If Isabel appears repressed, her limitations are attributable to James himself. Seeking escape from the confines of nineteenth-century realism, he had little interest in representing the mundane details of marriage. At the same time, divorce remained an unthinkable alternative, both for him and the protagonists he created. This impasse, as we shall see, likewise accounts for the structural gaps in *The Golden Bowl*.

The interpretive problems in *The Portrait of a Lady* are compounded by James's stereotyping of the other women characters. Despite his association of female figures with the muses of Romanticism, he could neither imagine nor completely endorse their liberation as a social reality. Mrs Touchett, who 'erect[s]' her differences with her husband 'into a law', seems invented by James for the purpose of illustrating what Isabel ought not to do (*PL*, I, 26). And his conception of Pansy as a victim also limits Isabel, who is deprived of a chance for effective agency. During her final visit to the convent, she offers Pansy the opportunity to escape: 'Will you come away with me now?' Pansy, however, replies that she must obey her father and Madame Merle: 'Only if you're here I shall do it more easily' (*PL*, II, 384, 386). Later, when Henrietta says to Isabel, 'I don't see why you promised little Miss Osmond to go back', Isabel can only respond, 'I'm not sure I myself see now . . . But I did then' (*PL*, II, 397–8). Although *The Portrait of a Lady* has been praised for its 'bold re-evaluation of what a woman married to a dishonorable man should do',[7] James was constrained by his prejudices from developing a plot sufficient to his theme. Hence he left his protagonist '*en l'air*'.

The typecasting of Henrietta is also revealing, especially to critics tempted to overestimate James's feminism. At first this friend serves as proof to Isabel 'that a woman might suffice to herself and be happy', and she emerges as the one who speaks for the option of escape: 'Leave your husband before the worst comes' (*PL*, I, 71; II, 304). Further, as James says in his Preface, Henrietta is allowed greater freedom than he had planned, since she appears in more episodes than are warranted by her function as a mere *ficelle* (*LC*-II, 1082–3). None the less, James re-establishes his control by means of irony and satire – a technique he subsequently used in *The Bostonians* to put talkative feminists in their place. In her roles of prying lady journalist and partisan of Goodwood, Henrietta becomes a meddler rather than a champion of freedom. The ultimate irony is her engagement to little Mr Bantling – a development which, 'to Isabel's sense', shows 'a want of originality' (*PL*, II, 400). Was James hinting at some self-criticism here? If so, he was more perceptive than many of his admirers.

Compared with *The Portrait of a Lady*, *The Golden Bowl* allows greater freedom to both characters and readers. Whereas Isabel, from the outset, lives in the structure visibly designed by James, Maggie becomes the protagonist only in volume two – a shift that makes her feel like a minor actress 'promoted to leading lady' (*GB*, II, 208). And the role she assumes is not simply that of a figure in a Jamesian fable; it is that of the Jamesian author himself, struggling to attain a balance between the mastery needed to execute a design and the diffidence required by respect for others' liberty. Her foil, Fanny Assingham, is the meddler turned bad novelist: having mistakenly 'fallen in love with the beautiful symmetry of [her] plan' for the two marriages, she becomes increasingly desperate as events spin out of her control (*GB*, I, 389). (Readers of volume one may even hope that the adultery will occur, so that the lovers may escape from the busybody.) Maggie, however, despite her 'lucid little plan' (*GB*, II, 27), permits others the latitude to act as they will. Instead of playing the part of the domineering wife, she descends into the 'labyrinth' with the errant prince (*GB*, II, 187) – a metaphor similar to the one James uses in his Preface to depict his own relationship with his characters (*LC*-II, 1323). She likewise refuses to intervene in her father's marriage, saying, 'I leave you to make of your own side of the matter what you can' (*GB*, II, 270). And, in two of the novel's most famous scenes, she helps Charlotte to act out her chosen lies – the falsehoods that enable the latter 'to rise to the occasion and be magnificent' (*GB*, II, 279).

Consistent with the ethos of liberty is James's effort to discard 'the muffled majesty of authorship' (*LC*-II, 1323). In *The Portrait of a Lady*, our sense of Isabel as a free character results, to a degree, from James's narrative control: we are told that 'she would be an easy victim of scientific criticism if she were not intended to awaken on the reader's part an impulse more tender and more purely expectant' (*PL*, I, 69). But, as Martha Nussbaum has noted, in *The Golden Bowl* 'the author places himself humanly in the world of his text and links us to himself as limited and human adventurers'.[8] Because of this effacement, readers may form their own estimates of Maggie, which may be less flattering than those of the implied author. Like Nussbaum, we may view her as an exemplar of clear vision and high intelligence;[9] or we may pity her as a victim of others' designs, especially those of the predacious Charlotte. Then again, we may regard her more sceptically as a manipulator. 'You're terrible', says Fanny at one point (*GB*, II, 115); and, indeed, there is something unsettling in the silence that causes others to reveal their guilt. Despite his often celebratory rhetoric, James seems less anxious to secure our good opinion of his protagonist.

But more troubling ambiguities stem from his use of Maggie's consciousness as the sole centre of volume two. Taking issue with Nussbaum, S. L. Goldberg and Geoffrey Harpham have questioned James's premise that the growth of perception is an end in itself, one that justifies the devaluation of plot.[10] And, even if we accept James's philosophy, we may ask whether Maggie affords us an adequate perspective on the subject of the novel, recorded in his notebooks as '*The Marriages*' (*CN*, 146). One peculiarity is that Maggie knows her husband so little, although her passion for him is vividly rendered. In the first chapter, he tells her, 'There are two parts of me.' The first, he explains, is made up of his family history, written 'in rows of volumes, in libraries . . . But there's another part, very much smaller doubtless, which, such as it is, represents my single self, the unknown, unimportant – unimportant save to *you* – personal quantity. About this you've found nothing' (*GB*, I, 9). Yet Maggie and the readers remain in the dark, because her strategy, once she discovers his unfaithfulness, is to allow him to wander around 'the closed dusky rooms' of Portland Place while she entertains the visitors at Fawns (*GB*, II, 293). In her imagination she hears his mute appeal:

Leave me my reserve; don't question it – it's all I have just now, don't you see? so that, if you'll make me the concession of letting me alone with it for as long a time as I require I promise you something or other, grown under cover of it, even though I don't yet quite make out what, as a return for your patience. (*GB*, II, 221)

This appeal obviously reinforces the theme that individuals need and deserve their liberty. But the absence of the Prince leaves readers with unanswerable questions – about the sacrifices Maggie makes '[f]or love' (*GB*, II, 116), about the almost magical process whereby she regains her husband's affections, and about the fundamental issue of whether such a marriage is worth saving. One suspects that James himself may have lost interest in Amerigo's conventional, fixed character when he became absorbed in portraying the princess as 'a creature consciously floating and shining in a warm summer sea' (*GB*, II, 263). Late in the novel, the narrator tells us that Amerigo's place is 'like something made for him beforehand by innumerable facts', whereas Maggie's 'improvised "post"' is marked only by the geography of 'the fundamental passions' (*GB*, II,

323–4). Curiously, too, the figure of Adam is aggrandized – especially when Maggie perceives him as 'a great and deep and high little man' (*GB*, II, 274) – while the prince fades into obscurity. If we are supposed to infer that Maggie should think more of her marriage and less of her filial ties, the structure of volume two is 'rum' indeed.

The story of Charlotte, as filtered through Maggie's limited perspective, poses additional problems for ethical critics. Nussbaum praises Maggie for acknowledging 'the suffering of Charlotte caused by her act' and for being willing 'to bear guilt' in consequence.[11] In fact, however, Charlotte's pain results primarily from the actions of her lover and her husband. Amerigo lies to her about Maggie's knowledge – a falsehood surmised by Maggie but not confirmed by the prince until the final chapter (*GB*, II, 213–14, 355). According to Nussbaum, his callousness is a 'tragic necessity',[12] but others may emphasize the gratuitous cruelty of his deception. Readers wishing to join this debate are reduced to speculating on scenes outside the text.

Then there is the mysterious figure of Adam, portrayed far more vividly as Maggie's father than as Charlotte's husband. Does he lead his wife to her doom with a 'silken halter' (*GB*, II, 287), or is this metaphor the product of Maggie's overworked imagination? Again, is Maggie right to conclude, optimistically, that Charlotte will play a 'great' role in American City – that she will not be 'wasted in the application of [Adam's] plan' (*GB*, II, 365)? Or has Maggie been deluded once more by her filial piety? We, as readers, are in a poor position to judge, because we know even less of Adam and Charlotte's marriage than we do of Amerigo and Maggie's. In volume one, 'The Prince', James departs from his compositional scheme to give us two remarkable chapters devoted to Adam and Charlotte (*GB*, I, 210–41) – episodes hinting that the two characters, notwithstanding their good intentions, will become mutual victims. But, in volume two, we are confined to the perceptions of Maggie, who reflects that 'the real "relation" between her father and his wife was a thing she knew nothing about and that in strictness was not of her concern' (*GB*, II, 138).

I concur with Goldberg, then, that Nussbaum's admiring discussion of this novel fails to account for the Ververs' – and James's – limitations.[13] On the one hand, James used too much architecture – at least in volume two, which 'abides rigidly by its law' of composition according to the standard set forth in the Preface (*LC*-II,

1324). Yet, on the other, he may have used too little. As he admitted, his own rereading of *The Golden Bowl* made him aware of 'many more of the shining fish afloat in the deep sea of [his] endeavour than the net of widest casting could pretend to gather in' (*LC*-II, 1338). Maggie is only one of James's marvellous sea creatures; and as he captures her, the others escape.

I do agree with Nussbaum that critics should return to 'the ethical and social questions that give literature its high importance in our lives'.[14] To focus exclusively on linguistic games is to succumb to the irresponsibility that James repudiated. We should be wary, however, of following Nussbaum in adopting the Prefaces as authoritative guides.[15] James's reviews, together with the novels themselves, reveal his ambivalence toward values that remain in conflict; and the clashing metaphors of the prefaces signal his acceptance of unreconciled oppositions. Thus he played his dual roles of formalist master and postmodern precursor without striving for theoretical consistency. And he took himself less seriously than have many of his admirers.

But recent theorists – especially the feminists and the cultural materialists – can foster our awareness of ideological motives that James himself may not have recognized. His own conscious concerns were more aesthetic than political. As he read the newspapers, he probably reflected on current issues; but he spent more time reading the fiction of his rivals and devising ways of improving on it. Fortunately for him, the nineteenth-century novel was a genre typically in need of refinement – 'a ponderous, shapeless, diffuse piece of machinery, "padded" to within an inch of its life, without style, without taste, without a touch of the divine spark, and effective, when it [was] effective, only by a sort of brutal dead-weight' (*LC*-I, 497).

None the less, we should also discern the political reasons for Jamesian delicacy. From Turgenev in particular, he learned valuable lessons concerning the limits of language and of masculine authority. Hence his unfinished endings and omitted scenes created the illusion of his characters' independence. But silence became a means of finessing dangerous issues, notably those of divorce and women's rights. His faith in consciousness has attracted many followers; but it served as a defence mechanism for a writer who often failed to answer the Tolstoyan question – 'What is to be done?' – and whose plotting suffered in consequence. Above all, his avoidance of banality

– especially the representation of domestic life – confirmed his own identity as a strong man, not a passive woman. Feminists must therefore deal with an anomaly: Isabel and Maggie are far more intelligible as Jamesian alter egos than as women coping with marital unhappiness.

Should we condemn James for the limitations of his gender and culture? Of course not. But we should acknowledge the differences, as well as the continuities, between his perspective and ours. His counsel to aspiring authors – 'Oh, do something from your point of view' (*LC*-1, 93) – also applies to ethical critics. We can pay tribute to his insights, and to his ongoing struggle to achieve them, without building an idol in our own image.

NOTES

1 See Naomi Schor, *George Sand and Idealism* (New York: Columbia University Press, 1993), 44.
2 Stephen Donadio, *Nietzsche, Henry James, and the Artistic Will* (New York: Oxford University Press, 1978), 16.
3 Ibid., 118.
4 Janet Adam Smith, ed, *Henry James and Robert Louis Stevenson: A Record of Friendship and Criticism* (London: Hart-Davis, 1948), 102.
5 Joseph Wiesenfarth, 'A Woman in *The Portrait of a Lady*', *Henry James Review*, 7 (1986), 18.
6 Sandra K Fischer, 'Isabel Archer and the Enclosed Chamber: A Phenomenological Reading', *Henry James Review*, 7 (1986), 48.
7 Paul Hadella, 'Rewriting Misogyny: *The Portrait of a Lady* and the Popular Fiction Debate', *American Literary Realism*, 26 (1994), 10.
8 Martha C. Nussbaum, *Love's Knowledge: Essays on Philosophy and Literature* (New York and Oxford: Oxford University Press, 1990), 194.
9 Ibid., 134
10 See S. L. Goldberg, *Agents and Lives: Moral Thinking in Literature* (Cambridge University Press, 1993), 301–2; Geoffrey Galt Harpham, *Getting It Right: Language, Literature, and Ethics* (University of Chicago Press, 1992), 43.
11 *Love's Knowledge*, 133, 135.
12 Ibid., 136.
13 See *Agents and Lives*, 299, 302.
14 *Love's Knowledge*, 168.
15 Ibid., 10.

CHAPTER 4

James and the shadow of the Roman Empire: manners and the consenting victim

Adrian Poole

Rome has served, for the West, as its greatest sign of historical necessity. Look, touch, believe: this truth seems engraved in the very stones of Rome, that history is not just what has been, but what always had to be. How comforting to contemplate the pastness of the past, to feel one's exemption from it, as Isabel Archer does, initially, as she takes the long stride from the Roman past to her own future in a single flight (*PL*, ch. 27). Or alternatively, for James himself, closer to home, how numbing to feel the estrangement, face to face with the grave of his sister Alice, the pen dropping helplessly from his hand, 'with what it meets of the ineffable, what it meets of the cold Medusa-face of life, of all the life *lived*, on every side' (*CN*, 240).

James was acutely attentive to the actions of memory and forgetting, and the powers that drive them on, in public and in private. The modern city could seem to him ruthlessly devoted to the very principle of forgetting. On the steps of the Capitol in Washington, an encounter with a trio of Indian braves wandering peaceably through the august precincts inspired him to imagine the very action of 'history' itself as a foreshortening and simplification, 'reducing to a single smooth stride the bloody footsteps of time': 'One rubbed one's eyes, but there, at its highest polish, shining in the beautiful day, was the brazen face of history, and there, all about one, immaculate, the printless pavements of the State' (*American Scene*, ch. 11). 'Printless' echoes the coinage Shakespeare finds for Prospero ('And ye that on the sands with printless foot / Do chase the ebbing Neptune'),[1] and, later in *The American Scene*, James will think of the way so many impressions, in his native land, simply cease to be, 'as soon as your back is turned – to fade, to pass away, to leave not a wreck behind' (ch. 14). As if the magic of the new world were to conjure up and wipe away in a single motion, smoothing and polishing an unmarkable surface. At least the old world had the decency or shame to preserve some rack and ruin, including the arch ruin of all – the great city which for George Eliot, looking through Dorothea's eyes, summed itself up as 'all this vast wreck of ambitious ideals'.[2]

Rome was much in the mind of James and others at the turn of the century, as the imperial powers, old and new, steeled themselves against each other. I wish to consider the role played in James's writing by the idea of Rome and empire and historical necessity, and I begin by picking up an observation of T. S. Eliot's that links James and the great poet of imperial Rome. On the face of it, this is an unlikely juxtaposition. Ransacking James for allusions to the *Aeneid* does not yield many spoils.[3] Rowland Mallett briefly recalls the Sibyl's assurance to Aeneas that the downward route is easy enough, when he shamefully thinks of smoothing the *descensus Averni* for Roderick Hudson (ch. 16). And the underworld does figure in one of James's revisions to this novel, when he darkens Rowland's thoughts about the danger that Christina poses to Roderick (ch. 9).[4] But allusions to classical literature are fairly scarce in James, and they rarely carry much weight.[5] He will have known the Dido to whom Matthew Arnold makes such memorable allusion near the end of 'The Scholar Gipsy', but he does not himself press her into service. Yet Virgil and James meet in the mind of T. S. Eliot, and this is far from a senseless coincidence.

It occurs in Eliot's 1944 paper, 'What is a Classic?'. He is pondering the maturities required of mind and of manners in the writer and his age, and he argues that Virgil was uniquely placed to meet these needs because of his position in history, at the still point of the turning world, the passage from the pagan era to the Christian. Yet Virgil still had to make himself a 'classic' by virtue of the way in which he seized his own world at its best and judged it by its own highest ideals. This makes Eliot think of James: 'House parties of the wealthy, in Edwardian England, were not exactly what we read of in the pages of Henry James: but Mr James's society was an idealization, of a kind, of *that* society, and not an anticipation of any other.'[6] 'An idealization, of a kind'. Of what kind, exactly? This is not the first time Eliot has struck such a note about James. Twenty years earlier he had risked using a dirty word when he wrote of James's 'romanticism'. This was, it turned out, a romanticism of which Eliot could approve; not the usual brand of sentimental evasion, but a driven and visionary idealism that looks its own world in the face and stares through it to something better beyond.

it was not the romanticism of those who dream because they are too lazy or too fearful to face the fact; it issues, rather, from the imperative insistence of an ideal which tormented him. He was possessed by the vision of an ideal society; he *saw* (not fancied) the relations between the members of such a society. And no one, in the end, has ever been more aware . . . of the disparity between possibility and fact.[7]

In other words, the 'idealization, of a kind' that Eliot attributes to James offers the contemporary world its own best possible face in the hope that it will be shamed rather than flattered. This is, as James himself might have said, a fond hope, and it is not surprising that he has been accused of overestimating the capacity of his readers for realizing that they ought to be feeling challenged and aroused rather than dazzled and beguiled, or, indeed, bored and exasperated. Virgil has had analogous detractors who see in him no more than an emperor's apologist. When the Sainte-Beuve so much admired by James chose to lecture on Virgil at the Collège de France in 1855, having accepted an appointment from the Emperor Napoleon III as Professor of Latin Poetry, he was shouted down by auditors eager to declare their opposition to all the lackeys of imperialism.[8] Idealization, of any kind, will have its dangers.

Eliot's motives in associating Virgil and James doubtless include the desire to position himself as Dante's heir, at the far end of the Christian era. But his immediate concern, in this 1944 essay, is with 'manners'. He admires in Virgil a 'refinement of manners . . . particularly in that test of manners, private and public conduct between the sexes'.[9] He singles out the great moment in the underworld when Aeneas meets the shade of Dido and suffers her magnificent rebuff; it is, says Eliot, 'not only one of the most poignant, but one of the most civilized passages in poetry'. It is not just that Dido behaves well, as we say, by not shouting and screaming but instead just using that most civilized of weapons, the snub – 'perhaps the most telling snub in all poetry'. What is really 'civilized' about the passage is Aeneas's response. He accepts her judgment of his behaviour, and not out of mere politeness, as who should say, 'well, you have every right to your feelings and even opinion'. No, according to Eliot, he really *does* accept her judgment of him: 'what matters most is, that Aeneas does not forgive himself'. This is a remarkable act of identification on Eliot's part. He suggests that Dido's behaviour may be a projection of Aeneas's own conscience, but Aeneas has become a projection of Eliot's conscience as he creates the burden of guilt to be shouldered by the bearer of history. Eliot makes Aeneas into the tragic character or even martyr so many readers have wanted to find in him, and failed. In fact, the words that Virgil makes Aeneas address to Dido are all to do with self-justification and self-exculpation. When she fails to answer him, Virgil tells us that he weeps, that he gazes after her, that he is shaken by the inequity of fate, and that he pities her.[10] Then he carries on. It is intriguing and frustrating that we do not get to hear more than this about what goes on inside him. But this is the kind of hero this epic needs, one with good manners.

Good manners, at least in Virgil and in Henry James, depend on not saying a lot of things, on assuming or hoping that other people will understand what you mean without needing to explain yourself. What Eliot admires in this scene is exactly the silence in which Dido and Aeneas collaborate, and into which he can then read his own meaning. He wants to believe that Aeneas and Dido agree over what is unsaid between them, but of course there is no means of knowing. This is what makes it such a 'Jamesian' moment. Readers of James, especially of the later James, are constantly being asked to interpret scenes like this, in which two (or more) characters exhibit the wonderful manners of their world, in refraining from the utterance of their own thoughts and feelings and the insistence that other people utter theirs, thus maintaining the illusion (or the ideal) that everyone knows everything without being told, whereas, in reality, as Eliot has it in his own 'Portrait of a Lady': 'we are really in the dark'.[11] To this extent Eliot is right to imply that there is something 'Jamesian' about Virgil's moment of confrontation, when violence is at least masked by the manners that permit or even encourage words and eyes to miss each other. But Eliot wants to see more than this. He wants Aeneas' manners, in accepting Dido's silence, to secrete a sense of guilt, a guilt that will enhance the nobility of serving the cause of historical necessity. This is one way of conceiving the founder of empire.

Virgil and James have this in common, that there is a recalcitrance to the way they represent their imperialists. And readers may want to read into James's imperialists the guilt that Eliot sees in Aeneas. But that is what they must do, read it *in*. They will not find it there already in the consciousness that James attributes to Strether and Milly Theale and Maggie Verver. The stealthy concussions around which the action revolves, in *The Ambassadors* and *The Wings of the*

Dove and *The Golden Bowl*, these invariably yield winners and losers. The winners are the ones who realize that the silence is not and cannot be equally shared, and who can manipulate the silence to their own best advantage. And forgive themselves for doing so, should this prove necessary – ruthlessly.

Eliot thought we could not escape the shadow of the Roman Empire. At the time he wrote *The Waste Land*, it was for him as it had been for many writers from around the turn of the century the end of empire rather than its birth that engaged his imagination. As William Vance's rich survey demonstrates, Rome held an absorbing fascination for American writers, artists, and intellectuals at least up until the 1920s, when Eliot's poem marks a watershed, in this respect as in many others. Vance observes that beneath the poem 'lie the history and mythology of imperial Rome, fragmented and transposed to our century in the dying British empire'.[12] The poem's epigraph has the same Cumaean Sibyl who foresaw the founding of Rome now plead for the death she has, like Tennyson's Tithonus, been denied. In my beginning is my end. And perhaps, beyond *The Waste Land*, vice versa.

Rome meant many things to James, but that was exactly the attraction of the place itself and all the matter it contained, an attraction that develops a particular intensity in the nineteenth century, and perhaps, even more particularly, as Vance suggests, for the American imagination: an enormity of signs, susceptible to all kinds of interpretation. Of one of its most spectacular creations or remains, the Colosseum, Vance suggests that American writings about it cumulatively reveal 'an ambivalent attitude towards imperial power, its rise, its glories and terrors, and its fall'. It becomes, he says, 'the Moby-Dick of architecture'.[13] James uses the architecture, of course, as all novelists were bound to, but it is significant that, when he recalls his first memory of visiting Rome in 1869, the initiatory moment that he chooses should be a dramatic one with human actors. He recalls rushing out into the street 'heedless of breakfast and open-mouthed only for visions', to be greeted by a vision of the Pope (*WWS*, I, 109). What impressed him was the instant effect of the Pope's presence on the world around him, the total submission and reverence he commanded. That is real power – or that *was* real power in 1869, before the new age dawned, the age of what James loftily calls 'the emphasised rule of the mob' (*WWS*, II, 165).

Rome was not least important to James for the role it played in two of the big fictions he inherited and chose to rewrite, *The Marble Faun* and *Middlemarch*. If one were limited to a single description of Rome's effect on him, one might borrow the phrase with which George Eliot credits Ladislaw, that Rome made his mind 'flexible with constant comparison'.[14] For James, as for Emerson and Hawthorne before him, and for the contemporary Conrad of *Heart of Darkness*, the modern equivalent of Rome could well seem to be London – unless perhaps it were Paris. And the modern equivalent of the Goths could well seem to be the Americans, especially as the century neared its end and they descended on Europe with their new wealth and power. In a notebook entry for 1895, the figure of 'Mrs Jack' (Isabella Stewart Gardner) induced in James a nightmare vision: 'The Americans looming up – dim, vast, portentous – in their millions – like gathering waves – the barbarians of the Roman Empire' (*CN*, 126). Unless the Americans were themselves the new Romans, advancing from their Republican era to a new imperialist age. Writing in 1905, Henry Adams recalls himself meditating in 1860 that 'Rome was actual; it was England; it was going to be America.'[15] He was scarcely alone in noticing the vast stride to empire that America had taken in the decades following the Civil War. His novelist friend set himself to measure some aspects of this stride in the phase of his writings inaugurated by the writing of *The Ambassadors* (begun in the autumn of 1900) and concluded with the publication of *The American Scene* (in 1907).

These writings draw deeply on the ideas and images of empire, and they pose all sorts of questions about the narrative of empire, the apparent inevitabilities of its beginnings and endings. The comparative method wrought into the texture of the writing means that Rome is only one of several sources. It is true that the 'question of an *Imperium*' and the image of London as the modern Rome figure vividly in the opening lines of *The Golden Bowl*, and that Fanny Assingham deputes herself to personify a *pax Britannica* (*GB*, Bk. 5, ch. 1). But there are always other examples to draw on, especially France and Paris. In an 1886 letter to Charles Eliot Norton, James likens 'the rotten and *collapsible*' state of the English upper class to 'that of the French aristocracy before the revolution – minus cleverness and conversation', repeating sentiments expressed in the recently published *The Princess Casamassima*. But James typically thinks of an alternative: 'Or perhaps it's more like the heavy, congested and depraved Roman world upon which the barbarians came down' (*HJL*, III, 146). Where empires are concerned, James's imagination moves freely between Rome and France. Louis Napoleon may have prompted Marx to his famous *mot* about history repeating itself – first time tragedy, second time farce – but, as Hillis Miller has observed, the French Revolution and First Empire had already, and self-consciously, repeated Roman history.[16]

Henry James's friend, Robert Louis Stevenson, thought it was possible to get out from under the shadow of Rome, and he was in a good position to claim he had succeeded when he wrote from the South Seas:

> To cross the Channel is, for a boy of twelve, to change heavens; to cross the Atlantic, for a man of twenty-four, is hardly to modify his diet. But I was now escaped out of the shadow of the Roman Empire, under whose toppling monuments we were all cradled, whose laws and letters are on every hand of us, constraining and preventing. I was now to see what men might be whose fathers had never studied Virgil, [and] had never been conquered by Caesar.[17]

Yet Stevenson had taken Virgil with him, as he exchanged old worlds for new, moving from Europe to America, from America to the Pacific islands. In March 1886, at Bournemouth, he reports himself 'overpowered' by reading *Aeneid* 5 and 6, the latter for the first time, and concludes: 'We are all damned small fry, and Virgil is one of the tops of human achievement';[18] eighteen months later in the Adirondacks he has progressed to *Aeneid* 7 (and is coincidentally reading *Roderick Hudson*);[19] a year later in Tahiti he affects to complain that the *Aeneid* is all he has to read.[20] And, in March 1889, he boasts to James from Honolulu of the grief-stricken letter his departure from Tahiti has provoked from his native friend Rui: 'My XIX century strikes here, and lies alongside of, something beautiful and ancient. I think the receipt of such a letter might humble – shall I say, even Mallock? – and for me, I would rather have received it than written *Redgauntlet* or the VIth *Aeneid*.'[21] Virgil was ringing in his imagination through the writing of *The Master of Ballantrae*, from December 1887 to May 1889, as the novel's four allusions to the *Aeneid* suggest.[22]

The fugitive Stevenson was not quite the scholar gipsy Arnold had in mind, and James responds to the challenge with some brilliant banter. Ponderous questions about the shadow of empire do not always have to be answered in the high Roman fashion, in the tones of a Virgil or an Arnold or a Henry Adams: 'You are indeed the male Cleopatra or buccaneering Pompadour of the Deep – the wandering Wanton of the Pacific. You swim into our ken with every provocation and prospect – and we have only time to open our arms to receive you when your immortal back is turned to us in the act of still more provoking flight' (*HJL*, III, 278). 'You are indeed the male Cleopatra': but James is himself adopting the idiom of the Shakespearean Cleopatra, who turns her back on the Roman language of tragedy and epic. There are all sorts of ways of turning away; Dido's is not the only style. James favoured the figure of the turned back for the artist's guardianship of a private and creative space, but it is an image for which Rowland Mallett revealingly reaches when he is trying to describe the power exerted by Christina Light: 'she probably has a way of turning her back which is the most maddening thing in the world. She's an actress' (*RH*, ch. 15). It is like James to be ludic in thinking about an artist's elusiveness, and he will not settle on a single image to pin Stevenson down. But it is notable that Cleopatra recurs when James's mind is on the stretch of empire and its limits. Cleopatra and Dido can easily melt into each other (as they seem to do in *The Waste Land*); they are the two signal representatives of a regal passion that at once threatens and, in defeat, confirms the narrative of Roman empire. Neither can simply be described as a victim, not least because readers and audiences of Virgil and Shakespeare have been tempted by the thought that it might be paltry to be Caesar and miserable to be Aeneas. (Norman Vance points out that the revival of Purcell's *Dido and Aeneas* after 1840 dealt a bad blow to Aeneas's reputation).[23] But, of the two, it is Cleopatra who, thanks to Shakespeare, retains in the anglophone imagination a power of self-renewal that her darker Carthaginian sister lacks. As Rowland Mallett says of Christina: 'She's an actress.'

The badinage with Stevenson contains another significant allusion: 'You swim into our ken.' James is fond of this image from Keats's sonnet 'On First Looking into Chapman's Homer', and here it is evidently spurred into play by the Pacific, at which stout Cortez stared with eagle eyes. Keats leaves himself happily undecided between stout Cortez and the gentler 'watcher of the skies' in the previous lines, and James is likely to have admired such irresolution. In his treacherous way, James whispers something to us about Adam Verver when he makes him think of the discovery of his imperial destiny as a Patron of Art in the terms of 'Keats's sonnet about stout

Cortez in the presence of the Pacific' (*GB*, Bk. 2, ch. 1). It is a revealingly partial reading of the poem that remembers it like this, and Adam does not inspire confidence in his capacity for patient wonder when we are further told that 'a couple of perusals of the immortal lines had sufficed to stamp them in his memory'. Adam is all set to 'rifle the Golden Isles', but he has already rifled the magical realm of poor Keats's poem. We meet a more diffident imperialist, perhaps another breed entirely, in the protagonist of *The Ambassadors*, who discovers in the scene on the river that Chad and Madame de Vionnet 'had so remarkably swum into Strether's ken' (Bk. 11, ch. 3). Keats's poem keeps a distance between the wondering watcher and the eagle-eyed conqueror, and it arrests the latter before he starts rifling the Golden Isles. But a novel is bound to court the questions that a poem can suspend, and Strether has more difficulty in postponing the crisis of his dealings with the worlds, new and old, between which he is – as his name amongst other things intimates – stretched.

Rome figures largely in James's early fiction, in *Roderick Hudson* and *Daisy Miller* and *The Portrait of a Lady* and some of the tales. Early on in the first-named he describes Rome as 'the immemorial city of convention' (*RH*, ch. 5), and much later he makes Rowland inform Mary Garland that what they see around them is 'the results of an immemorial, a complex and accumulated, civilisation' (ch. 17). (In 1879, it had just been 'an old and complex civilisation'.) The word 'immemorial' is a significant one for James, and the repetition of the word in the 1907 text helps to suggest a deepened sense that Rome is, before all others, the city of memory and forgetting, where origins are lost and found. This is what troubles Mary as she feels her grip on her own origins beginning to dissolve.

James's relations with Rome had been marked before 1907 by the much-postponed and never relished biography of William Wetmore Story, the ex-patriate sculptor and poet. The shadow of this work hovered over James from soon after Story's death in 1895, but by the time of his visit to Rome in 1899 he was committed to the task. (He had last been in Rome in 1894 to visit the grave of Constance Fenimore Woolson, the woman in his life, if there was one, with the best claims to the role of Dido; she was buried close to Story and his wife, and in 1899 James again paid his respects.) The Story book continued to loom during the composition of *The Ambassadors* and *The Wings of the Dove*, and eventually got written between the latter and *The Golden Bowl*, appearing at the same time as the delayed *Ambassadors* in the autumn of 1903. Along with the initial draft of *The Sense of the Past*, *The Sacred Fount*, and 'The Beast in the Jungle', it shares the distinction of arousing curiosity about its relations with the three great novels of these years. James's patent lack of interest in Story himself is compensated, if that is the right word, by the immense, burgeoning interest he takes, and makes the reader take, in the activity of his own memory, in anticipation, as it will turn out, of the sustained flight of the later autobiographical writings. 'The dawn of the American consciousness of the complicated world it was so persistently to annex' – this, James says, is his subject. And in this sense the work bears closely on the three novels in which he explores the high noon of this annexation, in contemporary Paris, and London, and Venice. Rome roused his sense of history, as a matter at once personal and immemorial, in the here and now and dead and gone.

James does not use Rome directly in the three big novels of these years (apart from Amerigo's Roman provenance). George Eliot had called Rome 'the city of visible history',[24] but the history that James most wanted to see was written in human faces and voices, especially women's. He wanted a history that was more than 'visible'; the word he chooses is 'visitable': 'I delight in a palpable imaginable *visitable* past' (*LC*-II, 1177). This is why he was intrigued by the matter out of which he drew *The Aspern Papers*, and why he was so attached to the old women on whose vivid presence and voice he all attentively hung: the Fanny Kemble whose uncommemorated death stirs him to such eloquence in the Preface to 'The Altar of the Dead', the Mrs Procter who gives rise to a fine passage in the Story biography. It was through such living witnesses that 'one sniffed up the essence of history' (*WWS*, I, 227). The public and official makers of history were all very well, but for the historian of manners, intent on what he had once called 'the reverse of the picture' ('The Story of a Year' (*T*, I, 30)), women were indispensable. Or, as he makes Strether think: 'there it was again – it took women, it took women' (*AB*, Bk. 12, ch. 2).

Rome sends James to Paris, as it were, as the other great city of memory and forgetting in which history is visible and visitable, in which he can set loose, so much more richly than in his earlier Parisian novel, some emissaries of the future world-rulers to see what they can make of it and get out of it. If one is looking for an Aeneas in the novel, it may seem to be Chad; and when Madame de

Vionnet terminally exhales to Strether, 'But think of me, think of me –!', she may sound like the Dido of Purcell's unforgettable 'Remember me'. But all such possible memories and repetitions are subject to ironic reflection. The most intense reflection and the finest ironies surround Strether's apprehensions of Madame de Vionnet. It is through her, beyond all the other helps and hindrances, the solicitations and distractions, that Strether hopes to reach 'the taste of history' (*AB*, Bk. 5, ch. 3).

What Strether 'gets' from Madame de Vionnet herself cannot be isolated from her surroundings, the scene of which she is the keynote, the ground of which she is the figure. On his first visit to her dwelling in the Rue de Bellechasse, what he finds there or what he 'makes out', in James's suggestive phrase, is 'some glory, some prosperity of the First Empire, some Napoleonic glamour, some dim lustre of the great legend' (Bk. 6, ch. 1). There is the 'immemorial polish' that one might expect from a modern-day Rome. There is the stamp of history impressed on the relics 'of a private order', such as make this sanctuary 'something quite different from Miss Gostrey's little museum of bargains and from Chad's lovely home; he recognized it as founded much more on old accumulations . . . than on any contemporary method of acquisition or form of curiosity'.[25] Most importantly for Strether's purposes, Madame de Vionnet, unlike Chad and Maria, has just sat 'beautifully passive under the spell of transmission – transmission from her father's line, he quite made up his mind – had only received, accepted, and been quiet'. If only inheritance could always be so magically smooth; if only Strether could match this woman's beautiful passivity.

He sees her on other grounds, at Chad's and in Notre Dame, but he sees her once more in her most personal milieu for a last farewell after the famous scene on the river. By now he has modified his sense of her passivity, and in the first and virtually silent of the relevant chapters (the movement from the silence of the first to the dialogue of the second will put him on the spot most effectively), he fantasizes his relation with her as that of an all-trusting infant and an all-capable mother: 'the spell of his luxury wouldn't be broken. He wouldn't have, that is, to become responsible' (Bk. 12, ch. 1). This time the spell will all be over him, but again it is coloured by the sense of history that ministers to his deepest needs. And into it is introduced, as an image for the role that Strether wishes to see Madame de Vionnet play, the heroic and doomed figure of Madame Roland.

She is not the first historic woman to lose her head in Strether's histrionic imaginings. The red ribbon that Maria Gostrey wears round her neck reminds him of Mary Stuart, and in this as in so many respects 'Maria' leads him on to 'Marie'.[26] Nor is it solely as a tragic and beheaded heroine that Strether finally wants to see her. She has become for him the choicest of the many impressions he has accumulated. For all Strether's emancipation from the ethos of Woollett, he still imagines Madame de Vionnet as a magician, the embodiment of European sorcery. In terms of James's own fictional career, her lineage stretches back to the Princess Casamassima, Christina Light; Madame Merle contributes something to this line, and so does the pivotal figure of Miriam Rooth. Behind Christina there stands another Miriam – Hawthorne's: the Miriam who sketches the alarming archetypes of Jael, Judith, and Herodias. (Roderick Hudson's bust of Christina Light encourages Gloriani to identify *her* as Herodias, though there are interesting variations between 1879 and 1907 (ch. 9).)[27] But then that is the point about such women, as Strether realizes; the source of Madame de Vionnet's fascination is that there will always be more 'behind': 'He felt what he had felt before with her, that there was always more behind what she showed, and more and more again behind that' (*AB*, Bk. 12, ch. 2). He does not want to imprison her in a single cell. He wants her to go on proliferating against the immemorial polish of her surroundings. Her ghostliness for him is that of an image that endlessly revives and fades. At Chad's party he had recognized that she reawoke in him 'the idea of the *femme du monde* in her habit as she lived' (Bk. 6, ch. 3). In recalling the ghost of Hamlet's father at the very brink of its final departure, this Shakespearean echo has the paradoxical effect of making Madame de Vionnet come and go at one and the same moment. (James uses it of the aged Miss Clairmont who provided the source for *The Aspern Papers* (*LC*-II, 1175).) Such an impossible resolution of contradictions makes Strether inevitably think, a few lines later, of Cleopatra, 'like Cleopatra in the play, indeed various and multifold'. One might apply to Strether's imagining of this woman a phrase that Hawthorne finds for the statue of Cleopatra created by his sculptor Kenyon: 'one of the images that men keep forever, finding a heat in them which does not cool down, throughout the centuries'.[28]

In other words Strether wants this woman ideally neither dead nor alive but somewhere midway, eternally swimming in and out of his ken, as her grey eyes move in and out of their talk, during the happiest moment they share over their memorable lunch by the Seine. Such wonderful impressions may seem to make life worth living, at least for Strether. But there is a price to be paid for them, and in this novel it is the woman who must do the paying.

This brings us back to manners. There is a lot of talk about manners good and bad and beautiful in this novel, as in most of James, not least in the final scene between Strether and Madame de Vionnet (Bk. 12, chs. 1 and 2). 'Caprices, he was sure she felt, were before anything else bad manners.' Strether's admiration for her depends on her 'bridging of intervals', her seemingly endless ability to 'present' things so as to make them right, natural, inevitable. And she returns the admiration for *his* good manners in accepting everything with which he has been presented. Yet there is a moment, the critical moment, at which 'manners' are reduced to the singular, to painfully intense effect. It is the only moment in the scene at which their eyes meet – 'and the next thing he knew he had uttered all his thought. "You're afraid for your life!".' It is her thought too, the unspoken out in the open between them, and it makes her break down. 'She sat and covered her face with her hands, giving up all attempt at a manner.' She recovers enough to thank him for never having snubbed her, and apologizes for forgetting her manners. But he has spoken the truth. They can never meet again, after this. She does not take the hand he offers her, for good-bye.

Might things have been otherwise? I have been annexing Stevenson's 'shadow of the Roman Empire' as the weightiest figure the West has found for the inevitability of history. That is the sum of what 'Rome' seems to mean: this is how it was, how it was always bound to be, how it *had* to be. It quietly dawns on the reader that the most frequent word in *The Ambassadors* is, after all, 'had'. This is one of the reasons why Chad is given his name, to rhyme with 'had' (the other reason perhaps being that it contains the word 'cad'). For example: 'She had made him better, she had made him best, she had made him anything one would; but it came to our friend with supreme eagerness that he was none the less only Chad. Strether had the sense that *he*, a little, had made him too.' As it follows the expansion of Strether's empire, the novel constantly looks forward to look back, nowhere more concentratedly than at the moment when Strether gathers himself for the final impact of Madame de Vionnet's presence: 'He knew in advance he should look back on the perception actually sharpest with him as on the view of something old, old, old, the oldest thing he had ever personally touched; . . .'. This in the end is what makes Madame de Vionnet serve as Strether's Dido, as it were, the sign of historical necessity, what had to be. 'Ah but you've *had* me!' are his last words to her, as he leaves her to her fate, and there may be some truth to this. But the way he has had *her* has been the story to which we have mainly attended.

His last words to her on the threshold are delivered 'with an emphasis that made an end'. One might wish to redress that emphasis and break the silence to which he consigns her by recalling the last words of the Madame Roland of whom she reminds him. As she mounted the scaffold, the inspirer of the Girondins and victim of the Terror left her last impression with the words: '*O liberté, que de crimes on commet en ton nom!*' *O liberté*, o pax romana, o pax britannica – and all the other great ideals of history, in the name of which so many crimes have been committed.

At its most inconceivable, history is the sum total of what is done, to which every doing contributes, including what is said and written and heard and read, in doorways, on scaffolds, wherever. What is not said is also an act or part of one, and writing represents the other sides of utterance and the intervals between, the shades and the shadows. James can seem the most shady of writers and hence, in his way, the most imperious. So one must ask, finally, what anyone is doing in reading him.

In a remarkable passage of the Story biography, James does indeed present the vision of an ideal society. It is the community of Anglo-Americans equalized and harmonized by the spirit of Rome, as by 'the master-conductor of a great harmonious band in which differences were disallowed' (*WWS*, II, 206). James recalls meeting for the first time the Matthew Arnold he had once idolized, and being happily disappointed: 'It was, on the Roman evening, as if, for all the world, we were *equally* great and happy, or still more, perhaps, equally nothing and nobody; we were related only to the enclosing fact of Rome, before which every one, it was easy to feel, bore himself with the same good manners' (*WWS*, II, 208). We do not have Arnold's version of the occasion, or indeed anyone else's, any more than, in *The American Scene*, anyone other than James is allowed to get a word in edgeways. This is 'good manners'? We should recall that scene on the Capitol in Washington. What James's Rome represents is another version, polished beyond belief, of 'the brazen face of history'. Call it rather the shameless power of writing, in the face of which one may well rub one's eyes, to brazen it out. This is, James declares, 'the sense of Rome', in defence of which he is prepared to 'brave even the imputation of making a mere Rome of words, talking of a Rome of my own which was no Rome of reality' (*WWS*, II, 209). The mock-modesty of 'mere' is rich, as if it were the question of a choice between those hoary old antagonists, reality and imagination.

More important, however, is the recognition that it is not the choice, on which many readings of James so lazily repose, between surrender to the power of his writing or defiance of it. James does indeed, if you like, build a veritable 'Rome of words', and within this fictive empire there is much submission and many victims. But the responsible reader is not subject to this empire, or not merely so, caught on its borders and forced to choose, inside or out. Reading James should mean being neither here nor there but both at once, as the inhabitants of Story's ideal Roman world could never be, bound as they were, however consentingly and even consciously, by such 'good manners'. They could not, after all, read this: 'They then, as it were, the good manners, became the form in which the noble influence was best recognised, so that you could fairly trace it from occasion to occasion, from one consenting victim to another. The victims may very well not have been themselves always conscious, but the conscious individual had them all, attentively, imaginatively, at his mercy' (*WWS*, II, 208–9). The polished force of James's writing requires a reader under the influence but ready to trace it, working all the while not just to stay conscious but to become more so.

It is an education, or should be, attending to the composition of a Rome of words, with all its shadows.

NOTES

1 *The Tempest*, The Riverside Shakespeare (Boston: Houghton, 1974), 5. 1. 345.
2 *Middlemarch* (Edinburgh: Blackwood, 1871–2), ch. 20.
3 Adeline Tintner and Bruce Fogelman have made a couple of important finds. Tintner considers the significance of an explicit reference in the late tale 'Crapy Cornelia' (1909) (*The Museum World of Henry James* (Ann Arbor: UMI Research Press, 1986), 192–4), and Fogelman uncarths a systematically ironic comparison to Aeneas and Dido in the story of John Marcher and May Bartram ('John Marcher's Journey for Know-

ledge: The Heroic Background of "The Beast in the Jungle",' *The Henry James Review*, 10.1 (Winter 1989), 68–73). He also dwells briefly on an overt quotation in 'The Figure in the Carpet', noted by Tintner along with two fleeting references in *The Princess Casamassima* and *The Wings of the Dove*.

4 In the first English edition of 1879, Roderick thinks 'that she was a complex, wilful, passionate, creature who might easily engulf a too confiding spirit in the eddies of her capricious temper'; in 1907 he thinks 'that she was a complex, wilful, passionate creature who might easily draw down a too confiding spirit into some strange underworld of unworthy sacrifice, not unfurnished with traces of others of the lost'.

5 Philip Horne points out to me that, in 1905, Charles Eliot Norton made this comment on James and W. D. Howells, that neither 'have been as good as they would have been if they had been trained with some acquaintance in childhood with Homer and Virgil and the historic stream of imagination in literature'. See Letter to Weir Mitchell, 22 December 1905, in Anna Robeson Burr, *Weir Mitchell: His Life and Letters*, 2nd edn (New York: Duffield, 1930), 308.

6 T. S. Eliot, 'What is a Classic?' (The Presidential Address to the Virgil Society in 1944), reprinted in *On Poetry and Poets* (London: Faber, 1957), 62.

7 T. S. Eliot, 'A Prediction in Regard to Three English Authors', *Vanity Fair*, February 1924; partially reprinted in *Henry James: A Collection of Critical Essays*, ed. Leon Edel (Englewood Cliffs: Prentice-Hall, 1963), 56.

8 See Norman Vance, 'Virgil and the Nineteenth Century', in *Virgil and His Influence*, ed. Charles Martindale (Bristol Classical, 1984), 175–6.

9 T. S. Eliot, 'What is a Classic?', 62.

10 The closing lines of the scene are as follows: 'nec minus Aeneas casu percussus iniquo / prosequitur lacrimis longe et miseratur euntem' (*Aeneid* 6. 475–6). In 1697, Dryden translates: 'Some pious Tears the pitying Heroe paid; / And follow'd with his Eyes the flitting Shade' (*The Poems of John Dryden*, ed. James Kinsley, vol. III (Oxford: Clarendon, 1958)); in 1983, Robert Fitzgerald translates, 'Aeneas still gazed after her in tears, / Shaken by her ill fate and pitying her' (New York: Random, 1983; Harmondsworth: Penguin, 1985). The phrase 'casu percussus iniquo' causes some difficulty; Dryden omits it and Fitzgerald calls the ill fate certainly 'hers'. Yet the inequity of fate is shared by Aeneas; in the immediately previous line and a half, Dido has sought and found her former husband, Sychaeus, 'Who answer'd all her Cares and equal'd all her Love' (Dryden). It is at least partly the words 'aequatque Sychaeus amorem' that shake Aeneas with the sense that fate is 'iniquo'.

11 *Collected Poems 1909–1962* (London: Faber, 1969), 21.

12 *America's Rome*, 2 vols. (New Haven: Yale University Press, 1989), vol. I, 387.

13 Vance, *America's Rome*, vol. 1, 45.
14 *Middlemarch*, ch. 22.
15 Henry Adams, *Novels, Mont Saint Michel, The Education* (New York: Library of America, 1983), 803.
16 *Hawthorne and History* (Oxford: Blackwell, 1991), 112.
17 *In the South Seas* (1896), ed. Sidney Colvin, Tusitala Edition, Vol. XX (London: Heinemann, 1924), 8.
18 R. L. Stevenson, *Letters*, 8 vols., ed. Bradford A. Booth and Ernest Mehew (New Haven: Yale University Press, 1995), vol. V, 235–6.
19 *Letters*, vol. VI, 86.
20 *Letters*, vol. VI, 237.
21 *Letters*, vol. VI, 274.
22 For the significance of Virgil to *The Master of Ballantrae*, see the Introduction to my edition of the novel for Penguin Classics (Harmondsworth: Penguin, 1996).
23 'Virgil and the Nineteenth Century', 180.
24 *Middlemarch*, ch 20.
25 'Accumulations': between 1879 and 1907, James revised the passage in *Roderick Hudson* that deals with the first impression made on Roderick by 'the immemorial city of convention' (ch. 5). Roderick is supposed to be one of those spirits who feel at home in Rome: in the earlier version these spirits possess 'a deep relish for the artificial element in life and the infinite superpositions of history'; in 1907, the object of their deep relish has partially changed to 'the element of accumulation in the human picture'.
26 Laurette Veza has some pertinent comments about Maria Gostrey and Madame de Vionnet in *Henry James: le champs du regard* (Paris: Table Ronde, 1989), 180: 'Si l'échafaud n'existait pas il faudrait l'inventer afin de couper la belle tête de ces dames qui lui sont si attachées – afin de sauver sa peau, son sang-froid. Ruban rouge, incision sanglante, vision du sourire exquis d'une tête condamnée au tranchant du couperet. Superbe revanche sur les multiples representations d'un Jean-Baptiste sacrifié à la traîtrise féminine. (T. S. Eliot ne l'oubliera pas.)' ['If the scaffold didn't exist one would have to invent it to cut off the beautiful heads of these ladies who are so attached to him [Strether] – to save his skin, his *sang-froid*. Red ribbon, bloody incision, vision of the exquisite smile of a head condemned to the blade. Magnificent revenge on the multiple representations of a John the Baptist sacrificed to woman's treachery. (T. S. Eliot will not forget it.)']
27 Gloriani reproves Roderick for only making a bust of Christina. In 1879, he says: 'If I could only have got hold of her I would have put her into a statue in spite of herself'; in 1907, he says, 'I would have pumped every inch of her empty.' The later version dwells on the idea of Christina as Herodias or Salome (there is some confusion between mother and daughter). Rowland sticks his nose in to suggest that

perhaps Gloriani imagines Christina with Roderick's head on her charger, but Gloriani has the sleazy last word: 'Ah it isn't a question of Hudson's "head"!'
28 Nathaniel Hawthorne, *The Marble Faun*, Centenary Edition, vol. IV (n.p.: Ohio State University Press, 1968), 127 (ch. 14). Hawthorne's statue is derived directly from one of Story's best-known works, as James himself notes (*WWS*, I, 358).

CHAPTER 5

'What Maisie knew': Henry James's Bildungsroman of the artist as queer moralist
Alfred Habegger

What Maisie Knew traces an exemplary path from pained and mystified powerlessness to expert, responsible knowing. Beginning as the poorly informed captive of others' wills, the heroine grows into a free moral agent, both wiser and abler than those who should have doomed her, in all probability, to evasive victimhood.

James told this basic story again and again, from *The Portrait of a Lady* to *The Golden Bowl*. The version we get in *Maisie*, however, is a very special case. James's one novel about a child's growing up was written at a time when he himself was painfully recrafting his career, style, and sense of audience, and also (not incidentally) moving out of London. He wrote with a sharp, mordant deliciousness that surpassed his previous bouquets of tightly packed flavours, and along with his new tonalities he brought in a level of sensational action he had mostly avoided. The book seems 'late', 'modern', particularly in assuming a metropolitan social scene characterized by publicity, loud contrasts, pervasive infidelities, and a degeneration of responsibility.

Twenty years earlier, when James's parents were still alive and he was surer of the world and his place in it, he expressed the view that 'it is good for [children] to feel that the people and things around them that appeal to their respect are beautiful and powerful specimens of what they seem to be' (*LC*-1, 196). Now, writing in the mid-1890s, he produced a book in which the only person who entertains this ideal is the alternately ignored and abused heroine of the opening chapters, who moves us precisely by her lavishly respectful study of the unworthy 'people and things' around her.

The question the novel tries to answer is how an impressionable young mind, immersed in, and saturated by, the shabby, the sinister, the queer, turns itself into something free, fine, noble, and upright. Queered from the start, with her mind constructed of elements that are only superficially regular ('squaring' someone being a key activity in the novel), Maisie is assigned the labour of making herself into something rather like the high gilt Virgin that arrests her attention in Boulogne-sur-mer. This, the task of post-Victorian self-fashioning, should be regarded as complicatedly civilized precisely because of the tacit understanding that the heroine must avoid putting on the crude and absolutist moral sense, the 'straighteners', of Mrs Wix.

We could put it this way: the problem Maisie is assigned is how to grow up without becoming either queer or straight.

I

In the *Oxford English Dictionary*, the earliest citation of *queer* meaning *homosexual* dates from 1922, six years after James's death. In the United States (though not, it seems, in Britain) this newer and more restricted meaning has virtually replaced the traditional and more general sense, which now feels obsolescent and unavailable and definitely unsmart. If an American wants to use *queer* in the older way, he or she may end up feeling a certain defiant self-consciousness. In spite of that liability, it is the old sense of the word that I am going to revert to in this chapter, a choice based on the belief that, for James, the word still carried its traditional range of meanings. The aim is to reconstitute all the nuances in his use of the word without letting the modern and relatively specialized sense overwhelm the many older flavours.

Some have argued that when James wrote *queer*, as he often did in the latter half of his life, he had in mind the modern and more specialized sense.[1] But James used the language of his time, not ours, and when the word shows up in his prose it seems to work in the old way – to invoke an oddness that is not felt to be desirable and that surpasses harmless eccentricity. *To live on queer street*: to reside in a poor and disreputable section of town. *To have a queer turn*: to faint, or to feel on the verge of fainting. The word had a very broad coverage and could be applied to the crooked, the left, the odd, the shabby, the sinister. Sometimes, more restrictedly, it designated the subtly indecent – the illegitimate mixture of the normal and the abnormal, such as the Countess's 'moustache that was – well, not so happy a feature as Sir Claude's' (247).[2]

It is important to see that the queerness of the people and things among whom and which Maisie must somehow grow up is not simply a product of her perception; the queerness is presented as inherent and endemic. Ida's bejewelled flat chest; her and Beale's combined twelve feet three of height; pretty Miss Overmore's seven sisters and arched eyebrows and the way she holds a fork 'with her little finger curled out' (19); Mrs Wix's rosette of grey hair looking 'like a large button' (31) on the back of her neck; the crushing of little Clara Matilda on the frightening sounding Harrow Road: all these details evoke aspects of London that would have been too familiar or ordinary to require amused or even sober comment. Yet Maisie's perspective on them does not so much create their interest as call attention to something that was already out there and really and truly bizarre, and which got ignored only because of a generalized perceptual callousness.

Similarly, while the shocking mistreatment of the heroine by her dreadful parents clearly represents an extreme (or artfully literary) picture of what it means to be a child, there is all the same something undeniably ordinary and real about certain aspects of Maisie's situation. We may not remember scenes from our own lives like the one where Beale's friends pinch Maisie's calves and laugh loudly at some joke she does not catch (and that students want explained), but we have surely observed small children serving as a pretext for an exchange of incomprehensible adult laughter. In the same way, the senselessness, unpredictability, and occasional violence that characterize the behaviour of most of the adults in the novel does not simply reflect their individual badnesses. These are also the *general* conditions of life that any small person has to learn to negotiate.

It is partly because James took a special interest in the predicament of a small person living with monstrous brutes (twelve feet three) that scenes of grabbing and pushing have a central place in Maisie's consciousness and maturation. To be a small child is to live with the awareness that you are liable to be forcibly picked up or shunted aside at any time. "Take her, Mrs Wix," [Ida] added . . . giving the child a push from which Maisie gathered that she wished to set Mrs Wix an example of energy' (28). 'You're too delicious, my own pet!', declared Mrs Beale, whereupon Maisie is 'involved in another hug' (163). 'Maisie felt Sir Claude immediately clutch her. "No, no – thank you: that won't do. She's mine"' (183). 'The next moment [Maisie] was on her mother's breast, where, amid a wilderness of trinkets, she felt as if she had suddenly been thrust, with a smash of glass, into a jeweller's shop-front, but only to be as suddenly ejected with a push and the brisk injunction: "Now go to the Captain!"' (185).

Conversely, to be grown up is to be exempt from the danger of sudden grabs and pushes. In the last chapter, where Sir Claude declares that Maisie is free, that he has somehow 'produced life' (458), the girl's new independence is made visible by his respectful physical handling of her. Whereas Mrs Beale 'threw herself upon' the girl, 'encircling her' (460), possessing her, Sir Claude 'held her in front of him, resting his hands very lightly on her shoulders'. Here, as Sir Claude stands behind Maisie, neither holding nor shoving, the weight or pressure of his hands rests 'very lightly'. The same adverbial point is made slightly later in this scene when we are told that 'his hands went up and down gently on her shoulders' (464). Other adults say they love or respect Maisie, but the way their hands move tells a different story. The meaning of Sir Claude's easy pats is that he both cares for his stepdaughter and makes no claims on her, leaving her, in his word, 'free'. Unlike the others, he neither shoves her from behind nor enfolds her from the front in order to block her free forward movement.

The reason Sir Claude proclaims Maisie's freedom is that she has just demonstrated her achieved moral adulthood by making a fine, hard decision. If the girl had her wishes, she would undoubtedly prefer to carry on with both Sir Claude and Mrs Wix. But being an adult in the world of James's novels means facing the necessity of right choice even as one is hedged in by unpleasant and often compromising constraints. Sir Claude has no desire to pair off with an ageing frump (as James designated Mrs Wix in his working notes), much preferring what the well-built Mrs Beale has to offer, in spite of her defects of character. Hence, because the rivalry between these women rules out any ongoing association with both of them, Sir Claude asks Maisie to desert Mrs Wix and share a life with him and Mrs Beale:

My idea would be a nice little place – somewhere in the South – where [Mrs Beale] and you would be together and as good as anyone else. And I should be as good too, don't you see? for I shouldn't live with you, but I should be close to you – just round the corner, and it would be just the same. My idea would be that it should all be perfectly open and frank. (432)

Maisie may be too young and inexperienced to recognize the shabby self-deceptions in this proposal, which nicely catches the dubious promise 'the South' (of France) has often held for northern Europeans – a paradisal union of respectability and erotic delight –

but she *has* had considerable experience by this point of Sir Claude's chronic irresponsibility. He has already broken his promises to visit her often or to take her to lectures. Flagrantly weak, he cannot tell the truth or be relied on. Maisie's counter-proposition shows great practical moral wisdom. When she tells him she will desert Mrs Wix only if *he* deserts Mrs Beale, she is imposing a condition that asks for a definite commitment in advance, that insists on reciprocity (and thus equality) as the basis for any future relationship, and that imposes the element of self-discipline that is missing from the other adult relationships in the novel. Although Sir Claude cannot meet Maisie's terms, being unable to give up Mrs Beale (and unwilling to brave the world's obvious opinion of a man who takes on the solitary guardianship of a stepdaughter), he admires her decision: 'He was rapidly recovering himself on this basis of fine appreciation. "She made her condition – with such a sense of what it should be! She made the only right one"' (461). This fervent endorsement is to be taken as an authoritative judgment of Maisie's painfully achieved moral growth.

Ironically, Maisie's ability to make 'the only right one' is predicated on the queerness of her world. Of course, we should grant what the Preface makes clear, that the girl's inborn 'dispositions [are] originally promising' (viii).[3] That is to say, the reciprocal commitment she asks of Sir Claude issues from a rare moral temper, loving, peaceable, conciliatory. Still, it is striking that her proposition exhibits the same form as all the other interested deals she has observed paired adults making. As far as Maisie is concerned, the basic rule of life is that A proposes to let B do what she wants provided B lets A do what *he* wants. But, because deal-breaking always follows deal-making, the only thing the novel's adults *really* do is to try to 'square' others after breaking some prior contract with them. This is the history that shapes the girl's moral intelligence, the history she simultaneously absorbs and escapes. The supreme irony is that, because of her originally good 'dispositions', and because she is still too innocent to grasp the complex schemes of sexual blackmail always going forward, *her* squaring proposition turns out to be 'the only right one'.

Those who want to read some degree of corruption into Maisie's final state are not only being much too literal and unironic, in this way sharing Mrs Wix's dark suspicions, they are also overlooking the early chapters' emphatic signals that the girl is *not* in peril of her soul, her vulnerability notwithstanding. Thus, although some of the Faranges' acquaintances are horrified by what Maisie's parents are likely to make of 'her little unspotted soul', we are assured that 'no one could conceive in advance that they would be able to make nothing ill' (5). James even invokes the classic guardian spirit of beset infancy: 'The child was provided for, thanks to a crafty godmother, a defunct aunt of Beale's, who had left her something in such a manner that the parents could appropriate only the income' (9). This sentence concludes the introductory chapter, which stands out from later chapters in lacking a number and not restricting us to Maisie's or anyone else's point of view. That is to say, the last thing the omniscient narrator puts in our hands before dropping us behind Maisie's eyes is a reassuring suggestion of something providential, a hint that the wise fairy-tale godmother, whose business is warding off evil, has already intervened. As we read on, we can feel that our heroine will not be allowed to incur any ultimate damage.

The Preface emphasizes the same point in reconstructing the novel's origins. James had first conceived of Maisie as the helpless victim of callously unloving parents (whose original surname, his notebooks show, was Hurter (*CN*, 77)). Then two ironies fired his imagination. One was that the heroine's innocence would act as a catalyst for further adulterous liaisons. The other was that the little girl would be 'saved . . . rather than coarsened, blurred, sterilised, by ignorance and pain'. Together, these two ironies would dovetail, goodness producing greater evil and bale producing only bliss. 'For satisfaction of the mind' – the author's symmetry-loving mind, the delighted reader's mind – 'the small expanding consciousness would have to be saved, have to become presentable as a register of impressions', this being 'the *full* ironic truth' that constituted the narrative's appeal for its creator. In developing this point, James's Preface plays with a metaphor that builds from a glimmering ray of light to 'the red dramatic spark that glowed at the core of my vision' (vi–vii).

Maisie, as we see, was inspired by the idea that a battered, ignored, uneducated child would *not* finally be damaged or deformed by a lack of appropriate care and love. Instead, she would succeed in becoming what her maker had always striven to be, an ideally conscious register of impressions. Put this way, the novel's *donnée* is seen to carry a heavy charge of fantasy and self-projection. The materials out of which the narrative was constructed were, to some extent, intensely private. Maisie's struggle bore a close and complicated relationship to the author's own habitual strivings and self-idealizations.

The novel has a profound autobiographical aspect, in other words, and once we recognize this we notice a range of ironies the Preface fails to note. One of these is that the author who was so excited by the story of an undamageable child had, in his sister's words, 'a physical repulsion from all personal disorder'.[4] James had an unusually powerful need for a life of civilized order and amenity, and when he eventually wrote his memoirs, telling the story of how he himself was formed within the circle of his immediate and extended family, he was anything but candid about his many close relatives who came to shameful or disastrous ends after being neglected in childhood. One of these was a first cousin, John Vanderburgh James, or 'Johnny', whose father, John Barber James, had 'no gift for control or for edification' (*SB*, 182). Following the father's suicide in 1856, Johnny was committed to the Bloomingdale Asylum, and, in 1858, the day after his twenty-third birthday, he too killed himself.[5] Another first cousin, Bob Temple, was an alcoholic sponger with a prison record and a dismal army career.[6] A third first cousin, Francis Burr James, was remembered by the novelist's sister-in-law 'as a pathetically neglected and bewildered boy with no education and very poor health'.[7] Albert Wyckoff, a second cousin and a near neighbour during the eight years of James's boyhood life in New York City, was an orphan who also apparently came to a bad end.[8] These relatives formed a small but well-defined sector of James's past at the time he wrote *Maisie* – the past that underlay his matured sense of what he wanted to make of himself and how he felt he ought to live.

If we think of *Maisie* not only as a creation of a rarefied or transcendent artistic imagination but also as a very human product of a man living in time, a man who gave a great deal of thought to how men and women should live, it appears that the book that organized James's creative energies at a crucial moment in his life is the kind of narrative that overturns, denies, the usual and the obvious. The point was, precisely, to make plausible what is neither natural nor true: the novel emerged from an impassioned effort to reverse what its author perfectly well knew happens to children who suffer severe neglect and abuse.

Of course, James himself understood he was going against expectations, that, indeed, being part of the fun of the thing. In dozens of ways his narrative puts the reader on notice that it is *not* to be taken as realism, as when we are assured in the second sentence of chapter one that Maisie is smarter than any kid ever. But, after we have accepted such premises for the pleasure of reading this smart and special book, may we not (several readings later) cast a cold eye on them and ask some hard questions about their moral significance?

First: what kind of writer, or rather *person*, is inspired by the prospect of showing that a mistreated child will grow up to be a genius of perception and moral choice? Further: what kind of preparatory history does it take in order to inspire this person to create such a book? Finally: what sort of moral act does writing the book amount to?

II

Before we can glimpse the answers to these closely related questions, we need a rough sense of the point James had reached on his life's trajectory at the time he composed *Maisie*. The key facts, I believe, are these. His parents had been dead for some fifteen years, and his sister Alice for five. His big, ambitious social novels of the 1880s had flopped. Because his latest and best play, *Guy Domville*, had also not been a success, he felt compelled to give up his old dream of writing for the stage. Approaching his mid-fifties, he was getting tired of London and would soon move to Lamb House in Rye. His style, 'manner', was changing in conspicuous ways. He was beginning to revisit his past, with an autobiographical impulse that would surface first in *William Wetmore Story and His Friends*, *The American Scene*, and the Prefaces, and would then culminate in *A Small Boy and Others* and *Notes of a Son and Brother*. There was a new kind of daring in his fiction. He wrote for *The Yellow Book*. He reversed his harsh early judgment of Walt Whitman.

The novels involving children that James produced in the century's last quinquennium – *The Other House*, *The Awkward Age*, *The Turn of the Screw* – give suggestive evidence, as Leon Edel was perhaps the first to see, of the author's deep preoccupation with his own origins in childhood. These novels all involve a child's unknowing exposure to danger, corruption, betrayal, cruelty. In his characteristically circumspect and self-protective way,[9] James was thinking about the hazards he had survived, and also, perhaps, about how his strange upbringing had turned him into a maker of a certain kind of art.

Broadly speaking, James's writings about his early years in his family reveal two opposed and unreconciled attitudes. On the one hand, he looked back with huge respect and affection, affection in particular for his manic and amazingly original father. It was as if there was something sacred about the past that made James anxiously protective and willing to write about it only in ennobling terms. Not once in his later decades did he have anything *detailed* to say about the mother whose favourite he had been and whom he deeply loved.

On the other hand, James sometimes signalled a distinct sense of shame about his early life at home. His autobiography recalls the moment in 1852 when Thackeray made an embarrassing remark about a certain many-buttoned jacket and the small boy picked up a stinging intimation 'that we were somehow *queer*'. The chapter that dredges up this recollection begins with the phrase, 'dimly queer and "pathetic"', applied to the author's late sense of early memories. Although James had been dazzled by the 'radiant and elegant' Second Empire of the mid-1850s, he was also troubled by an awareness that it was 'new and queer and perhaps even wrong' (*SB*, 88, 77, 347). In 1860, when Henry James, sen. took the family back to Newport so that William could study painting with William Morris Hunt, seventeen-year-old Henry jun. had been mortified by the need to explain this abrupt decision to the family's friends in Paris. So embarrassed was he by his father's appearance of being gauche, uninformed, and unstable that he eventually tried to expunge the family's movements in 1858–60 from the biographical record.

These two opposed feelings about his past – it was a supreme thing of its kind, it was too shameful to talk about – can be traced in part to Henry James, sen.'s startling instabilities. Like other children, Henry jun. never lost the lingering traces of a parent's unresolved conflicts. And, inevitably, this lack of resolution continued to shape the way the son wrote about his own past and that of his one and only successful child-character, Maisie.

What picture would we have of Maisie's early life and all its brutal zigzags if *she* had composed *her own* retrospective narration? Obviously, something very different from the actual novel, with its sophisticated and ironic handling of her point of view. My guess is that Maisie's own story would be a book on the order of her author's treatment of *his* early life in *A Small Boy and Others* – the story of the growth of a gifted and active imagination attended by a series of mysterious and mostly romanticized and artfully dignified disasters.[10] My purpose in proposing this hypothetical question and answer is to provoke a sense of the relationship between history and the moral imagination in James – to suggest that, if we want to get at the history that produced *Maisie*, and at the ways in which that history is enacted by the novel, we have to know some of the history behind *her author's* autobiographical books and how *they* enact *it*.

In making this point, I am drawing on my recent biography of Henry James, sen., whom I see as an incredibly energetic, mercurial, and contradictory man, far more rash and unsettled than Henry jun. wanted the world to realize. The father had several distinctly unrespectable friends in the late 1840s and early 1850s. He could not decide what kind of education he wanted his sons to receive, he clearly regarded William's educational needs as paramount in the family's various moves, and he often ignored the other children's educational needs, including Henry jun.'s. Born at a time when his father was desperately unhappy, the boy got divided messages right from the start. He was loved and protected, but he was also repeatedly exposed and neglected. There was little or no continuity in his schooling. His needs, interests, talents, and level of preparation were often badly misjudged: in 1854 he was enrolled in a too-advanced course on business arithmetic at a private school in New York (Forrest and Quackenbos, names he later misspelled (*SB*, 222)), and in 1860 he was sent to a cram school for polytechnic hopefuls in Geneva. Again and again, the father blithely altered course, as when he casually approved Henry's enrolling in Harvard in 1862 after having forbidden him from doing so in 1861.

While Sir Claude is definitely not a portrait of the father, both he and Henry sen. treat their wards with a similar and quite mystifying blend of attaching affection and undependability. A comparable parallel can be drawn between all the hugs Maisie incurs and the James parents' clinging to some of their children (not letting William attend Harvard by himself in 1859, having the two older boys move back into the family home in Boston in 1864, actually selecting William's wife in 1876). The family was so closely knit that one of Henry jun.'s favoured boyhood fantasies featured the orphaned child who is thrillingly alone and exposed (this, in fact, being the story he returned to in *Maisie*). At the same time, the four boys were often left to fight it out among themselves, and in other ways sensed a cold parental unconcern. James William Anderson has called attention to Mary James's emotional distance from William.[11] Robertson, the youngest son, sometimes wondered if he had been adopted. In the summer of 1863, the letters Henry sen. wrote following Wilkie's nearly fatal injury at Fort Wagner and preceding his return to Newport (his wounds being so serious he could not be moved beyond the vestibule) chiefly concern the reception of the father's recently published *Substance and Shadow*.[12] In Henry sen.'s earliest surviving letter mentioning the future novelist's 'considerable talent as a writer', he also questions 'whether he will ever accomplish much',[13] evidently regarding his son's gift as a baffling and unpromising sort of activity. Henry jun. never forgot that the first approval of his juvenile stories and poems came, not from the family circle, but from two boyfriends, Louis De Coppet in the summer of 1854 and Thomas Sergeant Perry in 1858–9. The one thing the boy liked to do most of all, indeed the only thing he was any good at, was not appreciated by his loving family until he began publishing in the mid-1860s.

The combined love and neglect visited on Henry help explain why he had a fairly miserable childhood, and also why his memoirs substantiated his misery in such an uncertain fashion that Leon Edel (whose account of his subject's childhood I believe to be the weakest part of the biography) was not convinced of it. There is a constant equivocation in the basic story James tells about his childhood. He makes it clear he failed at school, his parents did not think highly of his capacities, he had little to show for himself, he spent his time dawdling and gaping and observing, and much was wasted on him. At the same time, he stresses that nothing was wasted on him, that he was living in an exciting and fulfilling way by creating himself, cultivating those powers of observation that would turn him into his kind of writer. The equivocation is most in evidence when he claims that, even in his bad moments, he got a 'foretaste . . . of all the fun, confusedly speaking, that one was going to have, and the kind of life, always of the queer so-called inward sort, tremendously "sporting" in its way' (*SB*, 350). It is telling that the q-word crops up here, and does so as a qualifier of the all-important 'inward', and also that the latter word does not seem to be quite right, judging from the preceding 'so-called'. The quoted passage also, and perfectly, applies to Maisie's adjustments to *her* scares and shocks. She can not join the sporting life as played by Sir Claude and Mrs Beale and the others, but she still bests every one of them on the (so-called) inward turf.

How abuse and neglect turn you into the queer (so-called) inward sort, and how this sort is one of the best things you can be, though so exquisitely painful: that is the self-justifying argument James conducted in *What Maisie Knew* no less than in *A Small Boy and Others*. What we get in both the novel and the autobiography is the Bildungsroman of the artist as queer moralist, who triumphs by learning the trick of transforming painful subjection into a highly responsive and responsible kind of living (Maisie) or a highly ethical kind of art (James).

Returning to the questions I asked at the end of section 1, I would say that the kind of person who is inspired by the idea of showing how an abused child grows into a perceptual genius is one who has painfully remade himself again and again, and whose vast creative powers are bound up with a self-protective blindness to the terrors of his own past. This kind of artist – anxious, energetic, self-defining, endlessly resourceful – restages his own history by creating narratives in which the crucial issue is whether the protagonist should look squarely at the Medusa-face of life and in which the standing answer is no, absolutely not, the protagonist had better learn how to see obliquely, queerly.

As for the third question – what sort of moral act does writing *Maisie* amount to – that will become clearer if we transport ourselves to the site where Maisie and her maker approach one another most closely, the port of Boulogne-sur-mer, situated on what used to be the main cross-Channel route between London and Paris.

III

It is no mere accident of geography that the French seaport in which Maisie makes 'the only right' choice and proves herself free and grown-up also happens to be the place where, forty years earlier, her fourteen-year-old author had a close encounter with death and was then mysteriously transformed from a small boy to a youth. Boulogne is the scene of crisis, the decisive turning-point, in Maisie's life, just as it had been for James. It is also the place where she begins and ends her brief, happy exploration of France. For heroine and author, Boulogne is the place where part of you dies so that you can become someone else.

It was on August 23, 1857, that James came down with what was diagnosed as typhus.[14] Delirious at times, he was confined to his bed for almost two months. Only after he had begun to recover did his father admit to the boy's grandmother in Albany that the family had 'trembled more than once for the issue'. Curiously, when he finally tottered out of his room, it was discovered that, even though he had become 'excessively thin', he had also grown 'a half-head taller'.[15] During his protracted convalescence, which lasted several months, he was too weak to join the other boys at school, and he received instruction from a tutor remembered as old and unpleasant-smelling and spent much of his time reading fiction checked out from Merridew's English lending library. Thus, of the nine or ten months James spent in Boulogne, he was alone and reading for most of the time. His autobiographical account of this period conveys an impression of silence, ennui, exile (*SB*, 412–16).

The story of what happened to James's sense of himself at Boulogne has never been adequately reconstructed, in spite of many indications that his protracted and nearly fatal illness had a definitive impact on his imaginative life.[16] Not only did he fall out of step with his brothers and other boys at the precise moment in which he experienced a startling spurt in growth and ceased being a 'small boy', but he simultaneously became a more committed reader than ever and (in his father's words) 'an immense writer of novels and dramas'.[17] Certain conditions and events fed his imaginative life. He was struck by the shabby or *louche* appearance of many of the semi-permanent English residents. He never forgot his shock when he saw the newspaper announcing the verdict of innocence in the celebrated English murder trial of Madeleine Smith, accused of killing a lover with arsenic;[18] apparently the future author of 'A Tragedy of Error' expected a guilty verdict. In later years, he more than once recalled the unhappy Boulogne exile of Thackeray's Colonel Newcome.

James recounted his slow convalescence in the last chapter of *A Small Boy*, but, reversing chronology, saved for the last page and the concluding sentences the moment in which he fainted and fell.[19] He wanted the narrative of his boyhood to end with a sudden and dangerous loss of consciousness.

Present to me still is the fact of my sharper sense, after an hour or two, of my being there [in bed during the day] in distress and, as happened for the moment, alone; present to me are the sounds of the soft afternoon, the mild animation of the Boulogne street through the half-open windows; present to me above all the strange sense that something had begun that would make more difference to me, directly and indirectly, than anything had ever yet made. I might verily, on the spot, have seen, as in a fading of day and a change to something suddenly queer, the whole large extent of it. I must thus, much impressed but half scared, have wanted to appeal; to which end I tumbled, all too weakly, out of bed and wavered toward the bell just across the room. The question of whether I really reached and rang it was to remain lost afterwards in the strong sick whirl of everything about me, under which I fell into a lapse of consciousness that I shall conveniently here treat as a considerable gap. (*SB*, 418–19)

Memory, here, is intertwined with anticipatory, forward-looking reinterpretation. When the narrator supposes he caught a glimpse of his strangely altered future – the 'change to something suddenly queer' – he shifts from historic to conjectural verb forms ('might . . . have seen'). Then comes the swoon, and with it the end, the death, of childhood, along with a promised resurrection into 'something suddenly queer'. In this interval, in Henry sen.'s phrase, the boy became 'a half-head taller' – a phrase that evokes deformation even while speaking of maturing growth.

Maisie is much more than the story of a lonely child's developing richness of consciousness. It is also a scenario for the gradual erosion and disappearance of one kind of consciousness and the steady usurpation of another, more 'constructed' kind. What dies is a primitive sense of feeling and robust physicality and self. What takes its place is an artificial sense of awareness and fine responsibility that is meant to be an alternative to, but none the less mirrors, the world's queerness. Indeed, the novel inserts the new kind of consciousness into us as readers as we struggle to follow, construe, the queer narrative thread.

James's Preface to the novel contains a passage that ingeniously sums up the queer turn in both his and Maisie's story. After commenting on the girl's habit of wondering, and how her wonder 'embalm[s]' the objects surrounding her, he writes:

She wonders, in other words, to the end, to the death – the death of her childhood, properly speaking; after which (with the inevitable shift, sooner or later, of her point of view) her situation will change and become another affair, subject to other measurements and with a new centre altogether. (xi)

The clause I have italicized has two parts. The first, which concerns Maisie's bewildered effort to figure things out, tells us that she pursues this effort to the end, to the death. Here, James is playing with the hyperbolic usage in which one expresses a determination to persist in an endeavour until one kills oneself or is killed. Maisie, James says, writing with a degree of exaggeration, is going to kill herself by wondering. But also he is not exaggerating. Then comes the dash and the brief pause or hiatus it imposes. Or rather, let us say 'gap', using the word with which James would conclude *A Small Boy*, where the word designates both an interval of unconsciousness and the hiatus between the author's boyhood and youth. In both the autobiography and the work of fiction, syncope denotes a kind of death. In his Preface to the fictional narrative, however, James uses the interval represented by a dash to perform a sudden pivot, or saving equivocation. It is not *real* death after all, but, 'properly speaking', only the death of childhood. Thus, reverting to propriety, James turns his attention away from the tragedy of damaged childhood.

Because the kind of moral act that writing *Maisie* amounts to is one that recapitulates the writer's own formative ordeal, it turns out to be an exceedingly *specialized* moral act, as evasive as it is constructive. It makes a special case for a certain kind of survivor-mentality, and it goes in for smothered raptures and supreme, inward victories. It is because so much of James's writing leads up to these kinds of moral acts that it is a mistake to regard him as a sound moral guide, or to search within his writings for a rich Chaucerian or Balzacian representation of human excellence and degradation. Instead, the queerness of James's world installs itself in a queerly responsive narrative self, which wants, above all, to tell the peculiar story of its syncope and energetic self-creation.

NOTES

I am grateful to Gert Buelens and Pierre A. Walker for their critiques of earlier versions of this chapter.
1 See, for instance, Stevens's contribution to this volume, at pp. 145–6, note 10.
2 All citations from James by page number only are from the first American edition of *What Maisie Knew* (Chicago: Stone, 1897).
3 All citations from James by Roman numeral only are from the Preface to *What Maisie Knew, In the Cage, The Pupil*, New York Edition, 24 vols. (New York: Scribner's, 1907–9), vol. XI.
4 Alice James, *Diary* (Harmondsworth: Penguin, 1982), 192.
5 Alfred Habegger, *The Father: A Life of Henry James, Sr.* (New York: Farrar, Straus & Giroux, 1994), 356, 362, 381.

6 See Charles and Tess Hoffman, 'The Failed American Dream: Cousin Robert Temple and James's "Jolly Corner"', *Harvard Library Bulletin*, n.s. 1 (1990), 39–49; Habegger, *The Father*, 441, 492.
7 Henry James, III, Typed sheet headed '*Howard James*', Houghton Library, bMS Am 1092.9 (4600), folder 14.
8 Habegger, *The Father*, 301–2.
9 Fred Kaplan, *Henry James: The Imagination of Genius: A Biography* (New York: Morrow, 1992), *passim*. Leon Edel, *Henry James: The Treacherous Years, 1895–1901* (Philadelphia: Lippincott, 1969), 260–70.
10 A case in point occurs at the end of Chapter 16, where Maisie, reading a 'Jamesian' meaning into Sir Claude's punishing treatment of her, manages to 'rejoice' and feel 'the sweet sense of success' (201), just as she had done in the suddenly remembered episode where her mother threw her down the stairs. (The episode is not narrated; this is its only mention.) Her inner narrative places the emphasis not on the pain suffered at others' hands but on her conversion of the experience into ecstasy and triumph.
11 James William Anderson, 'In Search of Mary James', *Psychohistory Review*, 8 (1979), 63–70.
12 Habegger, *The Father*, 444.
13 Ibid., 395.
14 William James, Letter to Edgar Van Winkle, 4 September 1857, Houghton Library.
15 Henry James, sen., Letter to Catherine Barber James, 15 October [1857], Houghton Library.
16 Kaplan made partial use of William James's 1857–8 letters to Edgar Van Winkle, but neither he nor Edel (*Henry James: The Untried Years, 1843–1870*, vol. 1 of *The Life of Henry James* (Philadelphia: Lippincott, 1953), 132–36) was aware of the dispatches Henry James, sen. sent the *New York Tribune* during the family's residence in Boulogne. Other possible sources of information have yet to be looked into.
17 Henry James, sen., Letter to Catherine Barber James, 15 October [1857], Houghton Library.
18 Habegger, *The Father*, 437, 552.
19 In his second autobiographical volume, James would follow a similar tactic, concluding with Minny Temple's death and then interpreting it 'as the end of [his and William's] youth' (*NS*, 515).

CHAPTER 6

*The double narrative of 'The Beast in the Jungle':
ethical plot, ironical plot, and the play of power*

Michiel W. Heyns

Revising 'The Beast in the Jungle' for the New York edition, James was led to reflect: 'my attested predilection for poor sensitive gentlemen almost embarrasses me as I march!' (*AD*, ix). James's embarrassment, never very acute in recording his impressions of his own work, would probably have been more pronounced than this had he known what posterity was to make of his predilection; but as it stands, his assumed ruefulness is still useful as a reminder that yes, poor sensitive gentlemen do abound in James, their very sensitivity frequently serving as the privileged and controlling medium of the fiction. If James is, as Conrad suggested, the historian of fine consciences, the histories of these sensitive gentlemen would seem to be pre-eminently the Jamesian subject.[1]

But, at roughly the same time as writing his Prefaces, James was speaking, in 'The Story in It' (1902), for the narrative potential of a different kind of history – though 'speaking' is, as often, too crude a word for the indirection of James's method of utterance. He dramatizes his subject as a discussion amongst three people on the question of what constitutes a worthy 'subject' for a writer. Maud Blessingbourne, complaining of the 'poverty of the life' in the French novel she has just unenthusiastically finished, explains to her more worldly-wise companions: 'Well, I suppose I'm looking, more than anything else, for a decent woman' (*DM*, 422). The urbanely adulterous Colonel Voyt and Mrs Dyott are convinced that she is not likely to find a decent woman inhabiting 'pictures of passion' (*DM*, 422); as the Colonel patronizingly explains:

Behind these words we use – the adventure, the novel, the drama, the romance, the situation, in short, as we most comprehensively say – behind them all stands the same sharp fact which they all in their different ways represent ... The fact of a relation ... What is it but, with absolute directness, a question of interest, or, as people say, of the story? What's a situation undeveloped but a subject lost? If a relation stops, where's the story? If it doesn't stop, where's the innocence? (*DM*, 425–6)

Of course, neither party succeeds in convincing the other, and the end of the tale leaves Voyt and Mrs Dyott, though conceding that Maud is 'not wholly bereft of sense', smugly contemplating their own narrative possibilities, next to which Maud's potential story seems mild indeed:

Her consciousness . . . *was*, in the last analysis, a kind of shy romance. Not a romance like their own . . . but a small scared starved subjective satisfaction that would do her no harm and nobody else any good. Who but a duffer – he stuck to his contention – would see the shadow of a 'story' in it? (*DM*, 434–5)

Readers of James know the answer to that one, of course. The situation undeveloped is, almost obsessively, the Jamesian subject; and the 'shy romance' of the character, by implication female, whose passion is but a 'small scared starved subjective satisfaction', as compared with the full-blown passion of a consummated relationship, is the prime subject of any number of James tales and novels – for example, Catherine Sloper's timid infatuation, Fleda Vetch's high-minded devotion, even Daisy Miller's hardly shy but oddly reticent attachment. And, where the shy romance does not have even this limited narrative prominence, it may figure as a suppressed narrative behind the privileged male narrative of the sensitive gentleman: the untold tale of the apparently subordinated female character, for example Miss Tita in 'The Aspern Papers', Nanda Brookenham in *The Awkward Age*, or Milly Theale in *The Wings of the Dove*, in a sense constitutes the point of the narrative in which she dwells so humbly; without her, there would have been no story in it.

Referring to the genesis of 'The Story in It' in his Preface to the New York Edition, James quotes 'a distinguished friend, a novelist not to *our* manner either born or bred' as asking, in the vein of Colonel Voyt: 'A picture of life founded on the mere reserves and omissions and suppressions of life, what sort of a performance – for beauty, for interest, for tone – could *that* hope to be?' (*DM*, xxii, xxiii). James avoids, with the magisterial agility of his late style, a direct answer ('and of course, indeed, on all such ground, discussion, to be really luminous, would have to rest on some such perfect definition of terms as is not of this muddled world' (*DM*, xxiii)), but he clearly expects his works to speak for themselves. And, indeed, the almost contemporaneous 'The Beast in the Jungle' (1903) offers a textbook example of a 'picture of life founded on the mere reserves and omissions and suppressions of life'. Of the many situations undeveloped in James, that in 'The Beast in the Jungle' is, perhaps, the most *crucially* undeveloped, in that the failure of development proves to be the point of John Marcher's tale: as James outlines it in his Preface, 'He has indeed been marked and indeed suffered his fortune – which is precisely to have been the man in the world to whom nothing whatever was to happen' (*AD*, xi).

When read like this, the tale is an affecting enough account of a self-fulfilling prophecy, an egotism so blind as to miss its only opportunity to escape from its own self-absorption. But that is, quite literally, only half the story. What I have called the double narrative of 'The Beast in the Jungle' may be understood, though, of course, not as absolutely as my method of analysis proposes, as a primary but transgressive male plot, interconnected with a secondary plot of female desire.[2] If the ostensible dynamic of the tale is ethical, bent on confronting Marcher with the nullity of his own history, it also is more covertly directed at the vindication of May Bartram's desire. Recognizing at last the mystery of her passion, Marcher is brought simultaneously to a commensurate consciousness of his own blind selfishness: '*She* had lived – who could say now with what passion? – since she had loved him for himself; whereas he had never thought of her (ah, how it hugely glared at him!) but in the chill of his egotism and the light of her use' (*AD*, 126). '*She* had lived . . . whereas he . . . ': here, at the climax of the tale, the two interdependent strands of the narrative are at last explicitly related.

Recognizing the difference between May's fully 'lived' life and his own self-absorbed existence, Marcher forfeits also the comfortable conviction that their stories were but different centres of the same story: '*She* at least never spoke of the secret of his life except as "the real truth about you", and she had in fact a wonderful way of making it seem, as such, the secret of her own life too' (*AD*, 81). That turns out to be true only in a more complex sense than the free indirect style can accommodate at this point: if the secret of his life turns out to be that nothing was to have happened to him, then that *nothing* happens to him, as it were, through her: she becomes the opportunity not taken – '*she* was what he had missed' (*AD*, 125). The Beast in the Jungle is as much a creature of her story as an enactment of his history.

Narrative power, then, resides as much behind as in the narrative. In one obvious sense, Marcher is in control of the narrative: as the one loved, and, furthermore, as the male, he takes the initiative and makes the decisions. But his rather complacent assumption of power may blind us to the fact that he is perpetually at a disadvantage, from the very opening of the story: on their meeting again after a lapse of some ten years, '[i]t affected him as the sequel of something of which he had lost the beginning... he was also somehow aware – yet without a direct sign from her – that the young woman herself hadn't lost the thread' (*AD*, 62). Ariadne-like, May holds the clue to the labyrinth; and, Theseus-like, Marcher avails himself of the aid without recognizing that it bestows an obligation. He accepts cheerfully enough the inequality of memory, with all that it implies: 'He accepted her amendments, he enjoyed her corrections, though the moral of them was, she pointed out, that he *really* didn't remember the least thing about her' (*AD*, 65).

To be the one remembered may be gratifying to one's vanity; but to be the one who remembers is, as the social formula has it, to have the advantage of the other. And this advantage she retains: their friendship builds not only on her clearer recollection of their original meeting, but also on her continued control of information. If Marcher is self-absorbed, as he, of course, infuriatingly is, he is consistently aided and encouraged by May Bartram. In making his secret her own, she condescends him into the most abject dependence upon her:

He had a screw loose for her, but she liked him in spite of it and was practically, against the rest of the world, his kind wise keeper, unremunerated but fairly amused and, in the absence of other near ties, not disreputably occupied. The rest of the world of course thought him queer, but she, she only, knew how, and above all why, queer; which was precisely what enabled her to dispose the concealing veil in the right folds. She took his gaiety from him – since it had to pass with them for gaiety – as she took everything else; but she certainly so far justified by her unerring touch his finer sense of the degree to which he had ended by convincing her. *She* at least never spoke of the secret of his life except as 'the real truth about you', and she had in fact a wonderful way of making it seem, as such, the secret of her life too. That was in fine how he so constantly felt her as allowing for him; he couldn't on the whole call it anything else. He allowed for himself, but she, exactly, allowed still more; partly because, better placed for a sight of the matter, she traced his unhappy perversion through reaches of its course into which he could scarce follow it. (*AD*, 81)

A modern reader schooled, say, in Foucault would notice here the slightly ominous typification of her as 'his kind wise keeper': a labour of love, of course, but also a position of power, the dedication of an unpaid nanny. May's complete absorption in Marcher's history is not so much an extinction of her own self as an appropriation of his: her stifling self-abnegation relentlessly takes pity on the pathetic Marcher and takes possession of the helpless creature she has helped bring into being. '[S]he liked him in spite of it'; 'she, she only, knew'; 'he so constantly felt her allowing for him'; 'she traced his unhappy perversion' – it is surely not surprising that this infantilizing relationship never matures into sexual equality. Eve Kosofsky Sedgwick has analysed, amongst other elements, this passage, to support her contention that 'to the extent that Marcher's secret has *a* content, that content is homosexual'.[3] The semantic shifts that make available words like 'queer' and 'gaiety' to Sedgwick's analysis may be no more than fortuitous;[4] nevertheless, the fact that they seem so readily to fill the gaps in the story helps us to see that there *are* gaps to be filled: Marcher's passivity seems to demand a stronger explanation than the self-absorbed blindness and inertia that are proffered in the tale. The fissures in the tale, as it were, are made evident by their receptivity to anachronistic meaning. Thus, if we want to fill those gaps, Sedgwick's hypothesis has the virtue of doing so; but we may not want to go all the way with the implications of this reading as Sedgwick extends it to May's role: 'I hypothesize that what May Bartram would have liked for Marcher, the narrative she wished to nurture for him, would have been a progress from a vexed and gaping self-ignorance around his homosexual possibilities to a self-knowledge of them that would have freed him to find and enjoy a sexuality of whatever sort emerged.'[5] The problem with this hypothesis, as to a certain but lesser extent with Sedgwick's reading of Marcher's own role, is that it has nothing in the tale itself to lean on: it is a late-twentieth-century projection of the possibilities of the relationship. We can imagine a woman's reacting as generously as Sedgwick claims May does; but could James? Granting that a tale may be open to possibilities not consciously foreseen by its author, I would still find active resistance to Sedgwick's reading in the nature of the power James gives to May: as I argue below, that power seems to me to be derived exactly from a heterosexual imperative of which May is, in fact, the exponent in the tale.

But, if I find Sedgwick's reading of May too enlightened for the tale itself, there is much in her analysis that accords with my sense of May's power; for instance: 'As their relationship continues, the sense of power and of a marked, rather free-floating irony about May Bartram becomes stronger and stronger, even in proportion to Marcher's accelerating progress toward self-ignorance and toward a blindly selfish expropriation of her emotional labor.'[6] May has the advantage that knowledge gives to the *eiron*; if, in the mythical prototype of this tale of self-fulfilling prophecy, Oedipus is the dupe of his fate as determined by the gods, here Marcher is the dupe of a doom of which May keeps the secret. That irony is underlined and intensified by the comparison of May Bartram to a sphinx whose riddle Marcher fails to guess (*AD*, 98–9): Oedipus got right, at least, the riddle of the sphinx. Even while May and Marcher are ostensibly united in the common task of watching, she withholds, from her apparently subordinate situation, information denied to his greater self-sufficiency. She sees what he sees, but she also sees more than he, and what she sees is *him*: if he beguiles the world, she has access both to his mask and to his vision:

What it had come to was that he wore a mask painted with the social simper, out of the eye-holes of which there looked eyes of an expression not in the least matching the other features. This the stupid world, even after years, had never more than half-discovered. It was only May Bartram who had, and she achieved, by an art indescribable, the feat of at once – or perhaps it was only alternately – meeting the eyes from in front and mingling her own vision, as from over his shoulder, with their peep through the apertures.

So while they grew older together she did watch with him, and so she let this association give shape and colour to her own existence. Beneath *her* forms as well detachment had learned to sit, and behaviour had become for her, in the social sense, a false account of herself. There was but one account of her that would have been true all the while and that she could give straight to nobody, least of all to John Marcher. (*AD*, 82)

If 'this association' comes to constitute the centre of her existence, it is also a power base; the suppression of the 'one account of her that would have been true all the while' does not prevent its becoming the authorized account, towards the revelation of which the narrative drives. The narrative is, of course, 'his', in being, with very few exceptions, controlled by his perspective, but it is teleologically directed by her knowledge and her desire.

But her advantage lies not only in the more comprehensive

knowledge her situation makes possible. Being quite aware that his own appreciation of May is less ardent than might have been wished, Marcher, from the start, self-consciously attempts to meet her evident devotion with tokens of at least some reciprocal consideration, prompting him to fuss anxiously at his own motives: 'There was that in his situation, no doubt, that disposed him too much to see her as a mere confidant . . . he was careful to remember that she had also a life of her own, with things that might happen to *her*, things that in friendship one should likewise take account of' (*AD*, 77). This conveniently overlooks the fact that the most important thing to have happened to her was to have fallen in love with John Marcher. The judgement passed on Marcher is surprisingly elusive: it is clear, of course, that his concern 'to remember that she had also a life of her own' is really only a refinement of egotism, leaving him but the more free to avail himself of such of her services as he finds convenient. But it is not always easy to locate exactly the provenance of the judgement: partly originating in Marcher's own consciousness, the narrative voice yet preserves a crucial distance from his inadequate scruples. The ethical plot, which is to say the process by which he is brought to full vision, is entrusted partly to Marcher himself; but, to the extent that it is an ironic plot, its perspective must transcend his own – for instance, in the force that 'a life of her own' acquires by its anticipation of his climactic insight that '*She* had lived.' His 'occasional warnings against egotism' (*AD*, 90) are similarly inchoate:

> He had kept up, he felt, and very decently on the whole, his consciousness of the importance of not being selfish, and it was true that he had never sinned in that direction without promptly enough trying to press the scales the other way. He often repaired his fault, the season permitting, by inviting his friend to accompany him to the opera; and it not infrequently thus happened that, to show he didn't wish her to have but one sort of food for her mind, he was the cause of her appearing there with him a dozen nights in the month. It even happened that, seeing her home at such times, he occasionally went in with her to finish, as he called it, the evening, and, the better to make his point, sat down to the frugal but always careful little supper that awaited his pleasure. (*AD*, 90)

Marcher's moral squeamishness is self-evidently ineffectual, all the more selfish for his anxiety not to be in the wrong. The judgement, however, is formed in an unarticulated zone, somewhere between the free indirect rendering of Marcher's self-exculpations ('very decently on the whole', 'he often repaired his fault') and narrative statement ('he was the cause of her appearing there with him'). This is to say that we also need a vantage-point outside Marcher's own consciousness to judge his actions, the more so that the 'narrator' is, in fact, a subtly dissimulated *eiron*, a voice that seems frequently to be at one with Marcher's own consciousness, and that yet opens more perspectives than he is aware of. We may speculate, for instance, about the qualification implied by 'the season permitting': does it mean that Marcher's reparations were seasonal only? Or we may wonder, as Marcher apparently does not, what happens to the 'careful little supper' on those evenings that he does not choose to 'finish, as he called it, the evening' with May (and what did she call it, this frugal meal with the man she loved?). The ethical narrative which measures Marcher's self-deception does so by allowing us access, albeit only inferred access, to May Bartram's part of the narrative. We read more than Marcher into his own situation, and the more that we read is May's story.

Marcher's story, then, consists at least partly of his ignorance of the significance of his own history; and, to the extent that this is so, May's more comprehensive vision grants her the position of power in the tale. Standing, towards the end of her life, in her little drawing-room, he recognizes that 'the place was the written history of his whole middle life' (*AD*, 86), but he cannot see, as she now can, what the meaning of that history is. As keeper of his secret, May, even in the etiolated passivity of her last days, still has the advantage of him:

[S]he was the picture of a serene and exquisite but impenetrable sphinx . . . She was a sphinx, yet with her white petals and green fronds she might have been a lily too – only an artificial lily, wonderfully imitated and constantly kept, without dust or stain, though not exempt from a slight droop and a complexity of faint creases, under some clear glass bell. (*AD*, 98–9)

The disturbing compound image reinforces the power of the sphinx with the death-like virginity of an artificial, funeral-parlour lily. The images of the 'impenetrable sphinx' and the glass-covered lily are almost rebarbatively asexual: May Bartram, in withdrawing into the secret of her passion, becomes less of the sympathetic watcher-with-Marcher and more of the dispassionate watcher-of-Marcher. The sphinx, we remember, strangled those who could not guess her riddle. It is in the course of this meeting 'in that long fresh light of waning April days' that, as he later recognizes, '[t]he Beast had lurked indeed, and the Beast, at its hour, had sprung' (*AD*, 98, 126). By this interpretation, the spring of the Beast consists precisely of nothing:

> 'The door isn't shut. The door's open', said May Bartram.
> 'Then something's to come?'
> She waited once again, always with her cold sweet eyes on him. 'It's never too late.' She had, with her gliding step, diminished the distance between them, and she stood nearer to him, close to him, a minute, as if still charged with the unspoken. Her movement might have been for some finer emphasis of what she was at once hesitating and deciding to say . . . She only kept him waiting, however; that is he only waited. It had become suddenly, from her movement and attitude, beautiful and vivid to him that she had something more to give him; her wasted face delicately shone with it – it glittered almost as with the white lustre of silver in her expression. She was right, incontestably, for what he saw in her face was the truth, and strangely, without consequence, while their talk of it as dreadful was still in the air, she appeared to present it as inordinately soft. This, prompting bewilderment, made him but gape the more gratefully for her revelation, so that they continued for some minutes silent, her face shining at him, her contact imponderably pressing, and his stare all kind but all expectant. The end, none the less, was that what he had expected failed to come to him. Something else took place instead, which seemed to consist at first in the mere closing of her eyes. (*AD*, 105–6)

What we are most conscious of, of course, in reading this passage is the obtuse misapprehension of Marcher, and the humiliation of May, in his failing to see 'that what he had expected' was exactly the wrong thing: in assuming 'that she had something more to give him' he misses what she is offering him. The surface narrative dramatizes May's weakness and defeat, the failure of her pathetic attempt to get Marcher to see that what she is offering him is herself. As he recollects it later, as insight dawns upon him: 'It had sprung as he didn't guess; it had sprung as she hopelessly turned from him, and the mark, by the time he left her, had fallen where it *was* to fall' (*AD*, 126). In this narrative, the Beast is Marcher's selfish failure to respond to her offer; this implication issues in the insight that '[t]he escape would have been to love her; then, *then* he would have lived' (*AD*, 126).

But the scene not only constitutes an opportunity not taken, it is also a test failed. If, at this point, the failure presents itself to

Marcher as an impersonal effect of the state of things ('What he had expected failed to come to him'), afterwards he can see the failure as more specifically his: 'He had justified his fear and achieved his fate; he had failed, with the last exactitude, of all he was to fail of' (*AD*, 126). And, from this latter perspective, May's offer here is more than that: it is a challenge and a test, 'her contact imponderably pressing' being then a near-insistent appeal – which, incidentally, seems to me to militate against Sedgwick's interpretation of her motives. May's strength is indistinguishable from the weakness – as woman, as invalid – that forms the basis of her ethical and sexual claim. And, in failing May's test, he is delivered to the Beast. If the woman is the weaker in a relationship, in traditionally being denied the right to claim or express her desire, the male is subject to the conventions which assume that he will make love to a woman he 'sees' regularly. In short, the heterosexual premise establishes an ethical imperative that validates May's desire.

By the time of their last meeting, having failed in her attempt at bringing Marcher to recognize her secret and his remedy, May has become a figure of mystery and power; but, once again, her power is veiled by her weakness:

> She spoke as with the softness almost of a sick child, yet now at last, at the end of all, with the perfect straightness of a sibyl. She visibly knew that she knew, and the effect on him was of something co-ordinate, in its high character, with the law that had ruled him. It was the true voice of the law; so on her lips would the law itself have sounded. (*AD*, 110)

What the sibyl pronounces, almost epigrammatically, is that Marcher should not share her knowledge: 'You were to suffer your fate. That was not necessarily to know it' (*AD*, 113). The distinction between suffering one's fate and knowing it makes it possible for Marcher's history to consist paradoxically in the failure to enact his history: if, as Hillis Miller argues elsewhere in this volume, for James 'a true historical event does not belong to the order of cognition', then Marcher's failure to live can be truly historical without being known – and here Miller's distinction between 'two kinds of knowledge' would usefully extend Marcher's failure also to his not 'knowing' May in the 'blind bodily material' way 'that cannot be narrated', as opposed to the purely cognitive kind. This 'bodily' knowledge, dependent as it is upon May's presence for its fulfilment, Marcher will never have: he is now, as May tells him, on the other side of his situation: 'It's past. It's behind' (*AD*, 112). The beast has sprung without his knowing it, and without his knowing her.

After May's death, Marcher is left with only the sense 'that the Jungle had been threshed to vacancy and that the Beast had stolen away' (*AD*, 116); what remains of May is mainly the memory of her prohibition: 'She had told him, his friend, not to guess; she had forbidden him, so far as he might, to know, and she had even in a sort denied the power in him to learn' (*AD*, 117). May had, as we have seen, become stronger in knowledge as she became physically weaker; it is then appropriate that after her death she should be strongest of all, and, in forbidding him access to the knowledge she watched for with him, deny 'the power in him to learn'. In death, May commands more respect and authority than she did in life. Upon visiting her grave, he tries to extract her secret from her very tombstone:

> He stood for an hour, powerless to turn away and yet powerless to penetrate the darkness of death; fixing with his eyes her inscribed name and date, beating his forehead against the fact of the secret they kept, drawing his breath while he waited, as if some sense would in pity of him rise from the stones. He kneeled on the stones, however, in vain; they kept what they concealed; and if the face of the tomb did become a face for him it was because her two names became a pair of eyes that didn't know him. He gave them a last long look, but no palest light broke. (*AD*, 118)

What strikes one in reading these bleak passages is that May's withholding of information from Marcher, though presented as an act of mercy, very effectively punishes Marcher for his obtuseness during her life. Marcher is a man haunted by a secret he does not understand or share, 'powerless' alike to turn his back on it or to possess it. But the logic of the story demands that he should be brought to full knowledge of her love and of his selfishness. This necessity brings about the rather odd feature of the tale, namely that the Beast seems to spring twice. That narrative strand that is concerned with Marcher's failure to understand has its issue in the understated 'leap' that he is not even aware of as such, the leap that takes place during his penultimate visit to May; but that part of the plot intent upon bringing him to painful knowledge culminates in the far more dramatic leap in the graveyard. Here May's grave speaks to him more successfully than May herself ever did: 'he had before him in sharper incision than ever the open page of his story' (*AD*, 125). And his story turns out to have been the empty shell of hers: 'he had been the man of his time, *the* man, to whom nothing on earth was to have happened' (*AD*, 125). Not only did she have the life that he missed, she also had the key to his own failure: 'So *she* had seen it while he didn't, and so she served at this hour to drive the truth home' (*AD*, 125). It is of the nature of this 'driving' that it should be violent; knowledge, when it comes, is disruptive: 'This horror of waking - *this* was knowledge, knowledge under the breath of which the very tears in his eyes seemed to freeze' (*AD*, 126). The second leap of the beast, signalling her victory, is punitive: 'He saw the Jungle of his life and saw the lurking Beast; then, while he looked, perceived it, as by a stir of the air, rise, huge and hideous, for the leap that was to settle him' (*AD*, 126-7). And appropriately, since this time the beast is executing May's knowledge, Marcher flings himself face down upon her grave.

'The Beast in the Jungle' has, for obvious reasons, attracted more attention than its literary qualities alone may justify. It seems to hint at ultimate truths, at figures in the carpet, at clues and at riddles – in short, at Jamesian self-revelation and expiation. 'The final passage in James's story', says Leon Edel, 'rises to heights of passion, of tenderness, of guilt, of self-accusation. It is as if Marcher's revelation were his own.'[7] More recently, Fred Kaplan has called it 'his most powerful short story on the subject of sexual and marital inaction, confused sexual identity, and evasive personal self-deception'.[8] Like Edel, Kaplan does not draw any very clear distinction between James and his protagonist, and the reasons for Marcher's failure are, by implication, sought in James's life: 'Not once ever desiring her or any other woman, he has missed the opportunity to love May Bartram because of his incapacity to function heterosexually. His most effective defense against the potentially frightening, perhaps disabling confrontation with homoerotic desire has been the renunciation of physical sexual relationships entirely.'[9] This echoes, of course, Eve Kosofsky Sedgwick's confident pronouncement that 'to the extent that Marcher's secret has *a* content, that content is homosexual'.[10] Though Sedgwick bases her theory on internal evidence from the tale rather than on biographical projection, the homosexual possibilities she finds in the story are certainly compatible with what we know about James's life. It seems plausible that James would have known the pressure of emotional demands that he had not the resources to meet, and that claimed, whether consciously or not, the sanction of conventional morality. But the biographical hypothesis is more vexing than usual, because the evidence points in such different directions. Fairly clearly, James had a strongly homo-erotic side, commonly assumed to have been unconsummated; but, by the time he wrote 'The Beast in the Jungle', he seems to have achieved a reasonably happy accommodation, if not consummation, of this side of his nature in a number of ardent friendships with younger men. Though these often left him regretting the absence of the beloved, they could not have figured to James as so null as to constitute the nothing that happens to Marcher. If, in the pleasure of the relatively uninhibited expressions of affection he permitted himself in relation to his male friends, he was driven anew to relive the guilt he may have felt on the death of Constance Fenimore Woolson in 1894, then we might have expected the tale to make more of possible alternatives for Marcher, and less of his emotionally void life. On balance, it seems safest to assume that, as James maintained in 'The Art of Fiction' (1884), the artistic sensibility draws on generalized rather than specific experience: 'Experience is never limited, and it is never complete; it is an immense sensibility, a kind of huge spider-web of the finest silken threads suspended in the chamber of consciousness and catching every air-borne particle in its tissue' (*LC*-1, 52).

I am offering James's reflections not as an evasion of the tensions that, as Sedgwick has shown, are undeniably present in the tale, but as a description of Jamesian method versatile enough to be extended to works other than 'The Beast in the Jungle'. By my reading of the 'ethical' plot, Marcher takes his place with all those other sensitive gentlemen whose sensitivity is exercised at the expense of, usually, a woman: Winterbourne in 'Daisy Miller', the literary scholar in 'The Aspern Papers', Vanderbank in *The Awkward Age*, Chad Newsome in *The Ambassadors*, Merton Densher in *The Wings of the Dove* – and even, though this may stretch the concept of sensitivity unduly, Morris Townsend in 'Washington Square'.[11] But, where these works can all too readily be reduced to the woman-as-victim stereotype, 'The Beast in the Jungle' enables us to see that the alternative, 'female', narrative may be the privileged one, in holding the key to the surface narrative: in these other tales, too, though not in quite the same sense, '[t]he escape would have been to love her'. Not all the young gentlemen are equally sensitive, of course: Morris Townsend is not so much devastated as disappointed in his attempt to mend his fortunes with the now obdurate Catherine Sloper, and Chad

Newsome seems unlikely to spend much of his successful career regretting Madame de Vionnet and the Parisian life he has to sacrifice to Woollett. But, in so far as a judgement is passed on these males, it is passed in terms of the female desire they disregard or exploit. The publishing scoundrel loses the coveted Papers, and Miss Tita, no longer the keeper of the secret of the history of Jeffrey Aspern and 'the divine Julia', becomes the protagonist of her own 'shy romance'. The self-centred Winterbourne comes to acknowledge his own mistake in not recognizing at the time that Daisy Miller 'would have appreciated one's esteem', and the flirtatiousness of which he was so ready to take advantage comes to seem oddly touching in death. And, in perhaps the most compelling deployment of the plot principle granting power to the absent protagonist, Milly Theale, withdrawing into silence, her last letter unread, becomes, through that silence, stronger than she was in life. It is Milly's story that dominates the sombre closing scenes of the novel, as Merton Densher waits for news of her; and it is the power of that story that informs Kate's famous recognition: 'We shall never be again as we were.'

Those heroines not content to renounce, surrender by that token the power conferred on them by the ethical plot. As long as Fleda Vetch, in *The Spoils of Poynton*, keeps to her conviction that it would be wrong to exert any pressure on Owen Gereth, she retains the power of moral authority: being so consciously in the right, she seems stronger than Mrs Gereth and Mona. But, as soon as she makes a move to claim Owen, she loses that authority, without gaining anything in its place. Even the much-disputed status of Maggie Verver, in *The Golden Bowl*, owes something of its ambiguity to the discrepancy between her apparent status as wronged wife and her manifest power: where one critical school sees a brave woman claiming back her own, another sees a rich woman reasserting control over an errant possession. By my reading, Maggie Verver, in claiming her own fictional space and assuming control of her own desire, breaks ranks, and forfeits the ethical privilege shared by her otherwise underprivileged predecessors; that is, in openly appropriating power, she surrenders the more covert dominion of the disregarded women. I would argue that those critics who seek ethical grounds for Maggie's assumption of power at the end of the novel are failing to discriminate the power plot, with its inherent ruthlessness, from the ethical plot, with its scruples and renunciations. By the same token, much criticism of James fails to do justice to the sheer toughness of his imagination: he can see that if the meek are to inherit the earth they have to out-manoeuvre the arrogant.

Interestingly, one of James's last tales dramatizes exactly the situation developed, albeit belatedly and coercively. In 'The Bench of Desolation' (1909), Kate Cookham wreaks the revenge of all those disregarded Jamesian females, by ruining Herbert Dodd with the threat of a breach-of-promise suit. The story has its embarrassments, not least in James's writing down to his lower middle-class characters, but it does offer an interesting inversion, writ large, of the pattern I have been examining. Here, the overt power is in Kate Cookham's hands, as she squeezes poor Herbert dry; and, for much of the story, she is seen as a monster of vulgarity. She claims, as it were, on all her predecessors' behalf, compensation for not being loved – and she thrives on it. When, after the death of Dodds's wife and daughters, Kate returns, she seems like the successful counterpart of May Bartram: 'Withal, something said, she had flourished – he felt it, wincing at it, as that; she had had a life, a career, a history, something that her present waiting air and nervous consciousness couldn't prevent his noting there as a deeply latent assurance' (*CT*, XII, 392). Similarly, the terms in which her reappearance is heralded seem consciously to recall and revise John Marcher's devastating insight: 'Yes, he had come back there to flop, by long custom, upon the bench of desolation *as* the man in the whole place, precisely, to whom nothing worth more than tuppence could happen; whereupon, in the grey desert of his consciousness, the very earth had suddenly opened and flamed' (*CT*, XII, 392). Kate Cookham explains her past conduct as but the consequences of the frustration of her desire to take care of him: 'I wanted to take care of you – it was what I first wanted – and what you first consented to' (*CT*, XII, 406). It is as if James wanted, on the one hand, to exorcize the power of the slighted woman by making her claim her retribution and be frankly hated for it, and, on the other, to make amends to her by readmitting her to the ethical plot. The story lacks the tragic intensity of 'The Beast in the Jungle' – at most it aspires to a kind of lugubrious despondency – but it does offer an interesting adjunct to the earlier tale, in reversing, as it were, the direction of the narrative and the distribution of power.

We need not subscribe to Edel's heavy-handed biographical reduction of 'The Beast in the Jungle' to 'the deepest message of

[James's] egotism' in order to divine, in the repeated return to the 'undeveloped situation', a personal concern with the potential selfishness of a life shared with others only on the basis of a mutual 'watching'.[12] By my reading, however, an equilibrium is restored by the retributive redistribution of the artistic process: the self-absorbed is brought to experience, at first hand, as it were, the frustrated desire of the selfless. Of course, May Bartram, like Milly Theale and Miss Tita, hardly benefits by this redistribution; but, in terms of plot dynamics, and hence of the play of power in the tale, there is a radical realignment of force: these figures, though in their different ways practised upon in their tales, are not mere victims. Fictional representation in James is not a straightforward duplication of power relations: the ostensible centre of power is subordinated to a secondary narrative that controls the primary, in a relation that complicates any generalizations we might want to make about fictional representation and power. Put differently, the power of the beast is ultimately derived from the 'small scared starved subjective satisfaction' of an unacknowledged romance.

NOTES

1 Joseph Conrad, 'Henry James: An Appreciation', *Notes on Life and Letters* (London: Dent, 1905), 13–23; extract reprinted as 'The Historian of Fine Consciences', *The Question of Henry James: A Collection of Critical Essays*, ed. F. W. Dupee (New York: Holt, 1945; London: Wingate, 1947), 62–3.
2 My interpretation courts Eve Kosofsky Sedgwick's withering description of the 'hammeringly tendentious blur in virtualy all the James criticism', which 'assume[s] without any space for doubt that the moral point of the story is not only that May Bartram desired John Marcher but that John Marcher *should have desired* May Bartram' (*Epistemology of the Closet* (Berkeley: University of California Press, 1990), 198). Sedgwick interestingly suggests why this should not be so, and I discuss her reading in more detail below.
3 *Epistemology of the Closet*, 201
4 But see Habegger and Stevens, chapters 5 and 7, respectively, in this volume.
5 Sedgwick, *Epistemology of the Closet*, 207.
6 Ibid., 210.
7 *Henry James: The Master, 1901–1916*, vol. v of *The Life of Henry James* (London: Hart-Davis, 1972), 141.

8 *Henry James: The Imagination of Genius: A Biography* (London: Sceptre-Hodder, 1993), 456.
9 Ibid., 457–8.
10 *Epistemology of the Closet*, 201.
11 Even Lambert Strether, not normally seen as one of James's exploitative males, treats Maria Gostrey rather as Marcher does May, and makes very little of her evident desire to be more to him than an enlightened tourist guide. (But, as Holland has argued: 'By profitably possessing Maria, then leaving her, in the affair of art, the affair of memory and imagination, rather than in the affair of marriage which she hopes for, Strether enacts for James the exploitive sacrifice on which the novel is founded. Strether's renunciation, while a genuine tribute to his experience and a payment for it, is a substitute for the payment that might be made in the life of the emotions and in more complete commitments of behavior' (Laurence B. Holland, *The Expense of Vision: Essays on the Craft of Henry James* (Baltimore: Johns Hopkins University Press, 1982), 281). Oddly, Strether's famous injuction to Little Bilham to 'Live!' and his claim to have himself failed to do so, have not, as far as I know, been ascribed to an undeclared homosexual side – for which, given Strether's evident attraction to Chad (and even, at a stretch of the imagination, his friendship with Waymarsh!), there is at least more positive support than in Marcher's purely negative case.
12 *The Life of Henry James*, vol. v, 141.

CHAPTER 7

Homoeroticism, identity, and agency in James's late tales
Hugh Stevens

THE PLAY OF 'IDENTITY': 'MORA MONTRAVERS' AND OTHER TALES

Attention to historical pressures governing constructions of sexuality enables James's late tales to be read as responding to anxieties surrounding sexual identities in turn-of-the-century Britain and America. These tales attend to the construction of identities, rather than the expression of identities already constituted. In late James, identity is both burden and necessity, but, even as necessity, evanescent and intangible. The burden of Jamesian identity is the burden arising from relations which stop nowhere – if identity is predicated on the subject's placement in a chain, what James, in the Prefaces, calls a 'tangled web' (*LC*-II, 1300, 1338), then crucial to such a construction are the relations admitted by the subject and those relations the subject repudiates or cannot admit in a given context. The play of identity in James's late tales revolves around such problems, questioning the legitimacy of any received 'map of the social relations', asking after other ways relations might be configured (*GB*, II, 324).

James's late tales are highly ironic about the laws of prohibition governing their own production. Although they thematize respect for social decorum, they also zoom in on those parts of the body and bodily relations their very gentility would seem to require they ignore. In 'Mora Montravers' (1909), for instance, Jane and Sidney Traffle, a childless, middle-aged couple, become alarmed at the open manner in which their beautiful 'niece' Mora – the daughter of Jane's dead half-sister – has taken up residence with the no less beautiful painter Walter Puddick. Although they hope the relation between the two young people will be regularized through marriage, they feel it a shame that the 'grand air' of the name 'Montravers' should be lost for the 'vulgar name' (as Jane Traffle calls it), the 'unfortunate name' (as Puddick himself calls it), of Puddick. Wondering if this is also Mora's objection to matrimony, Jane notes that '[h]er reason – if it is her reason – is vulgarer still' (*CT*, XII, 278–9). Mora's name is so grand, presumably, because of its suggestion of crossing mountains, but what is so objectionable about Puddick? This question takes on considerable urgency. Given that one meaning of 'dick' given in an 1891 dictionary of slang is 'penis' (cited in the *OED Supplement*), the name has a striking closeness to 'put dick': Jane and Sidney seem eager to avoid the unfortunate combination 'Mora Put Dick'.[1] 'Puddick', then, has a coarseness to match that of another notorious name from James's late fiction, 'Fanny Assingham'.

Other names in the late tales overflowing with innuendo include, from 'The Papers', Sir A. B. C. Beadel-Muffet; Abel Taker, C. P. Addard, Mrs Magaw and Mrs Vanderplank from 'Fordham Castle'; Murray Brush from 'Julia Bride'; Captain Roper from 'The Bench of Desolation'; and, from 'A Round of Visits', Mark Monteith, Phil Bloodgood, and Newton Winch. James's self-consciousness in naming his characters is attested to by the proliferation of erotic *double entendres* in the lists of names he made in his notebooks:

> Counterpunt – Prime – Mossom – Birdle – Brash – Fresh – Flore (*CN*, 183)

> Server – Yateley – Lender – Casterton – Taker – Pouncer (*CN*, 187)

> Assingham – Padwick – Lutch – Marfle – Bross – Crapp – Didcock – Wichells – *Putchin* – Brind – Coxeter – Cockster – Angus – Surrey – Dickwinter (*CN*, 194; James's emphasis)

The sexual connotations of such names create an erotic register which subverts the text's genteel veneer, and suggest multiple possibilities which remain unconfirmed (but no less radical for their uncertainty).

This polyvalence necessarily affects our reading. Erotic suggestions account not only for the excitement of the characters, but also for the excitement generated in reading the tale. The reader joins James's characters in the role of voyeuristic detective. The drama of 'Mora Montravers' derives not from any direct portrayal of the sexual behaviour of Puddick and Mora, but from the attempts of Jane and Sidney to imagine such behaviour, and from the various investments (horror, fascination, vicarious pleasure) they make in their imaginings. What appears to be, on the elderly couple's part, a demand for decency, undergoes significant shifts as the tale unfolds.

Faced with Jane's insistence that he should marry Mora, Walter Puddick, who 'repudiate[s] absolutely' Jane's charge that his relationship with Mora is not innocent (*CT*, XII, 293), bursts into tears. These tears provide a pretext for Sidney to comfort Puddick: 'Into the hall he ushered him, and there – absurd, incoherent person as he had again to know himself for – vaguely yet reassuringly, with an arm about him, patted him on the back' (*CT*, XII, 296). This gesture ushers the two men into intimacy: 'while the closed door of the drawing-room and the shelter of the porch kept them unseen and unheard from within, they faced each other for the embarrassment that, as Traffle would have been quite ready to put it, they had in common' (*CT*, XII, 296). This hint that Traffle's interest in the young man might be more than 'platonic' is reinforced later in the story by an incident at Traffle's club, with which, as a result of 'the state of his own nerves', he is on 'fidgety terms':

his suspicion of his not remarkably carrying it off there was confirmed to him, disconcertingly ... by the free address of a fellow-member prone always to overdoing fellowship ... – 'I say, Traff, old man, what in the world, this time, have you got "on"?' It had never been anything but easy to answer the ass, and was easier than anything now – '"On"? You don't suppose I dress, do you, to come to meet *you*?' – yet the effect of the nasty little mirror of his unsatisfied state so flashed before him was to make him afresh wander wide. (*CT*, XII, 303)

Portraying with ease the intervention of homosexual panic into male clubland, James foregrounds the anxiety of legibility. Fearing that his own 'unsatisfied state' is visible to the 'fellow-member prone always to overdoing fellowship', Traffle recognizes himself in what he is rejecting.

Surprisingly, Jane Traffle, previously figured as morally stern, takes up an interest in Puddick, after a discussion during which she discovers much about the young man, who 'likes to talk to me, poor dear' (*CT*, XII, 323). Later she explains her interest to her husband:

'And you like to talk with *him*, obviously – since he appears so beautifully and quickly to have brought you round from your view of him as merely low.'

... 'I never thought him low ... but I admit ... I did think him wicked.'

'And it's now your opinion that people can be wicked without being low?'
... 'It depends ... on the kind.'
'On the kind of wickedness?'
'Yes, perhaps. And ... on the kind of people.' (*CT*, XII, 323)

As a result of the 'kind of wickedness' Puddick exhibits, and the 'kind of person' he represents, Jane comes to think of him as 'my poor ravaged, lacerated, pathetic nephew', and her newfound interest 'made her distinguishably happier ... than she had been for so many months' (*CT*, XII, 319–20, 327). Jane is revitalized by her fascination with the young man, and is sure that her interest in Puddick will be shared by her husband. Sidney does derive pleasure from Jane's entrée into what he had previously thought of as 'the essential impenetrability ... of an acutest young artist's *vie intime*' (*CT*, XII, 299). 'Lord, the fun some people did have!' he thinks as the story closes. 'Even Jane, with her conscientious new care – even Jane, unmistakably, was in for such a lot' (*CT*, XII, 333).

Read without what Eve Kosofsky Sedgwick calls 'the easy assumption ... that sexuality and heterosexuality are always exactly translatable into one another',[2] 'Mora Montravers' emerges as a pithy comedy in which a middle-aged couple project themselves into the life of a young Bohemian artist, whose work and modes of erotic expression offer them an excitement they had found lacking in their suburban existence – an existence figured as quartered in '"spare" rooms, dreary and unapplied ... quite as on some dull interminable visit' (*CT*, XII, 267–8). The story shows the extent of what was and was not possible for the late James.

In asking what James avoids in his fiction, reticence should not be equated with timidity. It is true that none of James's stories makes a direct characterization of any character's '(homo)sexuality', or assumes that 'sexuality' can be described by a particular label. Further, the fiction consistently refrains from describing any genital activity. These two (seemingly obvious) absences are important for the freedom of interpretation they allow, rather than for the way they restrict interpretation. It should not be assumed that James's avoidance of those reductive epithets 'homosexual' and 'heterosexual' is merely a consequence of the conditions in which he published his fiction. Rather, his fiction questions whether 'sexuality' can be reduced to two such circumscribed concepts. If James's late fiction registers that a homo/heterosexual definitional frame has come to dominate perceptions of 'sexuality', his interrogations of such definitional mechanisms focus on the violence and psychic difficulties such a frame can precipitate.

The late James, famous for his timidity, was, in fact, exploring new possibilities for eroticism in fiction. Across the late tales, James develops an erotic lexicon, invents a discursive eroticism in which sexual tensions and connections between fictional characters are not contained by a heterosexual frame. If the stories avoid description of sexual activity, the genitality of their language and of the erotic spaces they describe ironizes and critiques the standards of literary gentility to which they ostensibly conform. Moreover, through a series of well-honed puns, *double entendres*, and references to the spectres of homosexual blackmail, scandal, and suicide, the late tales nevertheless manage to thematize homoerotic desire and the fate of the 'homosexual'. If James develops the potential of fiction to represent homoerotic pleasures, and interrogates the (psychic and physical) violence accompanying visible expressions of delight in such pleasures, he can do so because of the development, in late nineteenth-century Britain, of a language in which a lack of specificity accompanied an excess of suggestion, of connotation.[3] James takes full advantage of such a set of reference points, which enable him to portray indecency without any threat to decency.

The thematization of homoeroticism in James's late tales is neither sporadic nor incidental. The anxieties arising from the violent repudiation of homoerotic bonds in the wake of the Wilde trials, and the pressures put on male friendship and constructions of masculinity by the creation of that abject figure, the 'homosexual', inform James's attention to the minutiae of late Victorian and Edwardian social transactions. James is actively questioning the terms of the construction of the 'homosexual'. If his late fiction expresses no optimism about an identity construction predicated on (homo)sexuality, it is attentive to the costs of a structure in which homoerotic bonds are necessarily subject to censure. For many of James's 'poor sensitive gentlemen' (*LC*-II, 1250), homosexual identity is a difficulty, even an impossibility. However, for these poor gentlemen, an 'identity' foreclosing the homoerotic is equally difficult, equally problematic. For them, to ignore or to acknowledge the homoerotic is a 'rum' choice, for both alternatives mean exposure to various forms of violence.[4]

'A RAGE OF PERSONALITY': SHIFTING IDENTITY IN 'THE JOLLY CORNER'

In 'The Jolly Corner', the 56-year-old Spencer Brydon returns after 33 years in Europe to New York, and renews his friendship with Alice Staverton, a woman with a 'slim mystifying grace of . . . appearance, which defied you to say if she were a fair young woman who looked older through trouble, or a fine smooth older one who looked young through successful indifference' (*CT*, XII, 197). Alice and Brydon are bonded through a shared eroticism of the closet, with its hushed secrets, its shame, its violence.

Brydon's life has been a Paterian 'surrender to sensations', and he is haunted by 'the queerest and deepest of his own lately most disguised and muffled vibrations', the thought of 'opening a door behind which he would have made sure of finding nothing . . . and yet coming, with a great suppressed start, on some quite erect confronting presence, something planted in the middle of the place and facing him through the dusk' (*CT*, XII, 210, 198). Here the story's debt to Stevenson's *Strange Case of Dr Jekyll and Mr Hyde* (1886) is evident: Stephen Heath has noted of *Dr Jekyll* that its 'organizing image . . . is the breaking down of doors, learning the secret behind them'.[5] Indeed, James's comments on *Jekyll and Hyde* anticipate the way in which he rewrites Stevenson. 'There is something almost impertinent in the way . . . Stevenson achieves his best efforts without the aid of the ladies', James writes, 'and *Doctor Jekyll* is a capital example of his heartless independence' (*LC*-1, 1252). 'The Jolly Corner' represents *Dr Jekyll* with the aid of the ladies: Alice Staverton and Mrs Muldoon (the woman who cleans the house) are feminine presences who enter the male space of Brydon's fantasy life. If Brydon has a 'homosexual secret' then Alice has 'staved' it in – 'to stave' meaning to burst or force a hole in something. Her easy ability to divine 'his strange sense' is experienced by Brydon as a liberation from the closet: 'her apparent understanding, with no protesting shock, no easy derision, touched him more deeply than anything yet, constituting for his stifled perversity, on the spot, an element that was like breathable air' (*CT*, XII, 206). With Alice, Brydon's 'secret' is truly 'open'. He talks of his past as his 'perverse young course', and notes:

I've not been edifying – I believe I'm thought in a hundred quarters to have been barely decent. I've followed strange paths and worshipped strange gods; it must have come to you again and again . . . that I was leading, at any time these thirty years, a selfish frivolous scandalous life. (*CT*, XII, 205)

Yet, in 'The Jolly Corner', Alice is not merely a sympathetic observer, but an active participant in Brydon's fantasy life. The fantasy of breaking into the closet, smashing down its door, is one they create together.

Their shared fantasy is of an encounter with Brydon's 'fictional' double, the person he would have been if he had stayed in America. Alice encounters this double in her dream life, whereas Brydon meets him in his childhood home, the 'house on the jolly corner, as he usually, and quite fondly, described it – the one in which he had first seen the light' (*CT*, XII, 194). For Brydon, it is a matter of anxiety which of his two selves would have been more depraved – the Brydon who has been 'blighted . . . for once and for ever' by being Europeanized, or the missing Brydon, who might have escaped his 'father's curse' by following 'the rank money-passion', to become a businessman 'quite splendid, quite huge, and monstrous . . . quite hideous and offensive' (*CT*, XII, 205).

Brydon's meeting with his spectral double is described in the middle section of the story, a section which does 'without the aid of the ladies'. Brydon has begun to visit the house with compulsive regularity, 'sometimes . . . twice in the twenty-four hours', and his life on the jolly corner takes on greater definition than his social life:

He was a dim secondary social success . . . He projected himself all day . . . into the other, the real, the waiting life; the life that, as soon as he heard behind him the click of his great house-door, began for him, on the jolly corner, as beguilingly as the slow opening bars of some rich music follows the tap of the conductor's wand. (*CT*, XII, 207, 208)

Brydon's attempt to track down his '*alter ego*' is eroticized, figured as the 'stalking of a creature more subtle, yet at bay perhaps more formidable, than any beast of the forest' (*CT*, XII, 209, 210). If any sexual scenario carries within it traces of other sexual scenarios, then the description of this chase combines several sexual narratives, to constitute an unstable semantic and erotic overload. Most obviously, the story charts a confluence of narcissism and homosexuality, a meeting of the two phases which, in Freud's sexual narrative, follow auto-eroticism and precede heterosexual object-choice.[6] In that the house is Brydon's childhood home, his return is also a return to his childhood past, to the ghosts of parental and ancestral authority.

Further, the house represents the human body, a spatial erotics, one of James's most 'bristling' architectural creations.[7] Brydon's progress up its 'ample back staircase', during which he feels 'the sense of a need to hold on to something, even after the manner of a man slipping and slipping on some awful incline' (*CT*, XII, 212, 214), might suggest anal penetration: this is achieved by a proliferation of *double entendres*. Brydon is shown to have a somewhat anxious 'phallic' relationship to a series of anal openings and passages. The house is compared to 'some great glass bowl, all precious concave crystal, set delicately humming by the play of a moist finger round its edge' (*CT*, XII, 209). It is full of 'embrasures' (defined in the *Collins English Dictionary* as 'opening[s] forming a door or a window, having splayed sides that increase the width of the opening in the interior'), 'nooks and corners, . . . closets and passages'; trying to leave, Brydon confronts the 'fan-tracery of the entrance' and notices how 'the thin admitted dawn, glimmering archwise over the whole outer door, made a semicircular margin, a cold silvery nimbus that seemed to play a little as he looked – to shift and expand and contract' (*CT*, XII, 210, 212, 223, 224).

The phallic nature of Brydon's trial is made evident in the demand he feels to remain at the top of the stairs, which appears to become a test of sexual prowess and perseverance:

He had *stiffened* his will against going; without this he would have made for the stairs, and it seemed to him that, still with his eyes closed, he would have descended them, would have known how, straight and swiftly *to the bottom* . . . He took out his watch – there was light for that: it was scarcely a quarter past one, and *he had never withdrawn so soon* . . . It would prove his courage – unless indeed the latter might most be proved by his budging at last from his place. What he mainly felt now was that, since he hadn't originally scuttled, he had his dignities – which had never in his life seemed so many – all to preserve and *to carry aloft*. This was before him in truth as *a physical image* . . . (*CT*, XII, 215; my emphasis)

The house's anality and masculinity are further intensified by contrasts of surface and texture. The proliferation of hard surfaces – the large black-and-white marble squares in the hall (on which 'the steel point of [Brydon's] stick' makes a 'dim reverberating tinkle'), 'the points of [Brydon's] evening shoes', even 'the hard silver of the autumn stars through the window-panes (*CT*, XII, 209, 211) – contrast with the 'extraordinary softness and faintly refreshing fragrance' of Alice Staverton's lap, 'an ample and perfect cushion' and the 'mantle of soft stuff lined with grey fur', which caress Brydon in the third section of the story (*CT*, xii, 226, 227). The 'ample back staircase' of the house not only seems anal, but takes on the nuance of a water-closet: Brydon thinks of it as a 'deep well . . . which might have been for queerness of colour, some watery underworld' (*CT*, xii, 212, 223–3). Descending the stairs (during which time '[h]e tried to think of something noble') Brydon reaches 'the glazed spaces of the vestibule . . . the bottom of the sea, which showed an illumination of its own and which he even saw paved . . . with the marble squares of his childhood' (*CT*, xii, 223).

The story thus shows a fascination with waste products, and links anal eroticism to childhood. In Freud's theory of sexuality, the 'polymorphously perverse' child takes pleasure in bodily zones which are later stigmatized. In *Three Essays on Sexuality*, Freud stresses 'the significance of anal eroticism', writing that 'the history of the first prohibition which a child comes across – the prohibition against getting pleasure from anal activity and its products – has a decisive effect on his whole development . . . From that time on, what is "anal" remains the symbol of everything that is to be repudiated and excluded from life.'[8] Here Freud insists on the inherence of the social in the psychic: for Brydon, anal fantasy represents both a psychic and a social threat.

'The Jolly Corner' merges the psychic consequences of a sexuality generated by prohibition (is a prior anal eroticism prohibited? Or does prohibition of the anus further eroticize it?) with the social regulation of sexuality. It emphasizes the surveillance of the 'fat Avenue "officer"', whom Brydon 'had hitherto only sought to avoid', but whose approach 'he would have welcomed positively' in order to dispel his fear (*CT*, xii, 208, 220). In pursuing his double, Brydon is aware 'of the value of Discretion', the need to remain concealed, yet also of the desire to see – he has an 'obsession of the presence encountered telescopically, . . . focussed and studied in diminished perspective' (*CT*, xii, 218, 217). His double demands that he show, reveal, confess: the door through which he hopes to see his double says to him, 'Show us how much you have!' (*CT*, xii, 218).

Desire merges with violence in the eventual meeting of Brydon and his double. This encounter posits sexuality as a shattering of self, or a phallicizing of the self in which sexual expression is a mode of power: the double is 'something all unnatural and dreadful, but to advance upon which was the condition for him either of liberation or of supreme defeat' (*CT*, XII, 224).⁹ He begins the scene in the position of hunter, yet ends by being attacked; and the very uncertainty of his role excites him: 'he was already trying to measure by how much more he himself might now be in peril of fear; so rejoicing that he could, in another form, actively inspire that fear, and simultaneously quaking for the form in which he might passively know it' (*CT*, XII, 214). Erotic tension derives from the uncertainty of Brydon's relation to his double: a radical wavering between masochism and sadism. Is the other an 'animal brought at last to bay', a 'trodden worm', '[h]arder pressed' by Brydon, or will Brydon be 'harder pressed still' by the figure resembling a 'black-vizored sentinel guarding a treasure', by 'the stranger . . . advanced as for aggression' (*CT*, XII, 213–4, 224, 226)?

Compulsive desire eradicates Brydon's subjectivity: he does not have the agency to say, 'I have this or that desire', but moves into a scenario whose excitement depends on the possibility of his agency or will being erased. The encounter is part of another narrative, an action not only intensely personal (it is called 'this completely personal act'), but also infused with the social and the historical (*CT*, XII, 217). His fantasy life shows the traces of 'history' in his preoccupation with the closet, in the close linkage between narcissism and homosexuality, in the association of homoeroticism with the threat of violence and psychic transgression. These forces come together in the violent denouement:

. . . the stranger, whoever he might be, evil, odious, blatant, vulgar, had advanced as for aggression, and he felt himself give ground. Then harder pressed still, sick with the force of his shock, and falling back as under the hot breath and the roused passion of a life larger than his own, a rage of personality before which his own collapsed, he felt the whole vision turn to darkness and his very feet give way. His head went round; he was going; he had gone. (*CT*, XII, 226)

What is at stake in this violent encounter? The ghost of the jolly corner inspires both fascination and disgust in Brydon, who cannot isolate or stabilize the terms of difference and resemblance linking them. Brydon calls him a 'brute, with his awful face . . . a black stranger' (*CT*, XII, 231), and this brute's repulsiveness stems from his 'vivid truth', his resemblance to a late nineteenth-century aesthete marked with sexual alterity:

Brydon, before him, took him in; with every fact of him now, in the higher light, hard and acute – his vivid truth, his grizzled bent head and white masking hands, his queer actuality of evening-dress, of dangling double eye-glass, of gleaming silk lappet and white linen, of pearl button and gold watch-guard and polished shoe. (*CT*, XII, 225)

The palpable difference between Brydon and his double, his 'hidden self', is that the 'brute' seems more strongly defined by sexual alterity. Brydon creates and is repulsed by a version of himself whose 'queer actuality' is readily apparent. The force of 'bent' and 'queer',[10] and the way Brydon's double is 'thrust . . . out of his frame' (as if emerging from the closet),[11] help explain Brydon's 'immense' 'revulsion', his '[h]orror', at the 'stranger . . . evil, odious, blatant, vulgar' (*CT*, XII, 225–6). Brydon's relationship to his spectral double illustrates the ambivalence the late nineteenth-century homosexual subject feels towards a fantasy of masculinity as violent, sexually abusive, and powerful, as this fantasy represents, all at once, an erotic object (the allure of 'rough trade'), a possible figure of identification, and also, in its possible homophobia, a threat.

'The Jolly Corner' ends with Brydon, the male hysteric, in the role of invalid, cared for by Alice Staverton, who takes the role of nurse, physician, or psychologist. That he should be tended by feminine hands emphasizes Brydon's passive, invalid status. If there is a hint of a sexual attachment between them, then the story – in which a homoerotic narcissism seems to give way to a socialized heterosexuality – would echo Freud's theory of sexuality. Alice appears to have a teleological presence, as the endpoint of a process of hypnotherapy for the male homosexual in which a masculine image is faded out while a feminine image is faded in.[12]

Such a reading misunderstands, however, the bond between them. Alice's involvement with Brydon is not one of desire, but one moving between identification and desire. Her attraction to Brydon is not in doubt – she repeats, quite pointedly, the question to him, 'How should I not have liked you?' – yet this desire is not motivated by Brydon as erotic object, but by his fraught narcissism. Whereas many late nineteenth-century sexologists proposed that homosexuality was a result of sexual inversion – that the female soul of the male homosexual loves the male object, and similarly the male soul of the female homosexual loves the female object – and thereby maintained the primacy of heterosexual desire, Alice's fascination with Brydon appears to suggest that heterosexuality can also be based on involvement in a primarily homosexual scene. She dreams about Brydon only as doubled:

> 'You dream about me at that rate?'
> 'Ah about *him*!' she smiled. (*CT*, XII, 206–7)

Alice kisses Brydon in 'cool charity and virtue', and the closing embrace of the story is almost chaste in comparison with the erotic ardour of Brydon's adventures on the jolly corner (*CT*, XII, 228). The erotic bond between them is not one of mutual desire, but one of shared identification in Brydon's scene. This opens up the possibility that Alice's identity is just as fractured, as 'multiple', as Brydon's – if not more so.

Yet her manner of identification in the scene differs from Brydon's. Alice is attracted to the 'black stranger' for his battle scars, the way 'he's grim, he's worn – and things have happened to him'; she likes and accepts him 'for the interest of his difference' (*CT*, XII, 232, 231). Alice does not pity Brydon – or his double – out of the workings of a liberal conscience; and it is precisely this effortless empathy that nourishes Brydon, the fact that she does not 'disown' the spectral double, that, as she tells Brydon, she is reconciled to him more than Brydon is himself: 'as *I* knew him – which you at last, confronted with him in his difference, so cruelly didn't, my dear – well, he must have been, you see, less dreadful to me' (*CT*, XII, 232). The story then responds imaginatively to the demands of identity. Whereas therapeutic responses to multiple personality, both at the turn of the century and today, 'assume a notion of the already-constituted ... subject, understood as comprising a functional plurality of component parts to which violence comes entirely from the outside to shatter its functional unity into dysfunctional multiplicity',[13] Alice strives to preserve the multiplicity of Brydon's identity/ies, without seeking integration. (She ends the story by murmuring 'he isn't – no, he isn't – *you*!' (*CT*, XII, 232)). The tale contrasts Brydon's rejection of the stranger with Alice's warm acceptance of him. As often in James's tales, the violent reactions felt by men towards a perceived homosexuality (in other men *or* in themselves) is not shared by his female characters, possibly because the female subject is not threatened by a loss of masculine entitlement. Yet there is more at stake. I have shown that the stern Jane Traffle, in 'Mora Montravers', softens and takes up a maternal interest in Walter Puddick after she learns about his 'interesting' state. If the paternal law institutes the taboo on homosexuality,[14] then the masculine subject of James's late fiction, in transgressing this taboo, makes a turn towards the maternal. This turn is thematized in 'The Altar of the Dead'.

LOVE, LOSS, AND THE IMPOSSIBILITY OF IDENTITY IN 'THE ALTAR OF THE DEAD'

The Preface to 'The Altar of the Dead' is unusual in that James shifts from aesthetic concerns to an overtly political issue. He complains that London society shows too great an indifference to the dead. Remembering the dead is not a 'morbid' or sentimental ritual, but a vital social task – yet 'to be caught in any rueful glance at [the dead] was to be branded at once as "morbid"'. 'The sense of the state of the dead is but part of the sense of the state of the living; and, congruously with that, life is cheated to almost the same degree of the finest homage (precisely this our possible friendships and intimacies) that we fain would render it' (*LC*-II, 1249).

Although James's Preface inveighs against what he calls 'the awful doom of general dishumanisation' (*LC*-II, 1248), his tale implies that, even within this pervasive malaise, different situations pose different challenges to mourning. Freud's 'Mourning and Melancholia' makes the classic remark that 'people never willingly abandon a libidinal position',[15] and conceives of melancholia as a state in which the subject can neither relinquish a hopeless libidinal position, nor transfer the highly cathected libido bound up in that position to another position. Compare with this the point James makes in the Preface: 'it was impossible for any critic or "creator" at all worth his wage not, as a matter of course, again and again to ask himself what may not become of individual sensibility, of the faculty and the fibre itself, when everything makes against the indulgence of it save as a conscious, and indeed highly emphasised, dead loss' (*LC*-II, 1247).

George Stransom, the tale's protagonist, is a subject who can only indulge his sensibility as 'a conscious, and indeed highly emphasised, dead loss'. Stransom is shocked to see that others mourn and then form other relations. Early in the tale he meets Paul Creston, who has remarried, and is disgusted at what he perceives as disloyalty to the first Mrs Creston, as a discrepancy between the cheerful man he meets and 'the different face, the wholly other face the poor man had shown him last, the blurred, ravaged mask bent over the open grave' (*CT*, IX, 234). 'Creston was not in mourning now', the tale continues, and Stransom's disposition to melancholia is hinted at by his refusal to accept what he perceives as the 'frivolity, the indecency' of mourning completed (*CT*, IX, 237).

Stransom's dismay is soon compounded by his discovering, from a newspaper article, the death of his former friend, Sir Acton Hague, KCB. Hague has died from 'the bite of a poisonous snake': the sexual innuendo attached to his mode of death is strengthened by a number of insinuations that punctuate the tale. Reading the article, Stransom feels 'relief at the absence of any mention of their quarrel, an incident accidentally tainted at the time, thanks to their joint immersion in large affairs, with a horrible publicity' (*CT*, IX, 237). As is common in James, business activity and financial connection have erotic overtones. The 'publicity' given their quarrel is a violation to intimate rather than professional bonds: Stransom feels he has suffered a 'wrong', an 'insult . . . blankly taken from the only man with whom he had ever been intimate; the friend, almost adored, of his University years, the subject, later, of his passionate loyalty' (*CT*, IX, 237). We have here some typical delicately nuanced Jamesian innuendos. Following a description of Kate Creston as 'the only *woman* for whom [Stransom] might perhaps have been unfaithful', Hague is referred to as 'the only *man* with whom he had ever been intimate' (*CT*, IX, 236–7; my emphasis). Further, the quarrel has mixed privacy and publicity: '[t]he shock of interests had been private, intensely so; but the action taken by Hague had been in the face of men' (*CT*, IX, 237). Already the question needs to be asked: was this scandal a (homo)sexual scandal?

Stransom transforms a chapel of a suburban Roman Catholic church into his own mourning-altar, an altar devoted in particular to his dead fiancée, Mary Antrim. Stransom is figured as a Christ-like 'shepherd of a huddled flock, with all a shepherd's vision of differences imperceptible' (*CT*, IX, 242). However, 'there were gaps in the constellation': '[t]he greatest blank in the shining page was the memory of Acton Hague, of which he inveterately tried to rid himself. For Acton Hague no flame could ever rise on any altar of his' (*CT*, IX, 243).

Stransom's involvement with his altar is strongly eroticized. His first entry into the church is figured as penetration, a lifting of veils (a 'leathern curtain' beyond which there is 'a glimpse of an avenue of gloom with a glow of tapers at the end') enabling him to quit 'the great grey suburb and come nearer to the warm centre' (*CT*, IX, 238, 239). He is at once struck by 'the sombre presence of a woman, in mourning unrelieved', and expresses a desire to occupy her position: 'He wished he could sink, like her, to the very bottom, be as motionless, as rapt in prostration' (*CT*, IX, 239). Stransom and the woman (who remains unnamed) form a bond in which 'they grew quite intimate' over 'the idea that they didn't care for each other'. Rather they are drawn to each other because they 'feel deeply together about certain things wholly distinct from themselves' (*CT*, IX, 248).

Ironically, they do not know how similar the 'certain things' they both care about are. Only when Stransom visits his friend's home after her aunt's death, and sees Hague's picture on the wall, does he realize that her candles have all been lit for Hague, just as Hague is the one person for whom he has refused to light a candle. The story develops into a contest for the right to mourn the dead man. The woman insists that Stransom 'give [Hague] his candle', thereby forgiving Hague and giving him the same status as Stransom's other mourned friends (*CT*, IX, 258). Stransom, meanwhile, realizing the depths of the woman's intimacy with Hague, experiences 'an ague in which he had to make an effort not to shake' (*CT*, IX, 258). He learns that the woman had not wanted him to learn from her aunt what Hague had done to her (*CT*, IX, 259). The unspeakability shrouding Acton Hague's injuries to them both – 'from Acton Hague any injury was credible', the woman 'convey[s] with exquisite mildness' – hints at a reciprocating symmetry in their stories (*CT*, IX, 255). Hague had ended their friendship 'in the face of men': it seems that Hague had publicly aired the suggestion of Stransom's homosexuality. This helps explain Stransom's relief that 'no mention of their quarrel' was made in the reports of Hague's death (*CT*, IX, 237). Similarly, the woman's fear that her aunt may betray something ignominious about Hague's treatment of her makes it seem possible that Hague had left her for a man. This possibility is supported by Stransom's consideration that 'of [Acton's] previous life she should have ascertained only what [Hague] had judged good to communicate. There were passages it was quite conceivable that even in moments of the tenderest expansion he should have withheld . . . A man, in her place, would have "looked up" the past – would even have consulted old newspapers' (*CT*, IX, 259).[16] Stransom 'made . . . out that this relation of Hague's, whatever it was, could only have been a deception finely practised. . . . Stransom knew enough of his other ties, of his obligations and appearances, not to say enough of his general character, to be sure there had been some infamy. In one way or another the poor woman had been coldly sacrificed' (*CT*, IX, 264).

That is to say, the condition of shared widowhood Stransom and the woman have been enjoying, while their mourned objects remained anonymous, collapses when they find they are both 'widow' to the same man. Each reminds the other of what they had found most disagreeable in Hague: his lack of commitment not only to their person, but to their gender. James's freedom is enhanced, not curtailed, by the daring of this schema. James can portray both characters' attachment to Hague indirectly: the story can convey that both attachments are erotic by showing how jealous the characters are of each other. 'Acton Hague was between them, that was the essence of the matter; and he was never so much between them as when they were face to face' (*CT*, IX, 263). Stransom wants to know everything about the woman's attachment to Hague, even if such knowledge should make him miserable: 'He had never for a moment admitted that he was in love with her; therefore nothing could have surprised him more than to discover that he was jealous. What but jealousy could give a man that sore, contentious wish to have the detail of what would make him suffer?' (*CT*, IX, 263).

As James's description of the woman makes clear, in any triangular rivalry the rival can always become the object of desire. If one's partner desires another, then mimesis, or identification, makes that other an object of both hatred and desire. The story notes that 'the woman with whom [Stransom] had had for years so fine a point of contact was a woman whom Acton Hague, of all men in the world, had more or less fashioned'. Freud's account of mourning and identity-formation in 'Mourning and Melancholia' is implicit in the story's claim that '[s]uch as she sat there to-day, she was ineffaceably stamped with [Hague]' (*CT*, IX, 260). Just when the demands of exclusive constructions of sexuality intervene in Stransom's and the woman's friendship, challenging both their claims on the dead Acton Hague, the instability of identity and desire propel them together. The self-sufficiency of Stransom's sexuality is undermined, as it is unclear who has first claim on his affections: his dead fiancée, Acton Hague, or the unnamed woman. Stransom's desire for Hague tips over into desire for the woman, to the extent that her identity is shaped by Hague; and, as a love-object of Hague's, she becomes an object of Stransom's desire through the workings of mimesis. Moreover, the woman's whole-hearted mourning for Hague is destabilized by Stransom's obviously peculiar relationship to him. What Judith Butler calls a 'heterosexual matrix' assumes the separability of identification and desire: for the boy, identification with the father initiates desire for the woman.[17] In the messy triangle of 'The Altar of the Dead', as in 'The Jolly Corner', desire and identification are hopelessly confused. How 'identity' might be shaped out of these entanglements is the very problem set up by the tale, the problem needing to be solved so that some kind of narrative resolution might be reached.

Stransom responds to the crisis by making what Freud calls, in discussions of hysteria, a 'flight into sickness'. 'His irritation took the form of melancholy', James writes, 'and his melancholy that of the conviction that his health had quite failed' (*CT*, IX, 266). Stransom's melancholy arises from the ambivalence obtaining between him and the loved object in a context where both affection and object are subject to shame. The difficulty of mourning Hague, the tale implies, is a difficulty arising from a particular social arrangement, a structure privileging certain bonds at the expense of other repudiated bonds.

Hence it is interesting that the story foregrounds a process of legitimization, centred on the church. The Catholic chapel gives Stransom the opportunity to establish 'rites more public', rites legitimized by the approval of the church's 'bland ecclesiastics' and the 'delightfully human' Bishop (*CT*, IX, 240). The Catholic Church is, of course, one of the most powerful western institutions involved in the supervision of kinship and the administration of mourning rituals. This constitutes the church's attraction to Stransom: it bestows on him a space 'consecrated to an ostensible and customary worship' (*CT*, IX, 241).

James's use of fantasy and camp enables him to address apparently contradictory demands – the demands of a social structure that Stransom's bond to Hague be refused legitimization, and the psychic demands that the bond be acknowledged so that Hague may be mourned. The altar bridges private and public, but does so in according public respect to private sentiments, rather than subjecting these sentiments to the scandalizing gaze of the press.

Stransom wants his altar to have the same qualities James wants to give the novel (according to the account he gives in the New York Prefaces): symmetry, harmony, a resolution of whole and component parts. He is striving for what Bersani calls a 'redemptive aesthetic', that is, a cultural symbolization seen as 'essentially reparative'.[18] 'Symmetry was harmony', Stransom notes, and 'harmony was of course everything. He took, in fancy, his composition to pieces, redistributing it into other lines, making other juxtapositions and contrasts. He shifted this and that candle, he made the spaces different, he effaced the disfigurement of a possible gap.' Yet he cannot avoid 'moments in which he . . . catch[es] a glimpse of the void so sensible to the woman who wandered in exile or sat where he had seen her with the portrait of Acton Hague'. To arrive at his 'conception of the total, the ideal' he is faced with the need of adding 'just another figure': ' "Just one more – to round it off; just one more, just one", continued to hum itself in his head.' This murmur, 'just one more', echoes repeatedly in the closing paragraphs of the tale (*CT*, IX, 268). Stransom's structure can only be complete if it incorporates the shameful, unspeakable attachment he wishes to exclude.

Ghost tale, fairy tale, 'The Altar of the Dead' moves from the non-performativity of Stransom's melancholia into that most performative and utopian of modes, camp. Stransom's last visit to his altar reads like a Sirkian melodrama, adorned with 'a passion of light' and 'a choir of angels' (*CT*, IX, 271). Anticipating later camp and homoerotic appropriations of Catholic iconography (most notorious in Ronald Firbank's fiction), James brings Stransom to the angel who can prepare him to accommodate Hague. His dead fiancée, Mary Antrim, in the guise of Virginal (and libidinal) Mother,

smiled at him from the glory of heaven – she brought the glory down with her to take him . . . he felt his buried face grow hot as with some communicated knowledge that had the force of a reproach. It suddenly made him contrast that very rapture with the bliss he had refused to another. This breath of the passion immortal was all that other had asked; the descent of Mary Antrim opened his spirit with a great compunctious throb for the descent of Acton Hague. (*CT*, IX, 270)

Mary's divine intervention and sanction enable him to accomplish the identification he has strongly craved, to attain the masochistic ecstasy of the 'prostrate figure . . . a woman in deep mourning, bowed in grief or in prayer' (*CT*, IX, 270). He is able to fulfil the desire he felt when he first saw the mourning woman, the desire to 'sink, like her, to the very bottom, be as motionless, as rapt in prostration' (*CT*, IX, 239).

In his portrayal of Stransom, then, James comments on the difficulties arising from a foreclosure of homoerotic possibilities, and examines the ills attending any construction of sexuality depending on repudiation and exclusion. A sexual identity cannot admit proscribed bonds without a sense of panic or shame: to acknowledge such bonds without anxiety would only be possible with what Judith Butler calls 'an alternative logic of kinship'.[19] James's fiction sets itself the task of imagining such an alternative logic. 'The Altar of the Dead' uses any tools it can find to tackle such a task – parodic subversion, fictional fantasy – and, in doing so, makes a break with its own narrative procedure, as it swings out of realism into comic and fantastic melodrama. This switch in mode enables the story to escape the law of prohibition governing its own production. George Stransom's 'great compunctious throb for the descent of Acton Hague' constitutes the performative enactment of a marriage ceremony joining two men in the arms of that omnipotent body which offers or denies recognition to human relationships: the Roman Catholic Church. If the tale implies that the very construction of a 'homosexual subject' is fraught with difficulty, it ascribes this difficulty not to an inherent pathology of homoerotic desire, but to the fact that such desire has no adequate symbolization. James is asking whether the stringent conditions of masculine entitlement in late Victorian culture can be reconciled with an acknowledgment of emotional and erotic affiliations such entitlement appears to foreclose: this question is a presiding concern in his late fiction.

NOTES

1. In 1939, Joyce could use 'pud' as a slang term for 'penis' in *Finnegans Wake*. I have not been able to verify whether this usage of 'pud' was current in 1909. Note also the pun on 'Puddock', a toad: Jane and Sidney's fears might represent a jokey reversal of 'The Frog Prince' (my thanks to one of the anonymous readers for CUP for this suggestion).
2. Eve Kosofsky Sedgwick, *Epistemology of the Closet* (Berkeley: University of California Press, 1990), 196–7.
3. Neil Bartlett's *Who Was That Man?: A Present For Mr Oscar Wilde* (London: Serpent's Tail, 1988) describes the simultaneous publicity and caution of (homo)erotic languages in late Victorian London. This book, Sedgwick's *Epistemology*, and Christopher Craft, 'Alias Bunbury: Desire

and Termination in *The Importance of Being Earnest*', *Representations*, 31 (1990), 19–46, are the best analyses of the discursive terrain of the 'closet' and the 'open secret'. For good descriptions of the historical conditions which engendered such lingual circuitousness, see Jeffrey Weeks, *Coming Out: Homosexual Politics in Britain from the Nineteenth Century to the Present* (1977, revised edn, London: Quartet, 1990) and *Sex, Politics and Society: The Regulation of Sexuality Since 1800* (London: Longman, 1981).

4 See also Sedgwick's 'The Beast in the Closet: James and the Writing of Homosexual Panic', *Epistemology of the Closet*, 182–212.

5 Stephen Heath, 'Psychopathia Sexualis: Stevenson's *Strange Case*', *Critical Quarterly*, 28 (1986), 95.

6 See, for example, Sigmund Freud, 'Notes on a Case of Paranoia' ('Schreber'), *Pelican Freud Library*, ed. Angela Richards (vols. 1–11) and Albert Dixon (vols. 12–15), 15 vols. (Harmondsworth: Penguin, 1973–86), vol. IX, 198.

7 James often eroticizes and genders buildings, and, when describing the church of Saint Julian at Tours in *A Little Tour in France*, writes, 'I have always thought there be a sex in fine buildings; and Saint Julian, with its noble nave, is of the gender of the name of its patron' (*CTW*-II, 36).

8 *Pelican Freud Library*, vol. VII, 104.

9 See Bersani for an examination of the fantasies surrounding active and passive sexuality, and the relationship between sexuality and politics. In what reads uncannily like a description of the eroticism of 'The Jolly Corner', Leo Bersani writes: '[i]t is possible to think of the sexual as, precisely, moving between a hyperbolic sense of self and a loss of all consciousness of self' ('Is the Rectum a Grave?', in *Aids: Cultural Analysis, Cultural Activism*, ed. Douglas Crimp (Cambridge: MIT, 1988), 218).

10 There is, of course, dispute as to whether 'queer' might have had homosexual connotations for James at the turn of the century. The *OED* lists 1922 as the first date of this usage, which would, however, almost certainly have enjoyed considerable oral circulation before occurring in writing. It may be that James uses 'queer' precisely because its connection with 'homosexual' is tentative and uncertain. This would account for his use of the word when writing about Symonds in letters, and would also mean that, in his published fiction, the word can bring officially 'repressed' connotations into the public sphere (hence bridging the gap between 'public' and 'private' in a manner recalling the obscene names James gives his characters). Recent commentators who have argued that 'queer' already had homosexual connotations in the late nineteenth century include Elaine Showalter, in *Sexual Anarchy: Gender and Culture at the Fin-de-Siècle* (New York: Viking, 1990), 111–12; Wayne Koestenbaum, in *Double Talk: The Erotics of Male Literary Collaboration* (New York and London: Routledge, 1989); and Joseph Bristow, in *Effeminate England: Homoerotic Writing After 1885* (Buckingham: Open University Press, 1995). Bristow writes that 'there were groups of men –

such as Henry James and E. M. Forster – who, in the 1890s and early 1900s, discreetly gave this epithet a homophile inflection', and discusses James's comment in a letter to J. A. Symonds that the latter's 'A Problem in Modern Ethics' is 'a queer place to plant the standard of duty' (3, 128–9, quoting *HJL*, III, 398).

Given that James wrote 'The Jolly Corner' in 1906, it is striking that there are three seemingly indisputable instances of 'queer' carrying a homosexual innuendo in E. M. Forster's *Maurice*, written in 1913 and 1914, only a few years later. The first occurs when Clive is attempting a delicate seduction of Maurice, using Plato as a romantic aid: '"But hadn't you been getting hold of me for months? Since first you saw me at Risley's in fact?"[, asks Clive.] "Don't ask me." "It's a queer business, anyway." "It's that." Clive laughed delightedly, and wriggled in his chair. "Maurice, the more I think it over the more certain I am that it's you who are the devil"' ((Harmondsworth: Penguin, 1972), 85). The second involves the Wildean Ridley discussing Tchaikovsky's Pathetic Symphony, which he calls the '"Symphonie Incestueuse et Pathétique". And he informed his young friend', the text continues, 'that Tchaikovsky had fallen in love with his own nephew, and dedicated his masterpiece to him. "I come to see all respectable London flock. Isn't it *supreme*!" "Queer things you know", said Maurice stuffily' (141). The third instance involves the newly heterosexual Clive disowning his homosexual past: 'He hated queerness, Cambridge, the Blue Room, certain glades in the park were – not tainted, there had been nothing disgraceful – but rendered subtly ridiculous' (152).

11 The suggestion that the double is placed in a 'frame' marks only one of the tale's debts to Wilde's *The Picture of Dorian Gray*.

12 Donna Przybylowicz argues that 'in [his] acceptance of Alice's love [Brydon] acknowledges sexual difference and desire' and 'returns to the intersubjective realm of the superego and social authority' (*Desire and Repression: The Dialectic of Self and Other in the Late Works of Henry James* (Tuscaloosa: University of Alabama Press, 1986), 124).

13 Ruth Leys, 'The Real Miss Beauchamp: The History and Sexual Politics of the Multiple Personality Concept', in *Feminists Theorize the Political*, ed. Judith Butler and Joan W. Scott (New York: Routledge, 1992), 197.

14 For a superb analysis of the taboo on homosexuality, see Judith Butler, *Gender Trouble: Feminism and the Subversion of Identity* (New York: Routledge, 1990), 59–72.

15 *Pelican Freud Library*, vol. XI, 253.

16 The representation of homosexual scandal in the press is discussed in Ed Cohen, *Talk on the Wilde Side: Towards a Genealogy of Male Sexualities* (New York: Routledge, 1993); it is also a theme in James's 1903 tale, 'The Papers'.

17 Butler, *Gender Trouble*, 60.
18 Leo Bersani, *The Culture of Redemption* (Cambridge: Harvard University Press, 1990), 7.
19 Butler, *Gender Trouble*, 39.

CHAPTER 8

'A provision full of responsibilities': senses of the past in Henry James's fourth phase
David McWhirter

Narratives of literary careers, like all historical narratives, are ideologically overdetermined constructs – a truth to which F. O. Matthiessen was by no means blind when he argued, in 1944, that Henry James's career should be understood as culminating 'in the intricate and fascinating designs of his final and major phase'.[1] Matthiessen's high valuation of the three novels James published at the beginning of the new century – *The Ambassadors*, *The Wings of the Dove*, and *The Golden Bowl* – was proffered (polemically, it is worth recalling) in the face of a reigning critical orthodoxy that for two decades had read James's *œuvre* as a cautionary, even pathetic tale of deracination, expatriation, and subsequent decline. For Matthiessen, of course, such a misreading of James – he singles out Van Wyck Brooks and Vernon Parrington in particular – was 'eloquent evidence of what happens when you divorce the study of content from form'.[2] It is hardly surprising, then, that recent historicist and cultural critics have, in their turn, resisted the story of James's career bequeathed them by Matthiessen and his formalist, New Critical descendants; following the lead of John Carlos Rowe, contemporary James criticism has, in fact, increasingly sought 'to question, destabilize, and render uncanny the high-modernist Henry James, whose destiny always seems to end in the intricacies of his late style and its retreat from life into the palace of art'.[3]

As Rowe would be the first to point out, there is no question here of returning to Brooks's and Parrington's blunt dismissal of James's later fictions. Rather, deconstructing the myth of 'The Master' and its teleological orientation toward a 'final and major phase' permits us to re-encounter the diversity of James's *œuvre*, including the variousness of the major-phase novels themselves, apart from the familiar career mapping in which each of his texts has for so long seemed to occupy a predetermined niche. I have suggested elsewhere, for example, how the habit of reading James's so-called 'experimental phase' metaleptically, as merely a troubled stage in a resolving master narrative of his career, has worked to obscure the uncanny suspense of knowledge, authority, genre, and gender embodied in the late 1890s fictions, as well as their idiosyncratic historicity.[4] My concern in the present essay is with those texts – principally *The American Scene* (1907), the New York Edition (1907–9), and James's autobiographical volumes, *A Small Boy and Others* (1913) and *Notes of a Son and Brother* (1914) – that hold the rather dubious distinction of having been written *after* their author's 'final phase'. As Ross Posnock has remarked, James's non-fiction works from the post-*Golden Bowl* period have persistently been 'segregated', marginalized, and 'minimized' as the 'eccentric' productions of an author past his prime – a distortion of the career, Posnock persuasively argues, that has 'muffled the subtle power of James's historical imagination'.[5] Posnock's focus on this 'second major phase (1907–14) of autobiography, cultural criticism, and aesthetics' is, in fact, part of a broad resurgence of critical interest in what has sometimes been called James's 'fourth phase'.[6] Abandoning Matthiessen's belief in the finality of the canonical major phase, James's critics have increasingly discerned, rightly I think, a James who is, like the America he encountered in 1904, never final, 'perpetually provisional' (*CTW*-1, 689). And if the fate of Matthiessen's final phase should make us wonder about the wisdom of compartmentalizing James's career into reified phases at all – perhaps we should view the career as one long, endlessly experimental phase – it also suggests that we ought to be wary of any attempt to impose a totalizing, conclusive narrative on James's post-*Golden Bowl* work.

That said, even the most cautious effort to generalize about these texts would have to characterize them as marked by James's pervasive desire to revisit his personal, cultural and literary pasts – by what Posnock has aptly described as a 'late recrudescence of revisionary energy'.[7] As my title for this chapter suggests, however, James's persistent re-engagement with the past – in the late non-fictional texts from *William Wetmore Story and His Friends* (1903) to the essays of 1914–15 collected in *Within the Rim*, as well as in such fictions as 'The Jolly Corner' and the unfinished novels, *The Sense of the Past* and *The Ivory Tower* – is anything but consistent in the modalities through which it senses, engages, and represents the past. In *A Small Boy and Others* and *Notes of a Son and Brother*, for example, the past is simultaneously too full and too empty, alternately figured as a rich 'hoard' or overflowing treasure-house of memories *and* as a place of curious blankness with 'so little . . . to "show"', a space of absences, defeats, and failures, of passions, affairs, and adventures that were somehow missed, of things left undone or at best done by others (*AU*, 41, 8). 'To knock at the door of the past was . . . to see it open to me quite wide', James insists (*AU*, 3); but for a 'chronicler' as 'memory-ridden' as James, that door opens to reveal not only a 'precious store of images', but also a 'strange process of waste', a family history of 'early deaths, arrested careers, broken promises, orphaned children' (*AU*, 358, 461, 8, 10). Similarly, if James's return to the America of his youth frequently reveals a past capable of producing an almost unstoppable proliferation of impressions, 'stories', and prose, it also at moments – as during James's visit to his family's cemetery plot in Cambridge – can, as he puts it, cause the pen to drop from his hands (*CN*, 240). One of the burdens of *The American Scene* is James's nostalgia for a past that America seems to him ceaselessly engaged in repudiating. Yet as Leon Edel notes, the Wellsian time-travel fantasy, *The Sense of the Past*, which James left unfinished at the time of his death, is driven by an almost obsessive fear of being trapped in the past.[8] In 'The Jolly Corner', the past is both something Spencer Brydon wants to repossess and something that he is in danger of being possessed by.

The varied, contradictory nature of James's responses to the past is also manifested in the New York Edition, a project that might, at first glance, appear to constitute a straightforward attempt to invest the past with the permanence and grandeur of a monument. By constructing a collected edition of his work that is in truth highly selective, for example, James preserves and thus canonizes some of his earlier texts while 'quietly disowning' – in effect repudiating – others.[9] If, in the Prefaces, he remembers the genesis of certain fictions in extraordinary detail, he forgets (or chooses to forget) almost entirely the beginnings of others: 'Renewing acquaintance with [*Roderick Hudson*] after a quarter of a century', James enjoys the 'revival of an all but extinct relation' (*LC*-II, 1039); 'a certain vagueness of remembrance in respect to the origin and growth of "The Tragic Muse"', in contrast, leaves him looking on the novel as 'a poor fatherless and motherless, a sort of unregistered and unacknowledged birth' for which he none-the-less assumes responsibility (*LC*-II, 1103). In still another case, that of *The Awkward Age*, James 'recall[s] with perfect ease the idea in which [his text] had its origin', but is 'half-moved to leave [it] undivulged' (*LC*-II, 1120). Most conspicuously, James's desire to enshrine the 'literary deeds' (*LC*-II, 1340) of his young manhood coexists uneasily with his practice of extensive revision, a practice which many critics have seen as an outrageous violation of the past.[10] In its monumentalizing aspirations, the New York Edition entombs and embalms the past; in its inclusions and omissions, its prefatorial rereadings, and in the revisions, it blithely transforms it.

When Posnock describes James's varied reactions to the American scene he encountered in 1904 – 'contempt, condescension, exhilaration, fear, respect, pleasure, and nostalgia'[11] – he also provides a catalogue of the senses of the past exhibited by James throughout the fourth phase. Yet, as Posnock points out, the polyphonic diversity of James's motives has typically been ignored. James's late non-fictional texts have traditionally – and reductively – been read as the 'works of an aging, genteel, celibate bachelor whose last books seem more absorbed in the consolations of memory than in anything else'.[12] Some critics have discerned in James's late impulse of return a more aggressive form of nostalgia that anticipates the reactionary agendas of his high-modernist descendants. Joel Porte thus reads James's 'intense concern with preserving' the past in *The American Scene* as the product of his horrified response to 'an ethnic invasion that seemed palpably to threaten the essentially uniform Anglo-Saxon Christian culture that was the staple of his fiction'.[13] Seen in this light, James's re-engagement with the past in the fourth phase becomes a strategy of resistance to the intrusions of a vulgar, decidedly ungenteel modernity that, not coincidentally, was increasingly unappreciative of, and even hostile to, high culture and the refinements of Jamesian fictional art. It is only a small step from this position to Michael Millgate's view of the entire fourth phase as a massive 'testamentary act', the product of an authority obsessively and at times ruthlessly shaping 'the image of himself that would be handed down to posterity'. Memory here becomes a wilful appropriation of the past by an 'imperial' consciousness,[14] an attempt to reshape and fix the past in a unified master narrative of identity and mastery: James seizes and distorts the past – rewriting the letters of his family and friends for his autobiographical volumes,[15] revising his early fictions to make them conform to the later style – in a proleptic effort to determine, once and for all, what Henry James was.

The disturbing implications of James's sense of the past identified by Porte, Millgate, and others – the racism and xenophobia inherent in James's revisionist idealizations of the American past; the exploitation of women implicit in his cavalier rewriting of Minnie Temple's letters;[16] the ideology of imperial authorship and autonomous identity that (in Millgate's view) informs the whole New York Edition enterprise – are difficult to ignore. Yet, as Posnock shows, the nostalgia Porte deplores is both indulged and critiqued in *The American Scene*, and is only one of the multiple, intersecting, counter-changing senses of the past deployed in that text. Similarly, if the New York Edition is undoubtedly, in some senses, an attempt at monolithic self-definition that imposes a suspect and subjugating unity on the past – the unity, in R.W.B. Lewis's words, 'of a completed *œuvre*'[17] – it also should be apprehended as a conscious experiment which deliberately brings a variety of different perspectives – the original texts, the revisions, the Prefaces, Coburn's photographic frontispieces, even the eloquent silence of the excluded novels and tales – into relation, without insisting that they converge on any monumental completedness, or on a single narrative of James's career.[18] Indeed, to see James as engaged in a single-minded effort to define the past – whether to preserve, idealize, control, or reinvent it – is to misapprehend the main thrust of his revisionary energy in the fourth phase.

The question for James is, I think, less 'what it was' than 'who I am'. And this latter question depends for James not on *a* sense of the past, on a totalizing narrative of what was, but on a capacity for establishing multiple, often contradictory lines of connection, relation, and responsiveness to the past. 'Nothing', James once asserted, 'is my *last word* about anything' (*HJL*, II, 221). But because the writing self of the fourth phase has for so long been seen as what Yeats once called a 'finished man',[19] critics have until recently been largely content to mine *The American Scene*, the *Autobiography*, and the New York Edition for biographical data and for clues to reading James's earlier, 'canonical' works of fiction.[20] This view of the elderly James, itself a product of the myth that his career culminated in the major phase, in its turn has promoted an excessively 'finished' reading of the past as it is manifested in the fourth-phase texts. Thus Leon Edel unblinkingly asserts that, after *The Golden Bowl*, James 'no longer needed [to write more novels]: He had finally resolved the questions, curious and passionate, that had kept him at his desk in his inquiry into the process of living. He could now go back to America and make his peace with it; and he could now build the altar of himself, collect and unify the work of a lifetime.'[21] Posnock, in contrast, describes the fourth phase as embodying a protean dialectic of memory and consciousness, a reading much closer to the grain of James's alternately excited, bewildered, sometimes even terrified reactions to the multiple past selves his astonishing 'reach of reminiscence' discovers in 'the ragbag of memory' he proceeds to 'empty... into these pages' (*AU*, 41). If, as James himself remarks, 'there are parts of one's past... that bask consentingly and serenely enough in the light of other days – which is but the intensity of thought... there are other parts that take it as with agitation and pain, a troubled consciousness that heaves as with the disorder of drinking it deeply in' (*LC*-II, 1174). It thus seems to me almost impossible to read the alienated, 'restless analyst' (*CTW*-1, 361) of *The American Scene* as 'mak[ing] his peace' with America, or to correlate Edel's genteel, almost funereal Master, intent on building an altar on the remains of a self and a career that are already collected, embalmed and buried, with James's image from *Notes of a Son and Brother* for his own exploratory, intensely curious relation to the past: 'It's like putting one's ear, doctor-fashion, to the breast of time – or say as the subtle savage puts his to the ground – and catching at its start some vibratory hum that has been going on more or less for the fifty years since' (*AU*, 482).

What James seeks, in other words, is not a completed image of the past, but a *modus operandi* for investigating the complex, unsettled and often unsettling, relationships between 'what it was' and 'who I am', for experiencing, as he says, 'the pleasure of finding the past – the Past above all – answered for to one's own touch' (*AU*, 74). James's desire to 'touch' the past – a persistent and highly cathected metaphor in the fourth phase texts to which I will return – helps to explain why he focuses his 'present revisiting, re-appropriating impulse' on what he calls, in the Preface to *The Aspern Papers*, 'a palpable imaginable *visitable* past' (*LC*-II, 1174, 1177). Commenting on the novella's germ in 'the long survival' of Mary Shelley's half-sister Jane Clairmont – 'had I happened to hear of her but a little sooner', he remarks, 'I might have seen her in the flesh' – James finds striking testimony 'for the reality and closeness of our relation to the past':

the case had the air of the past just in the degree in which that air, I confess, most appeals to me – when the region over which it hangs is far enough away without being too far.

I delight . . . in the nearer distances and the clearer mysteries, the marks and signs of a world we may reach over to as by making a long arm we grasp an object at the other end of our own table. The table is the one, the common expanse, and where we lean, so stretching, we find it firm and continuous. That, to my imagination, is the past fragrant of all, or of almost all, the poetry of the thing outlived and lost and gone, and yet in which the precious element of closeness, telling so of connexions but tasting so of differences, remains appreciable. With more moves back the element of the appreciable shrinks – just as the charm of looking over a garden-wall into another garden breaks down when successions of walls appear. The other gardens, those still beyond, may be there, but even by use of our longest ladder we are baffled and bewildered – the view is mainly of barriers. The one partition makes the place we have wondered about *other*, both richly and recogniseably so; but who shall pretend to impute an effect of composition to the twenty? We are divided of course between liking to feel the past strange and liking to feel it familiar; the difficulty is, for intensity, to catch it at the moment when the scales of the balance hang with the right evenness. (*LC*-II, 1177–8)

For James, then, this 'visitable past' – precisely the past he relentlessly explores in the late non-fictional works – is essential because it tells of both 'connexions' and 'differences'. Uncannily 'familiar' yet 'strange', both 'appreciable' and '*other*', the 'nearer distance', unlike those 'periods more protected by the "dignity" of history' (and hence inaccessible to 'the backward vision'), invites even as it resists James's efforts at repossession: its 'appeal resid[es] . . . in some deep associational force . . . more . . . than in a virtue more intrinsic' – in the multitudinous relations it provokes rather than in the facts it documents, in its continuity, as opposed to its identity, with his present 'intensity of thought' (*LC*-II, 1174–8).

In his recent consideration of 'the question of selfhood', suggestively entitled *Oneself as Another*, Paul Ricoeur stages a confrontation between two conceptions of personal identity: 'on one side, identity as *sameness* (Latin *idem*) . . . ; on the other, identity as *selfhood* (Latin *ipse*)'. 'Selfhood', Ricoeur insists, 'is not sameness', for it 'implies no assertion concerning some unchanging core of personality'[22] – nothing like the 'unity of being' that Blackmur, echoing Yeats, ascribes to the James of the New York Edition Prefaces, and that Millgate denounces in the fourth-phase project as a whole.[23] While both conceptions of identity depend on a sense of continuity with the past, *idem* or sameness identity attributes that permanence to a schema rooted 'in the category of substance' – to the persistence of an essential, selfsame *whatness* that Ricoeur construes in narratological terms as 'character': sameness identity conceives of 'change as happening to something which does not change'.[24] But there is, Ricoeur asserts, 'another model of permanence in time besides that of character. In narrative terms, it is that of keeping one's word in faithfulness to the word that has been given.' Ricoeur sees in 'this keeping [one's word]' that is the hallmark of selfhood or *ipse*-identity the emblematic figure of an identity that is the polar opposite of that depicted by the emblematic figure of character. 'Keeping one's word expresses a *self-constancy* which cannot be inscribed, as character was, within the dimension of something in general [i.e. as a substance] but solely within the dimension of "who?".'[25]

Ricoeur argues that identity in narrative oscillates 'between two limits: a lower limit, where permanence in time expresses the confusion of [sameness and selfhood]; and an upper limit, where [selfhood] poses the question of its identity without the aid and support of [sameness] or the *idem*'.[26] And it is at this upper limit – where the continuity of 'keeping one's word' unfolds without the support, and without the disabling immobilizations, of sameness – that James is exploring his own selfhood in the fourth phase. As Paul Armstrong remarks, James's fiction had always constituted 'a prolonged inquiry into the status of ethics in a world where norms have no foundation deeper than existence itself',[27] a formulation that suggests why 'the perseverance of faithfulness to a word that has been given' as a model for permanence in time informs James's characters' struggles to establish viable modalities of ethical selfhood throughout his career.[28] James, for example, frequently constructs his moral dramas around the choice a character makes in response to the words given in a letter or document: this motif – instanced in the incriminating 'scrap of paper' Christopher Newman destroys rather than uses at the end of *The American* (*AM*, 537), the 'precious papers' James's publishing scoundrel ruthlessly pursues in *The Aspern Papers* (*AP*, 143), and the posthumous letter from Milly Theale that Merton Densher refuses to open at the end of *The Wings of the Dove* – resonates in connection with James's own choices regarding the family letters he altered for the autobiographies and the fictions he revised for the New York Edition. More importantly, Densher's concern with the moral implications of simply *reading* Milly's bequest is not unconnected to the moment at the end of the novel when, having lied to Mrs Lowder that he is on his way to church, he is suddenly moved to fulfil his lie out of a desire 'not to have wasted his word' (*WD*, II, 361). For this odd gesture adumbrates the strange but moving ways in which Densher's sense of himself is increasingly determined by his need to keep the promises he has made unwillingly, perhaps even unwittingly, to Milly. Indeed, the centrality of 'keeping one's word' as the locus of ethical selfhood is focalized throughout James's work in his attention to the act of promising. Isabel Archer, for example, might be seen as moving from the conception of identity as sameness that she articulates in her famous conversation with Madame Merle to a new sense of self embodied in her decision to keep her promise to Pansy. Hyacinth Robinson, the protagonist of *The Princess Casamassima*, commits suicide in the face of an impossible choice between violating his promise to Paul Muniment (and to his revolutionary ideals) and keeping it. As these examples suggest, 'faithfulness to a word that has been given' is not, for James, a formula for moral rectitude, but a context for understanding the self as an ethical continuity. One can, like Densher, remain faithful to a lie. And Isabel's return to Rome has been lamented by many readers as an act of moral capitulation and self-betrayal. Hyacinth's case, moreover – the ethical quandary of a man whose evolving fidelity to his revolutionary commitment renders the literal fulfilment of his promise immoral in his own eyes – reminds us, in Ricoeur's words, that 'the obligation to maintain one's self in keeping one's promises is [always] in danger of solidifying into the Stoic rigidity of simple constancy, if it is not permeated by the desire to respond to an expectation, even to a request coming from another'.[29] Reduced to the 'rigidity of simple constancy', in other words, the promise (as 'in the forms of promising sanctioned by law – oaths, contracts and so on') becomes an 'obligation' in which the relation of 'solicitude' (defined as 'the dialogic structure of the ethical aim') 'is, as it were, obliterated, erased'.[30]

It is in this context, I think, that we should understand Maggie Verver's successful effort to remake her marriage in *The Golden Bowl*, not by clinging to what it was, even less so to what *she* was, but through a fidelity to her vow that requires a massive revision of her relationship with her husband – a revision that cannot occur without *his* responsive participation – and a remarkable reconfiguration of herself. Like his American admirer Marianne Moore, who speaks with characteristic wit of 'Marriage' as

> This institution,
> perhaps one should say enterprise,
> out of respect for which
> one says one need not change one's mind
> about a thing one has believed in,[31]

James transmutes the moral, legal, and institutional certitudes of marriage into a purely ethical question. For he recognizes that the ethical self, like that 'enchanting thing', 'the mind', as it is described by Moore in another poem, is 'not a Herod's oath that cannot change'[32] – that it must 'pose the question of its identity without the aid and support of [sameness]'. In *The American Scene*, the New York Edition, and the *Autobiography*, what we see is James exploring his *own* cultural, authorial, and personal identity under the sign of this revisionary model of selfhood – a process that increasingly affiliates him with what Posnock calls a 'politics of nonidentity'.[33] And James's *ipse* – his 'Here I am' as opposed to 'This is *what* I am' – finds the contexts for its articulation precisely in his multiplicitous, protean, always proliferating *senses* of the past, in his never final, always provisional quest for new circuits of connection and continuity with a past that remains *other*, and with *those* others – America; William, Henry Senior, Minnie Temple, but also that always watching 'small boy'; the authors of *Roderick Hudson* and 'Daisy Miller' and *The Tragic Muse*; his readers – who inhabit that past and constitute the self which apprehends it.

James's understanding of the self as a keeping of one's word – his 'faithfulness to the word that has been given' – is nowhere more urgently articulated than in his Preface to *The Golden Bowl*. Locating the 'incomparable luxury of the artist' in his 'essentially traceable' relation to his past – his 'literary deeds', but also his other 'vital or social performances' – James insists that '[i]t rests altogether with himself not to break with his values, not to "give away" his importances. Not to *be* disconnected, for the tradition of behaviour, he has but to feel that he is not; by his lightest touch the whole chain of relation and responsibility is reconstituted.' And yet, James concludes, of the 'tie that binds' us to our past deeds and values, 'we can make almost anything we like' – a freedom, I would argue, that is made possible precisely by his understanding of that tie as ethical, as a chosen self-constancy, not an ontological persistence of the same (*LC*-II, 1340). Thus, when Maggie Verver, having accepted the necessity of parting from her beloved father in order to save her marriage, asserts that they will nevertheless always have the past – 'a provision full of responsibilities' (*GB*, II, 255) – she anticipates the rich relation and responsiveness to the past that characterizes James's fourth phase as a whole. It is in this light, for example, that we can best appreciate Posnock's revisionist characterization of *The American Scene* as a profound act of civic responsibility, and that we can best understand James's critique of an American cultural identity that, as he sees it, wants 'nothing to do with continuity, responsibility, and transmission' (*CTW*-I, 365). James quarrels with America not because it has changed from what he knew – no 'tough reactionary', he 'accept[s the] ravage' (*CTW*-I, 734) – but because America has failed to take its own experimental, provisional identity seriously enough. America, in James's sense, is not faithful to its own promise. Indeed, with its 'perpetual repudiation of the past', America resembles nothing so much as an *ir*responsible child, 'living but in the sense of its hour and in the immediacy of its want', in a 'chronic state of besprinklement with the sawdust of its ripped-up dolls' (*CTW*-I, 400, 496–7).

James's stress on his 'responsibility' to the past seems very close to Ricoeur's strong definition of that term:

Self-constancy is for each person that manner of conducting himself or herself so that others can *count on* that person. Because someone is counting on me, I am *accountable for* my actions before another. The term 'responsibility' unites both meanings: 'counting on' and 'being accountable for'. It unites them, adding to them the idea of a *response* to the question 'Where are you?' asked by another who needs me. This response is the following: 'Here I am!' a response that is a statement of self-constancy.[34]

Something akin to this threefold relation to the other – solicitude; accountability; responsiveness – can be discerned in James's insistence, throughout *A Small Boy and Others* and *Notes of a Son and Brother*, that 'no particle that counts for memory or is appreciable to the spirit *can* be too tiny', that he should be 'ashamed, as of a cold impiety, to find any element altogether negligible': 'even the more broken things', he writes, 'give out touching human values' (*AU*, 10, 4, 30). 'Solicited' by the past, James responds by 'indulg[ing]' and 'cherish[ing]' the moment, 'woo[ing] it all back' in order to 'lose [him]self in wonder' at its differences from, and continuities with, the man he has become (*AU*, 25, 424, 4, 188, 8): 'strange enough', he muses, 'the "aesthetic" of artists who could desire but literally to reproduce' (*AU*, 66). But it is in James's most sustained act of faithfulness to the word that he had given – the New York Edition – that we can find as well his most moving response to the past's demand, 'Where are you?'. James grants his fullest care and solicitude to 'the old picture, the work of his hand': his sense of responsibility 'helps him', he writes in his Preface to *Roderick Hudson*, 'to live back into a forgotten state, into convictions, credulities too early spent perhaps'; 'it breathes upon the dead reasons of things . . . and makes them revive' (*LC*-II, 1045). But 'care', as James says elsewhere, is 'nothing if not active' (*LC*-II, 1341). And Ricoeur's alternative model of ethical identity – his conception of an active self-constancy that exists 'solely within the dimension of "who?"' – seems especially helpful in understanding James's revisions for the New York Edition: neither as an effort to adhere to original intentions, nor as an attempt to force the differences of the past to conform to present motivations, but as a fully responsible keeping of the promise of the words he gave so long ago. Revision is not, for James, rewriting, but a process of 'seeing it again', essentially a mode of rereading; it is a new relation that collapses the logic of identity by engaging the difference between the novelist's 'original tracks' and his 'present mode of motion' – a relation that does not imply a hierarchy of priority or validity or value, and which opens, James insists, 'a myriad more adequate channels' for interpretation and self-understanding (*LC*-II, 1330–3).[35] 'Literally to reproduce' his earlier texts without revising them would be to embalm them in the distanced sameness of '[t]he thing done and dismissed' – a policy, James points out, requiring the 'non-revisionists' to have 'in advance and on system stopped their ears, their eyes and even their very noses'. To rewrite them altogether would be equally unresponsive to the demand he imagines them as making: 'Actively believe in us and then you'll see!' James's third way is to seek a relationship with the earlier text: making himself radically available to its otherness, he practices an active care that 'breathe[s] upon the old catastrophes and accidents, the old wounds and mutilations and disfigurements', and that responds to the other's 'plaint' or 'sharpness of appeal' with the 'Here I am!' of his late style, a style 'that experience had at last made the only possible one' (*LC*-II, 1120, 1332–7). One recognizes here as well James's commitment, in the New York Edition, to still another aspect of Ricoeur's ethical selfhood: 'the obligation to safeguard the institution of language'.[36] As James would write in 'The Question of Our Speech', 'All life ... comes back to ... the medium through which we communicate with each other; for all life comes back to the question of our relations with each other. These relations are made possible, are verily constituted, by our speech.'[37]

My intention in arguing for the profoundly ethical nature of James's fourth phase project has not been to excuse or condone the specific judgments, the acts of deed and word, produced by his 'present revisiting, re-appropriating impulse' (*LC*-II, 1174). James's responses to the American immigrants he encounters in New York – those 'aliens' who both repel and fascinate him – are often as crude and uncaring as his magisterial assertions that American women are to blame for the debased condition of our speech. James himself, responding to the protest of his nephew Harry, judged his deviation from 'the ideal of documentary exactitude' in the matter of his family's letters to have been 'a mistake' (*HJL*, IV, 800). But to conclude, as Millgate does, that James's 'retouchings' of the letters reveal the 'characteristic imperiousness' of a 'monster of egotistical voracity'[38] is to dismiss the gravity of James's defense of the 'whole "ethic" and aesthetic (and indeed its aesthetic, however discredited [it appeared to his nephew], *was* simply its ethic)' that informed his revisionary strategy (*HJL*, IV, 800). It is also to stop one's eyes, ears, and possibly even one's nose to the deepest resonances of that metaphorics of touching and retouching that Millgate himself acknowledges as 'the crucial term' through which James understands his revisions. For Millgate, the 'suggestiveness' of these 'analogies from painting' does not 'cancel out the apparent triviality of such processes as, precisely, "beautification", their hint of Tennyson's "sad mechanic exercise", or, at best, of Turner at a Royal Academy "Varnishing Day" fettling up his paintings for actual exhibition'.[39] But, as several passages quoted in this chapter suggest, James seems to have conceived of this 'touch' – the force, we recall, that 'reconstitutes' the 'whole chain of relation and responsibility' – as a literal laying on of hands, even, at times, as a physical embrace. In contrast to the 'barbarous injunction' of the 'antirevisionists' – 'Hands off altogether on the nurse's part!' – James imagines himself as 'washing [the] wizened faces' and 'straightening [the] grizzled locks' of his earliest texts (*LC*-II, 1331). Indeed, the New York Edition Prefaces are especially striking in the persistence with which they figure the younger author, his early books, even the characters in those books, *as* persons, as others who are all but palpably present in the Edition's relational landscape.[40] Thus where Millgate sees in Henry's reworkings of William's letters mostly a suggestion of the novelist's 'growing age and declining powers',[41] James himself describes to his nephew an experience of careful and caring touching of the other:

And when I laid hands upon the letters to use as so many touches and tones in the picture I frankly confess I seemed to see them in a better, or at all events in another light . . . than those rough and rather illiterate copies I had from you showed at their face value. I found myself again in such close relation with your Father, such a revival of relation as I hadn't known since his death, and which was a passion of tenderness for doing the best thing by him that the material allowed, and which I seemed to feel him in the room and at my elbow asking me for as I worked and as he listened. It was as if he had said to me on seeing me lay my hands on the weak little relics of our common youth, 'Oh but you're not going to give me away, to hand me over, in my raggedness and my poor accidents, quite unhelped, unfriended, you're going to do the very best for me you *can*, aren't you, and since you appear to be making such claims for me you're going to let me seem to justify them as much as I possibly may?' And it was as if I kept spiritually replying to this that he might indeed trust me to handle him with the last tact and devotion . . .

And the case is really that if it had been for me, from the first, of that hands-off kind, by a foreseen necessity, that consideration would have begun, *could* only have begun, further back and warned me from *any* sort of reproduction. *That* really will have been my mistake, I feel – there it will have begun; in thinking that . . . any mere merciless transcript might have been possible to me. (*HJL*, IV, 802–3)

In the New York Edition Prefaces, James is rarely shy about proclaiming his exemplary triumphs, never reluctant to bask in the 'golden glow' of 'the supremely good' things which 'raise the artistic faith to its maximum', and with which 'it is one's theory of one's honour to be concerned' (*LC*-II, 1306). But James is perhaps even more eager – and this has been less frequently noticed – to embrace his literary errors and mistakes: the 'misplaced middles' and 'false measurements', 'the absent values, the palpable voids, the missing links, the mocking shadows, that reflect, taken together, the early bloom of one's good faith'. These 'fallibilities', James insists, 'after all had their sweetness, so that one would on the whole rather have kept them than parted with them'. Indeed:

Such cases are of course far from abnormal – so far from it that some acute mind ought surely to have worked out by this time the 'law' of the degree in which the artist's energy fairly depends on his fallibility. How much and how often, and in what connexions and with what almost infinite variety, must he be a dupe, that of his prime object, to be at all measurably a master, that of his actual substitute for it – or in other words at all appreciably to exist? (*LC*-II, 1122, 1294–5)

However one may judge the fallibilities, sweet and otherwise, that are inseparable from the achievement of James's revisionary fourth phase – and James himself insisted that 'any imaged prose' owes the fullest 'flower of its effect to the act and process of apprehension that so beautifully asks most from it. It then infallibly, and not less beautifully, most responds' (*LC*-II, 1339) – those fallibilities are never irresponsibilities of the 'hands-off kind', never the product of a complacent or a completed mastery. If 'the proved error is the base apologetic deed' (*LC*-II, 1341), James's mistakes always and richly signal his willingness to risk himself in the ethical encounter of relation and response to the other, in whom, paradoxically, he discovers who he is.

NOTES

1 F. O. Matthiessen, *Henry James: The Major Phase* (New York: Oxford University Press, 1944), xv.
2 Ibid., x.
3 John Carlos Rowe, *The Theoretical Dimensions of Henry James* (Madison: University of Wisconsin Press, 1984), 28.
4 See David McWhirter, 'What's Awkward About *The Awkward Age?*', in *Centuries' Ends, Narrative Means*, ed. Robert Newman (Stanford University Press, 1996), 212–21; and 'In the "Other House" of Fiction: Writing, Authority and Femininity in *The Turn of the Screw*', in *New Essays on Daisy Miller and The Turn of the Screw*, ed. Vivian R. Pollak (Cambridge University Press, 1993), 121–48.
5 Ross Posnock, *The Trial of Curiosity: Henry James, William James, and the Challenge of Modernity* (New York: Oxford University Press, 1991), vii. Readers familiar with Posnock's study will recognize the indebtedness of this essay to its groundbreaking reconfiguration of James's importance to our understanding of modern culture.
6 Ibid., 4. Recent book-length studies substantially or wholly devoted to James's post-major phase work include: Charles Caramello, *Henry James, Gertrude Stein, and the Biographical Act* (Chapel Hill: University of North Carolina Press, 1996); Beverly Haviland, *Henry James's Last Romance: Making Sense of the Past and the American Scene* (Cambridge University Press,

1997); Carol Holly, *Intensely Family: The Inheritance of Family Shame and the Autobiographies of Henry James* (Madison: University of Wisconsin Press, 1995); Philip Horne, *Henry James and Revision: The New York Edition* (Oxford: Clarendon Press, 1990); David McWhirter, ed., *Henry James's New York Edition: The Construction of Authorship* (Stanford University Press, 1995); Michael Millgate, *Testamentary Acts: Browning, Tennyson, James, Hardy* (Oxford: Clarendon Press, 1992); and Kenneth W. Warren, *Black and White Strangers: Race and American Literary Realism* (University of Chicago Press, 1993). Renewed interest in the fourth phase is also evidenced by the publication of new paperback editions of *The American Scene*, ed. John F. Sears (Harmondsworth: Penguin, 1994); and *Italian Hours*, ed. John Auchard (Harmondsworth: Penguin, 1995), the latter a collection of earlier travel essays revised and supplemented for publication in 1909.

7 Posnock, *The Trial of Curiosity*, 81.
8 Leon Edel, *Henry James: The Treacherous Years, 1895–1901*, vol. IV of *The Life of Henry James* (New York: Avon Books, 1978), 331.
9 Letter of Henry James to James B. Pinker, 6 June 1905, quoted in Michael Anesko, *'Friction With the Market': Henry James and the Profession of Authorship* (New York: Oxford University Press, 1986), 144.
10 One early reviewer of the New York Edition in fact judged James's revisions to be a morally indefensible violation of his works' integrity: 'Readers have asked with some heat whether an author's published work does not belong to the public. "Who am I that I should tamper with a classic?" asked a young writer when requested to revise a bit of his own work. Let Mr. James respect the classics, even from his own pen' ('Why Mr. James Revised', *The Literary Digest* 29 (August 21, 1909), 275–6). Hershel Parker, one of the most vocal of recent 'antirevisionists', essentially concurs; see *Flawed Texts and Verbal Icons: Literary Authority in American Fiction* (Evanston, Ill.: Northwestern University Press, 1984), 85–114.
11 Posnock, *The Trial of Curiosity*, 13.
12 Ibid., 4.
13 Joel Porte, 'Santayana's Masquerade', *Raritan* 7 (Autumn 1987), 141–2.
14 Michael Millgate, *Testamentary Acts*, 100–1.
15 William's son, Henry James, junior – much to his later chagrin – made available to James letters written by his father and other family members for inclusion in the 'Family Book' the novelist had promised his sister-in-law Alice he would write. The 'Family Book' ultimately became *A Small Boy and Others* and *Notes of a Son and Brother*. See Millgate's extensive discussion of the issues raised by what he calls James's 'cavalier' rewriting of the letters he received (*Testamentary Acts*, 91–6).
16 See Alfred Habegger, 'Henry James's Rewriting of Minnie Temple's Letters', *American Literature* 58 (May 1986), 166–7, 176. In terms similar to

Millgate's, Habegger condemns James's revisions of the family letters included in *Notes of a Son and Brother* – especially those written by Minnie Temple – as fraudulent fabrications.
17 R. W. B. Lewis, 'Foreword', *The Art of the Novel: Critical Prefaces by Henry James*, ed. R. P. Blackmur (Boston: Northeastern University Press, 1984), ix.
18 For a more extended discussion of the complex, conflicting motives at work in the New York Edition, see my 'Introduction' ('"The Whole Chain of Relation and Responsibility": Henry James and the New York Edition') to *Henry James's New York Edition*, 1–19.
19 William Butler Yeats, 'A Dialogue of Self and Soul', in *The Collected Poems of W. B. Yeats* (New York: Macmillan, 1956), 232.
20 Carol Holly describes her recent study of James's autobiographies – one 'grounded in the life of the autobiographer during the time in which he was writing his life story' – as in part a corrective to the 'partial and idealized account[s] of the elderly James' given by Leon Edel and others (Holly, *Intensely Family*, 6). The result is a portrait of the sexagenarian James – conflicted, unstable, professionally anxious – that diverges strikingly from previous images of a serene and confident 'Master'.
21 *Henry James: The Master, 1901–1916*, vol. v of *The Life of Henry James* (New York: Avon Books, 1972), 191.
22 Paul Ricoeur, *Oneself As Another*, trans. Kathleen Blamey (University of Chicago Press, 1992), 116, 2.
23 *Art of the Novel*, xvii.
24 *Oneself As Another*, 118.
25 Ibid., 123.
26 Ibid., 124.
27 Paul Armstrong, *The Phenomenology of Henry James* (Chapel Hill: University of North Carolina Press, 1983), 206.
28 Ricoeur, *Oneself As Another*, 123.
29 Ibid., 267. For a reading of *The Princess Casamassima* that focuses suggestively on the ethics of Hyacinth's promise in the context of his changing perceptions, see Martha C. Nussbaum, *Love's Knowledge: Essays on Philosophy and Literature* (New York: Oxford University Press, 1990), 195–219.
30 Ricoeur, *Oneself as Another*, 268, 218.
31 Marianne Moore, 'Marriage', *The Complete Poems of Marianne Moore* (Harmondsworth: Penguin Books, 1982), 62.
32 Marianne Moore, 'The Mind is an Enchanting Thing', ibid., 135.
33 *Trial of Curiosity*, 285.
34 Ricoeur, *Oneself As Another*, 165.
35 Julie Rivkin demonstrates how commentary on James's revisions has habitually favoured *either* the logic of original intentions *or* the claims of retroactive mastery, thus misreading the uniqueness of his revisionary

practice. See 'Doctoring the Text: Henry James and Revision', in *Henry James's New York Edition*, ed. David McWhirter.
36 Ricoeur, *Oneself As Another*, 124.
37 Henry James, *The Question of Our Speech. The Lesson of Balzac: Two Lectures* (Boston: Houghton Mifflin, 1905), 10.
38 *Testamentary Acts*, 96, 93.
39 Ibid., 88.
40 Eve Kosofsky Sedgwick argues persuasively that the 'love' figuratively enacted in the prefaces between the elderly James and his earlier writing selves is 'almost by definition homoerotic'. See 'Shame and Performativity: Henry James's New York Edition Prefaces', in *Henry James's New York Edition*, ed. David McWhirter, 215–16.
41 *Testamentary Acts*, 96.

CHAPTER 9

Possessing the American scene: race and vulgarity, seduction and judgment

Gert Buelens

STILL SEDUCED BY THE EXQUISITELY AMBIGUOUS?

Henry James studies today are as vibrant as they have ever been. Yet, no matter how great the fascination with the Jamesian text, a large number of readers cannot get rid of a sense of shame at their enjoyment of it. They feel that reading James is something of an evasion of the real work of the world. If earlier generations located that guilty feeling within the ivory tower that James's formal experimentation offered them, a technically more blasé generation has associated its unease more often with the politically ambiguous, or plainly incorrect, stance the Master adopts. This is particularly true with regard to *The American Scene*, at present one of the hottest texts in James studies. Noting 'the commonplace racial slurs punctuating' that text, Bryan Washington, for instance, has a hard time resisting the book's 'liberal, eminently civilized voice, sometimes sustained for pages at a time, [that] becomes so seductive, so powerful, that we forget (or want to forget) about the racial slurs, the cultural stereotypes . . .'.[1] Washington regrets that the primary subject of his book, James Baldwin, succumbed to the seduction and appeared to undertake an 'iterative valorization' of Henry James throughout his work.[2] 'If such writing [as *The American Scene*'s] is representative, symptomatic of James's nativism and of his elitism, then why did Baldwin, by contrast a progressive, bother to read him at all?'[3] Implicitly admitting an inability to come up with a satisfactory reply, Washington writes: 'There can be only speculation here, but . . . Baldwin almost certainly gave James the benefit of the doubt.'[4]

A similar sense of embarrassment troubles Kenneth Warren in the course of his engagement with James in *Black and White Strangers*. While resenting what he feels is undue pressure on the African-American critic to remain dedicated to 'a criticism and politics centered upon ... black difference', Warren does feel a need to confess that, at a 'mundane level, the time spent reading James ... is admittedly time away from the black-authored texts that have been neglected'.[5] 'If we are not to overvalue James's exquisitely ambiguous critiques of capitalism and racism [in *The American Scene*]', Warren has more recently wondered, 'how should we value him? Why, indeed, should we value him at all?'[6] Sounding as apologetic about his enthusiasm for James as Washington is with regard to Baldwin's discipleship, Warren goes on to offer his personal reasons for 'Still Reading Henry James' (as the title of his piece puts it). They are proffered in a strikingly diffident manner that I want to highlight by eliding, for now, the actual arguments (they appear in the attached footnote): 'Here, all I can do is to say that what makes James of continual interest to me is that ... And while answering this question is not the most pressing political issue of our time... And for those of us sometimes embarrassed by the fact that James has managed to stick around ... nothing more should be required than ...'[7] This diffidence is in sharp contrast to the terms Warren uses in discussing W. E. B. Du Bois, who

enacts the political drama of the intellect wrestling with the temptation to instrumentalize itself for the legitimation of the prevailing order. He performs for us the difficulty of thinking differently... [W]e are warned to be aware of how similar our own intellectual techniques may be to those we contest, but we are also able to find some self-justification in our predicament. Our sense of the difficulty of our enterprise also makes it clear why the hard intellectual work we do is 'necessary'.[8]

If with regard to James, 'all [Warren] can do is to *say* [something]', Du Bois with greater virility '*enacts* the political drama of ... *wrestling*'. Instead of merely chattering about it, Du Bois '*performs* ... the difficulty*'. Whereas a Jamesian question 'is *not* the *most pressing* issue', we do '*contest*' manfully when we are under the wings of Du Bois. If James can make 'us' feel 'embarrassed' we are fortunate to find some moral 'self-justification' thanks to Du Bois. In short, with Du Bois we feel reassured that our 'intellectual work' as literary critics is '*hard*', as a man's job should be, rather than '*exquisitely ambiguous*'.

The terms I have italicized show that there is a distinctly gendered side to the unease some critics register over James. A closer look at the *Henry James Review*'s 'Race Forum' suggests that the key 'political' objection voiced against *The American Scene*, and Jamesian realism in general, is actually that it is insufficiently masculine, and therefore immoral. Like the seductive snares of a wanton woman, the purple patches of James's irresponsible prose are in need of correction by the critics (if they are not to be guiltily enjoyed by the same). When contributors to the 'Race Forum' seek to redeem James from the charge of 'political incorrectness consequent on [his] failures of racial sympathy', they tend to replicate the gendered and moral assumptions of his censors, attempting to demonstrate that the Jamesian aesthetic responsibly performs serious cultural work worthy of comparison with real, hard politics.[9]

Consider Ross Posnock's 'Henry James and the Limits of Historicism'. Posnock reminds us that, for Kenneth Warren, *The American Scene*'s 'handling of the race problem falls dreadfully short of the clear denunciations of lynching and mob violence that prevailing conditions called for'.[10] As Posnock comments:

However one assesses the fairness of this judgment, it does carry force – its stark, obdurate literalism becomes the ceiling against which shatter all analogical arguments for James's openness as a cultural critic (including those found in my own work on James). One can revel in and demonstrate in ever-ingenious ways the subtleties of James's serpentine negotiation with otherness. But Warren's judgment will remain unmoved and unmovable.[11]

The privileged terms in Posnock's gloss perform a yoking of masculinity and morality: a moral 'judgment' regarding James's silence in the face of racist violence need not be considered in the light of 'fairness', but of 'force'. That is to say, the critical assessment of James's silence on (undesirable) violence itself becomes a form of (desirable) violence: it 'shatter[s]' 'arguments', it opposes to any attempt at 'negotiation with otherness' the 'unmoved and unmovable' violence of 'stark, obdurate' power. It is striking how easily these complimentary phrases could be associated with the very attitude that marked the lynchers and mobsters which *The American Scene* should have denounced. Refusing any 'negotiation with otherness', 'unmoved' by the suffering of black people, white autocratic men closed their ears to any liberal 'arguments for . . . openness' and were proud to 'remain . . . unmovable', applying the 'stark, obdurate literalism' of the lynching pole.[12] In a feminist vein, one could even find the 'literalis[t] . . . ceiling' reminiscent of the glass 'ceiling' – 'unmoved and unmovable' – that places a patriarchal 'reality check' on the upward mobility of women.

The passage seems to serve mainly as an act of white male

contrition. The bracketed aside suggests that the critic feels uncomfortable about having joined the women in 'revel[ling] in ... [Jamesian] subtleties', 'overestimat[ing] the range of James's empathic powers', while all along that work was so 'disappointing' to black people.[13] Yet, the essay's final paragraph does attempt to undertake a redemption of James from those intractable charges by appealing to such qualities as might stand the test of implacable scrutiny, such Jamesian strategies as even 'Du Bois might have admired and valued'.[14] *The American Scene*, Posnock argues, 'does possess an "alternate trajectory" ... commit[ted] to immersion, hazard, contingency, and ... this trajectory displays political power and even courage though not precisely of the sort Warren asks for [but] embracing what Du Bois called "a certain tingling challenge of risk" ... Henry James ... enact[s] a pragmatism that turns aesthetics from contemplation to action that cuts against the grain of capitalist efficiency and utility.'[15] Posnock's James is in the thick of the struggle, 'committ[ed]', 'immers[ed]', exposed to 'hazard', needing 'courage' in the face of a rousing 'challenge of risk', manfully 'cut[ting] against the grain', heroically turning mere aesthetics to 'action'. This James may truly assume an honourable place in the fight for 'political power'.

Even when critics are secure in their admiration of James's work, and do not feel called upon to defend his political correctness, they still tend to discuss *The American Scene* in terms of a rhetorical logic in which political progress is only to be expected from taking an active stand in a battle over power. For Sara Blair, of 'particular concern ... is James's pursuit of two entangled aims: to *contest* the nation-building *power* of emergent mass visual culture, and to create a space of cultural *agency*'.[16] The author of *The American Scene* is fired by a '*contestatory* and deeply social intention', demonstrates his 'performative em*battle*ment', and has a '*contestatory* interest in the framing of racial and national fate' (270). By the end of the book, Blair claims, James has achieved a '*posture* [that] intensifies his *contest for the power* of producing [part of] America's cultural design' and '*positions* himself so as to *contest*' other designing moves (271; emphasis added). The word 'contest' and all its derivations are chanted as a kind of mantra throughout the piece, sometimes twice in the same line (269), and, if James did not exactly take a firm stand on the question of Jim Crow racism, at least he 'position[ed] himself' in a properly radical fashion at a more general level (271). While the emphasis here is less on the hardness that needs to be mustered to succeed on the cultural battlefield, for this critic, too, politics is clearly the privileged term over aesthetics, as when Blair tries to defend 'James's notoriously aestheticized cultural politics' (265). Responding in the same issue of the *Henry James Review* to Posnock's challenge that her 'analogical arguments for James's openness' 'shatter' against the reality of his failure to condemn Southern lynchings, Blair admits that 'James indubitably preserves the "literary", the high cultural, as a space of social performance *at the cost* of more radical attacks on the politics of hierarchy, of race supremacy, of margin and center themselves.'[17] The italicized phrase again underlines the preferability of 'radical attack[ing]' as a means of working social change. The literary can only play second fiddle to the political on Blair's account, which turns out to be not so different from Posnock's once one attends to the way both try to invest the aesthetic with combative rhetorical force.[18]

OF CONTESTATION AND POLARIZATION

But what if we could regard the Jamesian literary, not as a means of performing *at the cost* of more radical attacks on a certain politics, but as *a more profitable* way of theorizing and practising the political? As one political scientist, Bonnie Honig, has recently argued, 'the test of democratic theory and politics is not so much their ability to resolve the most polarized issues but rather their ability to *relax the propensity to polarization*'.[19] Honig's book sets out to 'explore the sites, instruments and goals of . . . a *stealth politics* . . . noting how certain sites and forms of political action may work to reinscribe citizenship as a political *practice* rather than as a *(juridical) status*' (italics in original). As such, she differentiates her project from that of multiculturalists who 'see politics as a way to secure the necessary material and juridical conditions to protect existing [minority] identities . . . They seek to establish equal respect for existing groups, to give overdue recognition to previously neglected minorities.' The James critics reviewed above tend to locate their project within the context of an openly contestatory fight over status. A better James, to their mind, would have written about black people as full-fledged subjects possessing the same level of consciousness as his usual heroes and heroines. (This is Warren's main point, about which more below). And, of course, a better James would have taken a radical stand, aligning himself outspokenly with Southern blacks' rights to protection and equal respect. His failure to join liberals of the time (such as his brother William) in denouncing lynchings becomes, for these critics, a failure to pass what Honig calls the 'litmus tests that sort out who is with "us" and who is against'. What some political theorists are attempting to 'delineate and model' instead, according to Honig, is 'the proper democratic labours of translation and negotiation in order to prevent the development of polarization and litmus-testing'.

There is a striking parallel here with the recent work in moral philosophy of people like Annette Baier and Carol Gilligan. Baier's *Moral Prejudices* has rejected 'the more contractarian model [of philosophers like Kant and, more recently, Rawls], [in which] morality regulates and arbitrates where interests are opposed'. Instead, Baier wants to focus on the contemporary (and the specifically feminist) potential of Hume's philosophy. As she puts it, 'on a Humean view, as on [that of] Gilligan's [woman interviewees], morality's main task is *to rearrange situations so that interests are no longer so opposed*', in Honig's words, to relax the propensity to polarization.[20] There is, in Baier's work, a clear feminist undertone that such a concept of morality is more readily associated with the traditionally feminine qualities of caring, nurturing, responsiveness, rather than with the traditionally masculine ones of *lex dura*, violence and mutual distrust (necessitating the resort to 'contracts'). It should be clear that such a gentle philosophy does not imply a Buddhist withdrawal from social interaction into isolated contemplation. To the contrary, Baier emphasizes that her view of morality implies 'both an individual and a social task' (70). Whereas an appeal to the individual's discrete 'reason' is central to the contractarian tradition, the qualities privileged in Baier's account exist in a social field: 'What matters most, for judging moral wisdom, are [socially] corrected sentiments, imagination, and cooperative genius' (73). In an essay dealing with terrorism, entitled 'Violent Demonstrations', Baier warns against state violence in response to terrorist acts. Rather, emphasizing the importance of language to human transactions, Baier suggests that we look harder for 'the right tactful incantations for the ceremony of graduation into legitimacy [demanded by terrorists]. History surely can give us useful suggestions for tried and true face-saving diplomatic phrases' (222). Can we tackle 'violence', Baier wonders, by answering it with 'more verbal violence, and more moralizing or meta-moralizing [i.e. by moral philosophers like herself]' (223). But, since this is such uncharted territory, 'we all, like the terrorist, tend sometimes to fall back on homeopathic cures, and so on mere violence as a response to violence' (223). Are not those who would insist on measuring the Jamesian text by the standard of a 'stark, obdurate literalism' engaging in an act of verbal violence of the type that these philosophical considerations warn against? Calling on James to make a more 'violent demonstration' of his political correctness, they may miss the whole point of his 'tactful incantations', of his expertise at employing such 'face-saving diplomatic phrases' as are so badly needed in the reality of negotiation within democratic societies.

'READING FOR RACE IN JAMES'[21]

Up to this point, the burden of my argument has been on suspect rhetorical strategies in studies of James and race. Such an argument is itself open to at least two forms of criticism. One is to lay bare the extent to which my own case inevitably participates in the 'verbal violence' of contesting other readings of *The American Scene*. Another is to point out that *The American Scene* itself features a persona who takes pride in his manful, heroic adventures, mining for meaning against the odds, venturing into perilous voids.[22] There is some truth to such criticism, and it is clearly necessary to engage more closely with the substance of the criticism levelled at James's writing of race. Kenneth Warren's *Black and White Strangers* offers the greatest challenge here, because it is one of the few to go beyond charging James with the use of racial slurs and ethnic stereotyping.[23] What Warren does instead is to argue that the aesthetical values of Jamesian realism helped to create a climate in which Jim Crow racist laws could flourish.

Black and White Strangers finds fault with Jamesian realism on two related counts. One is that literary realism assumed as one of its aesthetical principles a continuity between the public and the private that allowed it to examine how 'human relationships' were being affected by the life of the nation.[24] In particular, realism tried to imagine 'the consequences that would ensue from an "extension of the field of democratic struggles to the whole of civil society"' (13). The problem with this aesthetic commitment, in Warren's view, is that it ate away at the basis of the liberal defence against the introduction of Jim Crow racist laws. That defence rested on the claim that the 'civil equality' (prior to Jim Crow), which ensured that black and white citizens could share public spaces (such as trains and streetcars), did not 'presume social equality', because it 'did not challenge [segregated] communal norms regarding marriage, the family, and education' (40). 'Jamesian narrative technique', Warren argues, 'underscored the difficulty of making discriminations' such as those between the public and the private, the civil and the social (41). James did make one distinction. While the white protagonists he portrays, such as Isabel Archer, emerge from a state of 'vulgarity' to one of 'consciousness', black characters are never enabled in this way. The second plank of Warren's critique of James is, then, that his African-Americans are and remain irredeemably vulgar, unable to achieve any insight into their situation. For some of James's characters, Warren argues, 'the mark of the most vulgarly unresponsive consciousness is the African American, a figure whose presence must be suppressed for any sense of social ease' (38). In this way, too, Jamesian realism seemed to prepare a sympathetic ground for 'the enforcement of Jim Crow laws' (38).

Walter Benn Michaels has formulated some persuasive criticism of Warren's account. Challenging Warren on his interpretation of how Jim Crow racism worked, Michaels claims that the latter rested on a perception of blackness as so fundamental a negative quality that 'vulgarity' was merely incidental to it. Granting Warren's point that James's 'connection of blacks to the vulgarization of civilized behavior'[25] 'expressed a certain prejudice against blacks', Michaels argues that 'it was only by *separating* blackness from vulgarity that American racism transcended its status as the expression of personal prejudice and achieved in Jim Crow its status as a principle of social organization'.[26] Listing some evidence from contemporary sources, Michaels concludes epigrammatically that 'the utopian vision of Jim Crow was not the separation of the genteel from the vulgar but the separation of the genteel white from the genteel black'.[27] If James is to be faulted in his writing of race, it would have to be on the ground of his 'never imagin[ing] . . . that the offense given by "hideous" women on public conveyances could be made political by being made racial and could thus become the object not only of horror but of legislation'.[28]

Michaels's essay does not explore another questionable aspect of Warren's argument: the separation that Warren finds in James between white protagonists, redeemable by consciousness, and black figures, marooned in a disabling and disturbing vulgarity. This distinction hides from view the host of white Jamesian characters (and, in *The American Scene*, 'types' of people) who are, and who remain, vulgar, or who are first perceived as cultivated only to prove irredeemably vulgar later on. Take, for instance *The Portrait of a Lady*, on which Warren has some otherwise brilliantly illuminating comments. As Warren correctly points out, 'Isabel must fulfill the type of the somewhat vulgar American heiress who would be "an easy victim of scientific criticism".'[29] Yet, it is, in an important sense, inaccurate to claim that she can go on to 'become the novel's true center' (29). To metaphorize Isabel's movement as one from 'vulgar "victim"' to 'true center' is to simplify the complicated relation between consciousness and forms of agency in this novel. To the extent that Isabel is indeed 'vulgar' in the first half of the book, it is not so much because she is, as Warren puts it, 'consign[ed] . . . for a time to vulgar usage' at the hands of Ralph Touchett, Madame Merle, and Gilbert Osmond, but because she has herself wielded a fortune about (30). Her vulgarity has consisted in a material, acquisitive form of agency. She has regarded the world as hers for the taking, and herself as its prime motor. Sensing no limits to her power, she has bestowed her fortune on Osmond, a man who possesses great civilization but not the money with which to translate his exquisite taste into the material possession of desirable objects. Isabel's later accession to consciousness does not just bring her the insight of hindsight that she has, in fact, been the object of the wily agency of others, but it also coincides with a loss of power in the present that moves her to the *margins* of the novel's *literal* (plotted) agency while placing her at the *centre* of its *moral* agency. That is where she remains, no longer initiating any action, but responding, in so far as her married circumstances allow, to the call of a dying Ralph Touchett and to the demands of the promise she had made to Pansy Osmond. Having transferred her fortune to Osmond, she has, in a sense, transferred her vulgarity to him.[30] Having lost the power of vulgarly material agency, she has gained in morally responsive agency.

The power of consciousness and conscience, in James, is always won at the cost of material power. Vulgarity and literal possession of the scene are associated with the latter; artistic interest and ghostly possession with the former. As long as Isabel seemed in full possession of her world, she was slightly vulgar, and we were meant to have second thoughts about her; when she has become a loser, she gains in psychological and moral value and becomes worthy of our full interest in her.[31] It is as though the romance that had first been staged between Isabel and Osmond, for the benefit of a disapproving audience, is now enacted between Isabel and an emotionally involved reader. Interesting, conscious characters in James are invariably associated with loss and deprivation. Consider the following examples also from works discussed elsewhere in this volume: Strether's insistence at the end of *The Ambassadors* '[n]ot, out of the whole affair, to have got anything for myself'; James's desire to show that Maisie would be, in the words of the Preface to *What Maisie Knew*, 'saved . . . rather than coarsened, blurred, sterilised, by ignorance and pain'; or even the rival mourner's ability in 'The Beast in the Jungle' to make Marcher wonder: 'What had the man *had* to make him, by the loss of it, so bleed and yet live?'

Tony Tanner has commented illuminatingly on the Jamesian predilection not just for persons, but for places that have a 'helpless, bereaved, amputated look': 'Absence rather than presence; shadow rather than substance . . . these are central preferences for James.'[32] Tanner illustrates this with quotations from *English Hours*, including a passage in which it is the absence of vulgarity that is singled out for praise by James. I cite the extract more fully here: The 'desolate, exquisite Dunwich . . . is not even the ghost of its dead self . . . All the *grossness* of its positive life is now at the bottom of the German Ocean . . . Few things are so melancholy – and *so redeemed from mere ugliness by sadness*' (*CTW*-1, 255, emphasis added). The coastline at Dunwich has barely been able to withstand the assault of the ocean, whose 'sawlike action gives it, for the fancy, an interest, a sort of mystery, that more than makes up for what it may have surrendered . . . [H]alf the secret of the impression, and what I may really call, I think, the source of the *distinction*, is this very visibility of the mutilation . . . There is a presence in what is missing' (*CTW*-1, 256, emphasis added).

It is the 'exquisite' 'interest', 'mystery', and 'distinction' of lost possession that James would have loved to find on the American scene. It is grossness that he finds instead. The grossness not just of African Americans and immigrants, on whom more in a moment, but the grossness of the 'too much', no matter who is causing the excess. The more directly quantitative connotations of the term 'grossness' convey better what is wrong with this attribute from James's viewpoint than its synonym vulgarity (though that, too, is frequently invoked in *The American Scene*, yet never directly applied there to the African American). The trouble with the 'ubiquitous commercial traveller', for instance, is his insistence 'on a category . . . which . . . loomed so large as to threaten to block out of view almost every other object' (*CTW*-1, 703). The 'obvious "bagman"' or 'lusty "drummer"', as James also calls him, constitutes a specimen 'of something I had surely never yet so *undisputedly* encountered' (*CTW*-1, 702–3, italics in original). What makes this type of person so 'extraordinarily base and vulgar' is its ability to take sole possession of the scene, here formed by 'the Southern trains and inns' (*CTW*-1, 702–3). Recalling how, as a type, 'the brawny peddler' was a familiar enough picture around the world, James wonders how it can here 'usurp a value out of proportion to all other values', how it can present 'so lurid a vision of its triumph . . . the sight of the type in completely unchallenged possession' (*CTW*-1, 703). Note that we are here discussing a type of vulgar person encountered in the South, yet, *pace* Warren's *Black and White Strangers*, marked by no biological or anthropological difference from the writer. The defining characteristic of the drummer is rather his preoccupation with 'getting the better of his fellow-man over a "trade"' (*CTW*-1, 705).

Crucially, there is not even the faintest suggestion that the problem of the bagman's vulgarly excessive command of the scene could be solved by *removing* him from the scene. If we are to see James's distaste for vulgarity as logically leading to social measures that would *exclude* certain people from civil society (as Jim Crow laws did) then it should, at the very least, be possible to read James's vulgar classes as problems in and of themselves. This cannot be done. One has a sense that blaming travelling salesmen for their vulgarity would be, for James, a vulgarly obvious response, as superficial and gross as the crudity of the bagmen itself. Intent on deriving interest from whatever experience or impression, including unpleasurable ones, James's 'imagination' instead allows the men to turn into 'something like victims and martyrs, creatures touchingly, tragically doomed. For they hadn't *asked*, when one reflected, to be almost the only figures in the social landscape . . . They hadn't actively usurped the appearance of carrying on life without aid of any sort from other *kinds* of persons, other types, presences, classes' (*CTW*-1, 705, italics in original). And what solution could the bagmen's suppression bring to the Jamesian order of things in any case? It would simply create another 'lonely waste', a 'boundless gaping void', adding to the emptiness of the American scene that allows such people to assume unchallenged autocratic possession in the first place (*CTW*-1, 638). The conclusion James draws from his observation of the drummer is that: 'No kind of person – that was the admonition – is a very good kind, and still less a very pleasing kind, when its education has not been made to some extent by contact with other kinds, by a sense of the existence of other kinds, and, to that degree, by a certain relation with them' (*CTW*-1, 705). It is a conclusion that he goes on to apply immediately to the similar spectacle of 'the American girl as encountered in the great glare of her publicity, her uncorrected, unrelated state' (*CTW*-1, 708). Her 'crude youth and crude presumption' are as little her fault as the bagmen's usurpation is theirs. James imagines her complaining inwardly:

Ah . . . what do I know, helpless chit as I can but be, about manners or tone, about proportion or perspective, about modesty or mystery, about a condition of things that involves, for the interest and the grace of life, other forms of existence than this poor little mine . . . All I want . . . is . . . that my parents and my brothers and my male cousins should consent to exist otherwise than occultly, undiscoverably, or, as I suppose you'd call it, irresponsibly. (*CTW*-1, 708–9)

The social problem that James is addressing in the case of the drummer and the American girl is one that is not to be solved by regulating the behaviour of those now vulgarly presuming too much, and certainly not by barring them from participation in the social scene. If it is to be solved at all, then it will be by ensuring that others now somehow absent from the scene emerge from hiding and start to act as a counterweight. 'By what combination of other presences', the American girl reflects, 'ever am I disburdened, ever relegated and reduced, ever restored . . . to my right relation to the whole?' (*CTW*-1, 708). Because such 'other presences' are 'irresponsibly' absent, it will not do to cast blame on the girl for her overbearing presence on the scene, no matter how disturbing that fact may be to the social ease of the observer.

Far from intimating that such gross types as the bagman and the American girl should be removed from the scene, James even succeeds in deriving from their case some of the interest he seeks on the American scene. Pursuing their 'victim[ization]', their 'doomed' condition, to the point where he can begin to feel sympathetic of the bagmen's situation, he reflects: 'They had the helpless weakness and, I think even, somewhere in dim depths . . . the vaguely troubled sense of it . . . I positively at last thought of them as appealing from this embarrassment' (*CTW*-1, 706). This reflection comes at the very end of a lengthy consideration of the commercial travellers' vulgarity. James manages, at last, to impute to these gross excrescences of the American landscape the timid stirrings of a consciousness, and hence the feeble foundation of a romantic interest that he could take in them. The poor people are 'helpless', 'vaguely troubled', and are mutely 'appealing' to their interpreter for sympathy in their 'embarrassment'. The appeal ultimately succeeds in suspending the damning ethical judgment of their 'sordid and ravenous habit' that he had begun by registering so disgustedly (*CTW*-1, 703). Similarly, the American girl's lament is eventually summed up as 'the questioning wail of the maiden's ultimate distressed consciousness', reaching the analyst '[f]aintly and from far away, as through dense interpositions' (*CTW*-1, 709). In these two cases, it is possible to retrieve some romantic interest, and show a degree of moral understanding in the face of vulgarity, by ascribing to the types in such unchallenged possession of the scene a secret desire to surrender their crudely overpowering position.

'THE SOUTHERN BLACK . . . "IN POSSESSION OF HIS RIGHTS AS A MAN"' (*CTW*-1, 662)

Why is it impossible for James to render the African American the same service? After all, at first sight the similarities between the vulgar types James encounters seem quite striking. 'One understood at a glance' he reports with regard to the 'Southern black', 'how he must loom, how he must count, in a community in which . . . there were comparatively so few other things' (*CTW*-1, 662). The terms James here uses are entirely reminiscent of those he invoked to describe the drummer, who 'loomed so large as to threaten to block out of view almost every other object' (*CTW*-1, 703). If the bagman is 'extraordinarily base and vulgar' and 'in completely unchallenged possession' (*CTW*-1, 702–3), 'the Southern black' is 'ragged and rudimentary, yet all portentous' (*CTW*-1, 662) and can strike 'with every degree of violence that . . . note of the negro really at home' (*CTW*-1, 664). While the Pullman is dominated by the 'lusty "drummer"' (*CTW*-1, 702), the 'shabby and sordid' scene James now overlooks is peopled by African Americans 'more numerous than the whites' in quantity and 'the lustier race' in quality (*CTW*-1, 681).[33]

Yet, there is a major difference between the grossly excessive presence of the African American and that of the other vulgar types encountered on the scene. The former's has been *won* in the course of a civil war that *defeated* the 'Confederate soldier' (*CTW*-1, 668). Having been so recently achieved, and at the cost of such a bloody war, the violent 'note of the negro really at home' (*CTW*-1, 664) can hardly be interpreted as a merely superficial tune, loudly masking a mutely victimized undertone of the sort that could be imputed to the drummer and the girl. In the post-Civil War situation that James addresses, it is not the African American, 'all portentous and "in possession of his rights as a man"', who strikes him as susceptible of the romantic interest of lost possession, but his antagonist, the formerly undisputed lord and master of the South, now disabused of his 'artlessly perverse [dream]' (*CTW*-1, 662, 661).[34] If Jamesian consciousness is to be detected in this situation, it is most likely to be discovered among the ones who *lost* the war, rather than those who seem to have benefited from its violence by an accession to 'rights'.[35] James manages to muster 'a sort of ingenuity of tenderness' on behalf of the thus 'afflicted South' (*CTW*-1, 663), at last crediting it with a 'haunting consciousness' and regarding its members 'as such passive, such pathetic victims of fate' (*CTW*-1, 662).

'[I]ngenuity' is, truly, what is required here of James. For Henry James, as for his present-day critics, the more 'obvious' response in the South would have been to rehearse the Union's contestation of the Confederacy – as James to some extent does when he mentions the sacrifice of humaneness 'in the interest of slave-produced Cotton', or wonders at the 'provinciality' needed to that end, likening it to that of 'lone and primitive islanders' (*CTW*-1, 661). Dwelling on such matters would have been much more obvious than undertaking what one critic has called this 'bizarre reversal in the positions and physical vulnerabilities of the races'.[36] 'The issue of slavery', Kaplan writes, 'had transformed the James family [in 1861] from mild supporters of the Democratic party into enthusiastic advocates of Lincoln and the newly formed Republicans'.[37] Two of Henry's brothers, Bob and Wilkie, enlisted in the Union army in 1862–3. Both saw active duty on the Confederate battlefields as officers in 'all-black' Massachusetts regiments. Wilky was seriously wounded and retained a limp for the rest of his life.[38] Henry, like his elder brother William, did not join his younger brothers at the time, though both he and William, according to a letter of Henry Sen.'s quoted by Kaplan, had 'vituperate[d]' their father 'beyond measure' in the summer of 1861 because he refused to let them join Lincoln's volunteer troops.[39]

James had not forgotten the family heritage by the time he came to write *The American Scene*. Visiting Richmond, he recalls that the 'Confederate capital had grown lurid, fuliginous, vividly tragic' for him 'as long ago as at the outbreak of the Civil War' (*CTW*-1, 657). It is surely no coincidence that one of the very few conversations to be reported throughout the book, and one of its few face-to-face meetings, takes place with 'a son of the new South', who recounts the heroism of his soldier father, culminating in 'a desperate evasion of capture, or worse, by the lucky smashing of the skull of a Union soldier' (*CTW*-1, 672–3). It is as if James were seeking out quite deliberately such a confrontation with the enemy of yore, as though he were at pains to place himself in a situation that would approximate as closely as possible the polarized positions that had pertained at the time of the Civil War, and in which his brothers had participated with manful action. Not content with this recollected brutality, James eggs the young man on to the point where he fully reveals the 'lively interest of [his] type' (*CTW*-1, 672). 'I complimented him', James informs us, 'on his exact knowledge of these old, unhappy, far-off things, and it was his candid response that was charmingly suggestive. "Oh, I should be ready to do them all over again myself!" And . . . as if it behoved even the least blatant of Northerners to understand: "That's the kind of Southerner *I* am!"' (*CTW*-1, 673). The obvious, 'blatant' response to this, given James's background, would be one of horrified ethical revulsion: 'Haven't they learned a thing, then? Clearly, they are still in need of a violent lesson from the North: I must denounce them!' The less obvious Jamesian response: 'I allowed that he was a capital kind of Southerner . . . He was a fine contemporary young American, incapable, so to speak, of hurting a Northern fly – *as* Northern; but whose consciousness would have been poor and unfurnished without this cool platonic passion. With what other pattern . . . *could* he have adorned its bare walls?' (*CTW*-1, 673).

Instead of answering like with like, meeting 'this cool platonic passion' in a polarizing way with hot denunciation, the Jamesian response closely approximates, I feel, what Honig calls 'the proper democratic labours of translation and negotiation'.[40] James translates, through the (conventionally feminine) act of flirtation (gently teasing the one-time enemy until he displays his violent disposition), the Virginian's staunch stand (manful, in conventional terms) into a (conventionally feminine) 'pattern' that '[ ]furnish[es]', 'adorn[s] [the] bare walls' of the other's 'consciousness'. James is able to negotiate a ground, romantic both in literary and in erotic terms, on which he feels able to meet the other outside the realm of violent confrontation and ethical denunciation. In the romantically coloured encounter with the Virginian, what takes place is a nonviolent interaction in which each retains the integrity of their (version of the) past. It is a type of social interaction which belies the common sociological assumption (seemingly shared by most of James's literary critics) that 'where persons of different culture interact, one would expect these differences to be reduced, since interaction both requires and generates a *congruence of codes and values* – in other words, a similarity or community of culture'.[41] Rather, the Jamesian participant in the interaction North–South *translates the other's* codes and values (I am proud of my father's forceful defense of Southern honour) in such a way into *his own* language of codes and values (his cool platonic passion adorns the bare walls of a provincial consciousness) that he can be genuinely interested in the other, while keeping to himself the heavily ironic basis of his interest, which would be provocatively hurtful to the other if apparent. That this does not, for James, imply a 'community of culture', let alone a shared ethical system, is amply borne out in the immediate sequel, where his musings on the 'very handsome . . . young Virginian' are brought to the conclusion that, 'though he wouldn't have hurt a Northern fly, there were things (ah, we had touched on some of these!) that, all fair, engaging, smiling, as he stood there, he would have done to a Southern negro' (*CTW*-1, 673).

Does James's act of translation and negotiation have any effect on the Virginian, though? Not in the 'contestatory' sense in which most commentators on James and race would like to have seen him assume agency. The exchange has not extinguished the opponent's 'passion'; there is not even any claim on James's part that he would somehow have shown the man that Northerners need no longer be hated. However, an earlier paragraph in the same chapter of *The American Scene* describes the alternative of active political intervention in terms that demonstrate how suspicious James felt of the efficacy of 'preaching, southward, a sweet reasonableness about [the African American]. Nothing was less contestable, of course, than that such a sweet reasonableness might play, in the whole situation, a beautiful part; but nothing, also, was on reflection more obvious than that the counsel of perfection, in such a case, would never prove oil upon the waters' (*CTW*-1, 662–3). In other words, when James, faced with the Virginian, failed to denounce lynchings, he was aware of the confrontational alternative available to the Northerner, but quite consciously chose not to adopt it because he was convinced that contestation was more likely to sharpen an already polarized situation. Instead, we could say – though I would not claim this as James's conscious intention – he enables the Confederate scion to relive the wound of history (as the other experiences it) and to enunciate the violence of that recollected event in a safely contained, staged, verbal context. It is no good, James implies, to preach reasonableness when cool passion is still exerting its sway. Let us first create an environment in which the opponent can feel that there is no need to insist on the reality of his version of history – on its stark, obdurate literalism; let us offer that other a chance to turn spectral the wound that he now still cultivates out of bitter resentment.[42] Once such oil is on the waters, perhaps reasonableness and justice can begin to be achieved. As an event recounted in narrative, then, James's encounter with the Virginian could be said to constitute a form of (largely unintended) agency that contributes to the defusion of a violently tense political situation, and thus prepares the ground for the democratic work of translation and negotiation.

It is possible to stress, with Warren, that the Jamesian form of agency described here was so premature as to be morally untenable in the type of society in which he was writing. James, that argument goes, could do no more than 'raise[ ] . . . the question of what kinds of values a society more democratic and egalitarian than the one he himself lived in might be capable of producing'.[43] The fundamental assumption when criticizing 'James on race' is that the society in which we, critics, are located has advanced on the diachronic line of human progress that links it to James's. There are no longer Jim

Crow laws; lynchings are a thing of the past; African Americans are now themselves critics reading James, etc. So it is possible to measure Henry James and his contemporaries (William James, Du Bois) by the standard of such progress. We have gone a long way towards realizing the democratic promise of the French Revolution and are closer to the Enlightenment ideals of liberty, equality, and fraternity. To read the location of our culture in this way, however, is to be blind to the extent that these values have been realized, and continue to be realized, at the cost of the serfdom, inequality, and violence inflicted on those somehow placed outside the democratic and egalitarian realm. Consider the Founding Fathers of the American Republic, who subscribed to democratic values, yet relied on indentured servants to generate their wealth. But also consider, more uncomfortably, the fact that the word-processors on which we write our enlightened essays have, more likely than not, been made cheap enough for our purses by having been produced in the semi-slavery of 'developing' countries. Consider, in so far as such information is not jealously guarded, the sources of the wealth that has made our Ivy League universities such desirable places to study or work. Or consider the subsistence wages paid to those who care for our preschool children while we carry out our 'hard intellectual work'. Modern, democratic, enlightened society is pervasively dependent on work performed in conditions that are 'incommensurable' with humanistic values.[44] As such, present-day Western society may not be all that different from James's: it may simply have succeeded in reorganizing inequality so that it exists less on the (all too visible) hierarchical axis *within* democratic society and has become concentrated in the (less visible) geo-economical axis leading *outside* that community. To criticize James's 'blindness' to the reality of violent inequality may therefore be an act of considerable hypocrisy; and to dismiss his non-violent forms of agency as idealistic may itself imply an idealistic belief that we should first remove violence and inequality *before* we can abandon contestatory strategies.

Regarded from the Jamesian perspective I have here been tracing, violent forms of relationality may, however, be a major obstacle to achieving a truly democratic society. What is required to make a success of the latter is the work of language (as is implied by Honig's rhetorical choice of 'translation' and 'negotiation') and, perhaps less obviously, manners. This quality – the antithesis of vulgarity – has been most usually associated with the ruling classes in a stratified society – the type of hierarchical society that a humanist democracy is thought to supersede. The assumption is that manners are a luxury that can be afforded by the aristocrat, whose very civilization criminally depends on the violent exploitation (and often suppression) of the vulgar labourer, left exposed to the literality of the world of work and unequal power. To the extent that a society becomes more democratic, power is more evenly shared, and manners disappear along with other vicious marks of distinction. Yet, James's reflections on the American scene (and his work in general) may well suggest that democracy cannot dispense with manners.[45] It is manners and Baier's 'face-saving diplomatic phrases' that stand between us and the more 'obvious', vulgarly literal and violent ways of possessing the scene. Manners, in the sense of the roles we play in different situations, moreover, resist any belief in a fully self-possessed ego and imply instead an alertness 'to the agitation of otherness, of the alien'; manners thus underpin the 'relational perspective' that, as Ian Bell has put it, 'so powerfully informs James's social and aesthetic imagination'.[46]

'HE RESTS IN IT AT LAST AS AN ABSOLUTE LUXURY'

There is a further twist to the plotting of race, vulgarity, seduction, and judgment in *The American Scene*. 'What happens', we could summarize this final complication, 'when language and manners provide no relational bridge between members of a democracy? Does violence automatically ensue?' The answer is to be found in the fascinating New York sections of the narrative. Faced there with 'the question of intercourse and contact' to a degree of difficulty that he does not encounter elsewhere, the 'restless analyst' has to admit 'to the reflection that the country is too large . . . to be dealt with as [he is] trying . . . to deal with it' (*CTW*-1, 457). In the terms that we have been activating, the gross assault of a vast and impenetrable reality defies the usual Jamesian attempt to derive romantic interest in the face of apparent vulgarity. The immigrant is the root of the trouble, the immigrant in 'this general first grossness of alienism', with this sense of being '*at home*', 'all solidly' in possession of the scene (*CTW*-1, 460). How can a 'personal relation' be established with an immigrant who meets a question with a 'blank' 'stare', because there is no common language between the two, and who, 'even on the Armenian basis, [did not appear] to expect brotherhood' (*CTW*-1, 454–5)? Overall, the New York immigrant presents to James a 'neutral and colourless image' (*CTW*-1, 462). 'What *does* become', he wonders, 'of the various positive properties . . . the good manners [which he had possessed in the Old World] . . .? [I]f they are not extinguished, into what pathless tracts of the native atmosphere do they . . . so all undiscoverably . . . melt?' (*CTW*-1, 462–3). Here, James can neither retrieve, 'for any complacency of the romantic', the buried qualities of the foreigner as he had been in Europe, nor can he impute to the immigrant any secret desire to feel less overpoweringly at home. What else has he or she come for? Like the African American, immigrants present the spectacle of recently achieved possession of the scene; in the Jamesian scheme, they belong with the proud winners.

If, in the South, the African American had further suffered from strong competition for James's emotional and intellectual sympathy in the shape of the defeated Confederacy, no such rival is available for the immigrant on the New York scene. Perhaps this accounts for the very different Jamesian response; perhaps also the fact that the immigrant's 'infusion' into the American scene has a more immediately tangible effect on the nature of 'such a term as the "American" character?' than the apparently more specific situation of the emancipated black. '[W]hat type', James wonders, 'as the result of such a prodigious amalgam, such a hotch-potch of racial ingredients, is to be conceived as shaping itself?'

The challenge to speculation, fed thus by a thousand sources, is so intense as to be, as I say, irritating; but practically, beyond doubt, I should also say, you take refuge from it – since your case would otherwise be hard; and you find your relief not in the least in any direct satisfaction or solution, but absolutely in that blest general drop of the immediate need of conclusions, or rather in that blest general feeling for the impossibility of them . . .

It is more than a comfort . . . this accepted vision of the too-defiant numerosity and quantity – the effect of which is so to multiply the possibilities, so to open, by the million, contingent doors and windows. he rests in it at last as an absolute luxury, converting it into a substitute, into *the* constant substitute, for many luxuries that are absent. He doesn't *know*, he can't *say*, before the facts, and he doesn't even want to know or to say; the facts themselves loom, before the understanding, in too large a mass for a mere mouthful: it is as if the syllables were too numerous to make a legible word. The *il*legible word, accordingly, the great inscrutable answer to questions, hangs in the vast American sky, to his imagination, as something fantastic and *abracadabrant*, belonging to no known language . . . (*CTW*-1, 456)

Overwhelmed by the 'hotch-potch of racial ingredients', James surrenders to the violence of this 'too-defiant numerosity and quantity'. The sheer quantity of surface impressions opens a 'million' 'doors and windows' each of which could lead to such mysterious depths as might redeem the grossness of the alien, yet whose 'large . . . mass' itself blocks any attempt at 'understanding'. The reality of 'the facts themselves', in all their literal presence, silences the 'restless analyst': 'he can't *say*'. Deprived of a ground for negotiation, he has to 'accept[ ]' the '*il*legible word . . . as something fantastic and *abracadabrant*, belonging to no known language' and hence untranslatable: materially resistant to incorporation in the interpreter's own language of codes and values. It is, moreover, impossible, under the circumstances, to retain any basis for judgment. As James puts it:

[he] feels justified of the inward, the philosophic, escape into the immensity . . . There is too much of the whole thing, he sighs, for the personal relation with it; and yet he would desire no inch less . . . Diminution of quantity, even by that inch, might mark the difference of his having to begin to recognize from afar . . . the gleam of some propriety of opinion . . . Goodness be thanked, accordingly, for the bigness. The state of flat fatigue [that he experiences here] . . . is not an opinion . . . it belongs to the order of mere sensation and impression; and as to these . . .: he may have as many of each as he can carry. (*CTW*-1, 457–8)

If the first of these two long extracts had still expressed a degree of irritation, their movement has clearly been towards a much more affirmative embrace of the unintelligible situation. Addressing, in the second extract, the impossibility of ethical judgment ('some propriety of opinion'), James sighingly accepts even that.

The rhetoric of both of these longer extracts is remarkably sensual. Compared to the teasing that marks the exchange with the handsome Virginian (an exchange that could rely on language and manners), the mutely silencing and grossly immense immigrant scene seems to produce a different type of erotically charged response. '[E]scap[ing] into the immensity', into a 'quantity' that does not 'mark . . . difference', one could say that the narrator here experiences a loss of ego boundaries produced by an overpowering presence. If the sexual economy implicitly at stake in the Virginian encounter had been conventional enough, that of the New York one seems unsettlingly masochistic in nature. It offers 'an absolute luxury' in which the narrator can undergo a 'blest general drop' of intellect ('conclusions') and judgment ('opinion') and enjoy sensual 'feeling', 'mere sensation', 'flat' 'relief'. The violent onslaught of a polyethnic democracy cannot here be met by the 'ingenuity of tenderness' through which other vulgarities could be endowed with romantic interest. Yet, even so, James's reaction is emphatically not that of ethical revulsion. Once again, he will not meet violence with violence, but rather surrenders his own identity in a bodily fusion with the alien scene around him: 'I seem to recall winter days, harsh, dusky, sloshy winter afternoons, in the densely-packed East-side street-cars, as an especially intimate surrender' (*CTW*-1, 460).

In the New York scenes, the Jamesian narrator retains no sense of his own identity. '[W]inc[ing] in the light of the question of intercourse and contact', he stops trying to respond at a rational level and surrenders to the materiality of bodily intimacy itself. No longer seeking romantic depth, James allows himself to be possessed by the alien scene, accepts his own translation by that scene into no more than a syllable contributing to 'the great inscrutable answer to questions [that] hangs in the vast American sky' (*CTW*-1, 456). The Jamesian presence here merely acts as one of the extensional definitions of 'this very equality of condition that . . . made the whole medium so strange' (*CTW*-1, 460). Fusing with this 'too-defiant scale of numerosity and quantity', James is absorbed into the vulgarity that he elsewhere deplores and simply becomes one of its extensional definitions, serving to affirm its domineering power. Since there is not even an inch to 'mark the difference' between narrator and scene, the distance required for any ethical, or romantic, address is missing from the situation. It is as if the narrator has here been able 'irresponsibly to escape' (*CTW*-1, 463) into an oceanic feeling of sensual, luxurious wholeness associated with the (pre-social) womb.[47] Indeed, 'he would desire no inch less', if this utopia could be maintained. The enigma that had elsewhere been the focus of James's cognitive and affective interest in people and scenes – the ghost of loss that may be penetrated behind a vulgarly possessive façade, say – here encompasses James to the point where his own discriminating consciousness is lost, where he can no longer teasingly seduce or be seduced but disappears as a centre of consciousness and site of agency. The only locus of consciousness left in this intriguing situation must be the reader, who can, if he or she be so inclined, try and probe the vulgar display for enigmatic interest

– who can participate, as a distinct individual, in a relation of seduction and judgment with the text of the American scene.[48]

Considered in the context of *The American Scene* as a whole, moreover, James seems to imply that a social existence, as a member of a democracy, necessitates an emergence from states of luxury and requires the assumption of an identity that has boundaries, that can observe distinctions between itself and the other. This is the basis of both romantic love and moral agency (each of which presupposes individuation). But, as the exchange with the Virginian demonstrates, to ensure that erotic and moral addresses remain properly non-violent, identity needs to be staged rather than affirmed; and manners will play an invaluable part in enabling the indispensable work of negotiation in a democratic society. Language, finally, may serve as a vital tool in the ghostly reliving of the wounds of history, rather than the perpetuation of the cycle of action and reaction that keeps violence eternally alive – literature may thus offer a site for that *non-violent enacting of history* on which the future of democracy depends.

NOTES

I am indebted to William Boelhower, Ortwin de Graef, Øyunn Hestetun, and, in particular, Bart Eeckhout for advice at the conceptual stages of this chapter.

1 Bryan R. Washington, *The Politics of Exile: Ideology in Henry James, F. Scott Fitzgerald, and James Baldwin* (Boston: Northeastern University Press, 1995), 116, 120.
2 Ibid., 18.
3 Ibid., 19.
4 Ibid., 121.
5 Kenneth Warren, *Black and White Strangers: Race and American Literary Realism* (University of Chicago Press, 1993), 141.
6 Kenneth Warren, 'Still Reading Henry James?', *Henry James Review*, 16 (1995), 284.
7 Ibid. The first elided part reads: 'he raises, again and again, the question of what kinds of values a society more democratic and egalitarian than the one he himself lived in might be capable of producing'; the second begins: 'it is clear that calls for the further democratization of our social and political orders often seem to elicit a Hyacinth Robinson-like fear'; the third continues: 'a reminder that the production and reproduction of value is never simply a repudiation of the past but rather a critical engagement with it'.
8 Ibid., 283–4.

9 Sara Blair, 'Response: Writing Culture and Henry James', *Henry James Review*, 16 (1995), 279.
10 Warren, *Black and White Strangers*, 113.
11 Ross Posnock, 'Henry James and the Limits of Historicism', *Henry James Review*, 16 (1995), 276.
12 Recall Warren's observation that it was one of the insights of Du Bois 'how similar our own intellectual techniques may be to those we contest' ('Still Reading', 283).
13 Posnock, 'Henry James', 276.
14 Ibid.
15 Ibid.
16 Sara Blair, 'Documenting America: Racial Theater in *The American Scene*', *Henry James Review*, 16 (1995), 265. Further page references appear in the text of the present paragraph.
17 Blair, 'Response', 281 (emphasis added).
18 Equally problematical is Mark Seltzer's account of *The American Scene* in *Henry James and the Art of Power*, a book Winfried Fluck critically discusses at some length in chapter 1 of the present volume. Let me just note here that Seltzer seems unable to decide whether the wish to 'disown[ ] the shame of power' that forms the focus of his book is actually James's or his own. Challenging 'this opposing of art and power ... even on the part of the most politically conscious critics', for instance, Seltzer reiterates his alternative claim in a revealing fashion: 'in my account of *The Golden Bowl* I have tried to show that desire is not in fact subversive of the "world of capitalism" but is instead constitutive of its power; the novel displays a radical entanglement between the *movements* of desire and the *moves* of power' (emphasis added). For Seltzer, if 'desire (the literary), can be thought of as susceptible to (neutral) movements, power operates in (sinister) moves. 'James's later work', he goes on, 'traces the "positive" and not merely the repressive character of power relations'. Ironically, Seltzer first has to establish that power relations are self-evidently repressive (contrast the distancing quotation marks around '"positive"' with the unmarked 'repressive'), before he can go on to ascribe to James the 'gesture of disowning the shame of power' ((Ithaca: Cornell University Press, 1984), 139).
19 Bonnie Honig, '"No Place Like Home": Democracy and the Politics of Foreignness', draft MS (Princeton University Press, forthcoming), (italics in original).
20 Annette Baier, *Moral Prejudices: Essays on Ethics*, 2nd edn (Cambridge, Mass.: Harvard University Press, 1995), 70 (emphasis added). Further page references appear in the text of the present paragraph.
21 Susan Griffin, 'Introduction', *Henry James Review*, 16 (1995), 247.
22 For the best statement of this point of view, see Ross Posnock's *The Trial of Curiosity: Henry James, William James, and the Challenge of Modernity* (New York: Oxford University Press, 1991), esp. chapter 4: '"The Religion of

Doing": Breaking the Aura of Henry James' (80–104). I engage more fully with Posnock's important book in my *Henry James: Style, Ethics and History: A Bibliographical Essay* (Brussels: Center for American Studies, 1996), esp. 44–7, 51, and 58.

23 Enough has been said about the poverty of Bryan Washington's study, which is only topped by Eli Ben-Joseph's supposedly 'interdisciplinary' but, in fact, mechanical listing of all politically incorrect topoi in James (*Aesthetic Persuasion: Henry James, the Jews and Race* (Lanham: University Press of America, 1996), 172). Sara Blair's *Henry James and the Writing of Race and Nation* (New York: Cambridge University Press, 1996) extends her 'contestatory' defence of James's record on race to other works besides *The American Scene*. A valuable essay by Jonathan Freedman was brought to my attention too late to engage fully with its argument here ('Henry James and the Discourses of Antisemitism', in *Between Race and Culture: Representations of "the Jew" in English and American Literature*, ed. Bryan Cheyette (Stanford University Press, 1996), 62–83).

24 Warren, *Black and White Strangers*, 41. Further page references appear in the text of the present paragraph.

25 Ibid., 124.

26 Walter Benn Michaels, 'Jim Crow Henry James', *Henry James Review*, 16 (1995), 288.

27 Ibid.

28 Ibid., 290.

29 Warren, *Black and White Strangers*, 29. Further page references appear in the text of the present paragraph.

30 Osmond's relation to vulgarity has always been intimate. Even when he had no money to back up his own domineering view of the world, he was obsessively preoccupied with 'the baseness and shabbiness of life', with 'the infinite vulgarity of things', which had spared only 'some three or four very exalted people whom he envied'. It is only by keeping 'this base, ignoble world ... for ever in [his] eye' that he can 'extract from it some recognition of [his] own superiority'. In the course of the fireside chapter, Isabel recognizes that this relation to vulgarity constitutes not 'a noble indifference, an exquisite independence', but a pathological dependence: 'He was unable to live without it' (*Henry James: Novels 1881–1886*, ed. William T. Stafford (New York: Library of America, 1985), 634–5).

31 She is by this point also ready to see a ghost at Gardencourt, as Ralph had predicted she might 'if she should live to suffer enough' (ibid., 787).

32 Tony Tanner, *Henry James and the Art of Nonfiction* (Athens: University of Georgia Press, 1995), 9.

33 Note how the close proximity of 'the lustier race' and the 'lusty "drummer"' make it problematical to charge James with essentialist racial characterizations.

34 The fact that James reads the contemporary South so consistently as a

present-day 'enunciation' of the 'event' of the Civil War can, for one part, be more fruitfully understood within the framework of Homi Bhabha's postcolonial cultural theory (cf. *The Location of Culture* (London: Routledge, 1994), 254); for another, it is, as David McWhirter argues in chapter 8 of the present volume, tied to James's insistent revisiting of his private history.

35 Laurence Holland, otherwise one of the most brilliantly perceptive of James critics, is not at his best in the rather summarizing account of *The American Scene* added as an Appendix to *The Expense of Vision: Essays on the Craft of Henry James* (Baltimore: Johns Hopkins University Press, 1982). His observation that 'James has to use the irony of quotation marks, indicating the failure of fulfillment yet, when speaking of the black "in possession of his rights as a man"' (430) lacks the necessary subtlety for reading the charge of 'possession' in James.

36 Eric Haralson, 'The Person Sitting in Darkness: James in the American South', *Henry James Review*, 16 (1995), 251.

37 Fred Kaplan, *Henry James: The Imagination of Genius: A Biography* (New York: Morrow, 1992), 53.

38 Ibid., 58–60.

39 Ibid., 54.

40 Honig, 'No Place Like Home', 37.

41 Fredrik Barth, Introduction, *Ethnic Groups and Boundaries: The Social Organization of Culture Difference* (Bergen: Universitetsforlaget and Boston: Little, 1969); reprinted in *Theories of Ethnicity: A Classical Reader*, ed. Werner Sollors (New York University Press, 1996), 301 (emphasis added).

42 I borrow the phrase 'turning spectral the wound of history' from Homi Bhabha's lecture at the 1996 English Institute: 'The Nearness of You: Proximity, Anxiety, and the Emergence of Minority' (Harvard University, 13 October 1996).

43 Warren, 'Still Reading', 284.

44 Bhabha, *Location of Culture*, 250.

45 The contractarian model of a 'morality [that] regulates and arbitrates where interests are opposed' (Baier, *Moral Prejudices*, 70) seems to derive from one aspect of the relations between aristocrats, to use a shorthand term. To the extent that the latter were driven by a desire to acquire a greater part of the 'scene' at the cost of their competitors, contracts are one, generally written, form of check on the acquisition of further territory; manners are another, unspoken one. Henry James's work offers access to that uncontractual realm of forms, manners as tools in the service of curbing power. It is this realm, too, that moral philosophers such as Baier are now focusing on.

46 Ian F. A. Bell, *Henry James and the Past: Readings into Time* (London: Macmillan, 1991), 11.

47 There is a similar moment in *The Ambassadors*, when, as Adrian Poole

writes in chapter 4 of the present volume, Strether 'fantasizes his relation with [Marie de Vionnet] as that of an all-trusting infant and an all-capable mother: "the spell of his luxury wouldn't be broken. He wouldn't have, that is, to become responsible" (Bk. 12, ch. 1)'. For a fascinating alternative reading of the 'democratic ebb and flow' of James's 'oceanic experience' in *The American Scene*, see William Boelhower, 'The Landscape of Democratic Sovereignty: Whitman and James Go Awalking', in *Modern American Landscapes*, ed. Mick Gidley and Robert Lawson-Peebles (Amsterdam: VU University Press, 1995), 43–76 (phrases quoted from 62).

48 The analytical framework and some of the terminology of the present paragraph were inspired by Leo Bersani's lecture at the 1996 English Institute: 'Caravaggio's Secrets' (Harvard University, 12 October 1996).

CHAPTER 10

History, narrative, and responsibility: speech acts in 'The Aspern Papers'

J. Hillis Miller

I

The relation between history and narrative seems at first glance fairly straightforward. History and narration have been inseparably associated in literary theory and in our everyday assumptions at least since Aristotle. In the *Poetics*, Aristotle prefers a probable fiction to an improbable history as the plot for a tragedy. Though narration is not the only way to represent history, it is certainly one of the major ways. We tend to assume that historical events occurred as a concatenated sequence that can be retold now as a story of some kind: first this happened and then that happened, and so on. Some form of causal or rationalizable connection is presumed. This will explain what happened and make it understandable. Narrative will tell the truth about history. Both narrative and history belong to the regime of truth. Narration is one of the chief ways to account for history, to take account of it, to rationalize and explain it, to find out its reason or ground. Fictional narrations, on the other hand, have 'historically', at least in the West, tended to present themselves in the guise of histories, as in Fielding's title, *The History of Tom Jones*, or in Thackeray's full title for *Henry Esmond: The History of Henry Esmond, Esq., A Colonel in the Service of Her Majesty Q. Anne, Written by Himself,* or in Henry James's remark, in his essay on Anthony Trollope, that, unless a fictional narration maintains the illusion of its historicity, it has no ground to stand on: 'It is impossible to imagine what a novelist takes himself to be unless he regard himself as an historian and his narrative as a history. It is only as an historian that he has the smallest *locus standi*' (*LC*-1, 1343).[1] That figure of the *locus standi* returns in Henry James's story, 'The Aspern Papers'. The motif appears there, as I shall show, in various figures arguing that biographical knowledge forms an indispensable ground for measuring literature's value. This intimate and unbreakable connection between narrative and history in the Western tradition seems unproblematic enough.

Raising questions about 'responsibility', however, adds a complication. This further wrinkle may upset the presumed symmetry between narrative and history. If both narrative and history are of the order of truth, responsibility is of the order of doing, of ethics, of performative rather than of constative uses of language. Do narrative and history in any way involve questions of responsibility, of obligation, of ethical response to an imperative demand? I shall try to explore this question by considering Henry James's novella of 1886, 'The Aspern Papers'.

II

To whom is the narrator of this story talking or writing? As in all such cases of first-person narration, it is not easy to answer that question. A first-person narration differs from third-person narration, with its convention of an anonymous narrating voice. In the case of a first-person narration like 'The Aspern Papers', it is as though we as readers, or, better, I as reader, since it is an intimate and singular experience, had been made the overhearer of a murmuring internal voice of narration that is going over and over the facts of the case as remembered, trying to put them in order, above all trying to justify itself. This voice speaks in response to a demand for an accounting. Someone, it seems, has said to the storyteller: 'Account for yourself'. The narrator of 'The Aspern Papers' speaks as a witness. As James's Preface to *The Golden Bowl* says, he is 'witness of the destruction of "The Aspern Papers"' (*GB*, I, vii). James's odd capitalization and punctuation here identify the Aspern papers themselves and the story of that title. In what way the story itself is 'destroyed' remains to be seen. The reader, in any case, is put by the narrator's deposition in the position of the conscience, the judge or jury. It is as if we had demanded this accounting and had taken upon ourselves the responsibility of evaluating it for plausibility and credibility, then judging it. We have to pronounce, 'Guilty' or 'Innocent'. If the verdict is 'Guilty', we must decide on what punishment should be meted out. Or rather 'I' am put in that position. The call is addressed to me, personally. I alone must act, must respond. I cannot let anyone else read for me. Perhaps, for example, I might think, the narrator is punished enough by being forced to think over and over what he has done, for the story ends with his statement of suffering: 'When I look at it [the picture of Jeffrey Aspern] I can scarcely bear my loss – I mean of the precious papers' (143).[2] Or the reader might be led to ask whether the narrator must be held responsible for moral stupidity, for not having understood correctly the relation between narration and history. What is the proper punishment for that crime? So I must carefully sift the evidence, read between the lines, put two and two together. The effect of this is to make me read carefully (or it should be), paying attention to tiny details of language, to any other clues the narrator may give, perhaps in spite of himself. If he is that notorious personnage, the 'unreliable narrator', then James may be speaking to me, ironically, through gaps and lapses in the narrator's language.

As in all such cases, I am myself on trial, for I am in danger of being unjust, or insensitive, or inattentive. I may have missed something crucial. James excels in putting the reader in that situation, in putting the reader on trial. If the narrator has, it may be, treated Juliana and Tina badly, I may be in danger of treating *him* badly, of judging him wrongly. If he behaved badly, how should he have behaved? Where did he go wrong? How would I have behaved in his place? And, of course, beneath all that, or around it, I am judging James, whom I know is the author of the tale I am reading. Can I trust him as a moral guide or as someone who tells the truth about the human situation?

Is this putting of the reader on trial characteristic of James's stories and novels, or is it peculiar to this one or to a group like this one? Do all James's works put on the reader this heavy responsibility of judging, with an implied penalty if he or she makes an error? I think it can be said to be a general characteristic. In each story by James, the characters behave in a certain way and the story comes out in a certain way. The reader is asked to evaluate that behaviour and that outcome morally. Usually the reader is asked especially to judge some climactic decision and act, almost always some act of (apparent) renunciation, of giving up, almost always a sexual renunciation. In 'The Aspern Papers', the narrator refuses Miss Tina's offer of herself in marriage. That precipitates the denouement. In *The Portrait of a Lady*, the heroine, Isabel Archer, returns to her cruel and egotistical husband, Gilbert Osmond. In *The Ambassadors*, Strether refuses to 'get anything out of it for himself', that is, he refuses Maria Gostrey's offer of herself. In *The Golden Bowl* Maggie condones her husband's adultery with her stepmother. In *The Awkward Age,* Vanderbank refuses to marry Nanda. In all these diverse cases, the reader must pass judgment on the protagonist's decisive, life-determining act.

James always gives the reader abundant, even superabundant, evidence, lots of rope with which to hang himself or herself. But, unfortunately, the evidence is always in one way or another indirect. The rule is that James never tells me in so many words what I should conclude, how I should evaluate and judge the characters. This exasperates some readers, for example Wayne Booth in *The Rhetoric of Fiction*. It is as though James were saying, with a faint ironic smile on his face, 'Here is all the evidence. I have kept nothing back. I have even given you, it may sometimes seem to you, a tedious superfluity of evidence. Now it is up to you to judge.' This is analogous to one of the imaginary visions the narrator of 'The Aspern Papers' has when he looks at the portrait of the dead poet Jeffrey Aspern, whose life so obsesses him: 'I only privately consulted Jeffrey Aspern's delightful eyes with my own (they were so young and brilliant, and yet so wise, so full of vision) . . . He seemed to smile at me with friendly mockery, as if he were amused at my case. I had got into a pickle for him – as if he needed it! He was unsatisfactory, for the only moment since I had known him' (*AP,* 97). Many readers have found James himself elusive and mocking. To read James is to be put in the pickle of being made responsible for judgment when the grounds for judgment are not at all certain. The reader is put on trial in a way that is not wholly pleasant. Certainly, it is not relaxed or merely receptive. The reader's state is not at all consonant with the idea that the pleasures of reading James are pure irresponsible pleasures of aesthetic form, the pleasures of passive admiration. This is the case even though James himself, in the Prefaces to his work, often promises just that, in the form of what he calls 'amusement'.[3]

III

Well, what is the evidence on which to base a responsible judgment of what 'The Aspern Papers' has to say about history and narration?

The Preface to this story (written for the 1909 New York Edition of James's work) stresses in several ways the relation of the story to history. Thinking about its genesis brings back to James the history of his own past life in Italy, 'the inexhaustible charm of Roman and Florentine memories', not to speak of the 'old Venice' of the story itself (*AP,* vi). Moreover, the story had its genesis, James says, in the way 'history, "literary history" we in this connexion call it, had in an out-of-the-way corner of the great garden of life thrown off a curious flower that I was to feel worth gathering as soon as I saw it' (*AP,* v). This is James's characteristically oblique way of saying that 'The Aspern Papers' is based on a historical episode. This was the survival into the late nineteenth century in Florence of Jane Clairmont, 'for a while the intimate friend of Byron and the mother of his daughter' (*AP,* vii) and the attempt by a man from Boston, Captain Edward Silsbee, to become a lodger in her house and thereby get hold of documents about Shelley and Byron she was thought to possess.

James's account of how he came to write 'The Aspern Papers' leads him to some general reflections about history and narrative. The anecdote about Jane Clairmont appealed to him as the subject of a story, he says, because it was just far enough in the past, but not too far: 'And then the case had the air of the past just in the degree in which that air, I confess, most appeals to me – when the region over which it hangs is far enough away without being too far' (*AP,* ix). The eloquent passage that follows develops and explains this appeal. Such a nearby past is visitable, recoverable. It combines strangeness and familiarity in just the right proportions, whereas a more distant past cannot be visited and reappropriated by the writer, thereby made into a narrative. Too many other historical periods intervene and baffle the imaginative writer's attempts at an intimate recovery:

I delight in a palpable imaginable *visitable* past – in the nearer distances and the clearer mysteries, the marks and signs of a world we may reach over to as by making a long arm we grasp an object at the other end of our own table. The table is the one, the common expanse, and where we lean, so stretching, we find it firm and continuous. That, to my imagination, is the past fragrant of all, or of almost all, the poetry of the thing outlived and lost and gone, and yet in which the precious element of closeness, telling so of connexions but tasting so of differences, remains appreciable. With more moves back the element of the appreciable shrinks – just as the charm of looking over a garden-wall into another garden breaks down when successions of walls appear. The other gardens, those still beyond, may be there, but even by use of our longest ladder we are baffled and bewildered – the view is mainly a view of barriers. The one partition makes the place we have wondered about *other*, both richly and recogniseably so; but who shall pretend to impute an effect of composition to the twenty? We are divided of course between liking to feel the past strange and liking to feel it familiar; the difficulty is, for intensity, to catch it at the moment when the scales of the balance hang with the right evenness. (*AP*, x)

This passage seems to promise that 'The Aspern Papers' will be a narrative about a successful visiting of the early nineteenth century, the time when Byron and Shelley lived in Italy. That James's definition of such a past (familiar and yet strange) corresponds exactly to Freud's definition of the uncanny (*das Unheimliche*) might give the reader pause. It would define such a recovery of the past as a raising of ghosts, the return of something repressed, something exposed and yet hidden, something known that nevertheless ought to be kept secret. This definition of the near past as an uncanny mixture of familiarity and strangeness may connect this story in some obscure way with James's ghost stories, such as 'The Jolly Corner' and 'The Turn of the Screw'. That, however, may be a false association, since what James here emphasizes is the possible successful recovery of history through narration. There seems nothing uncanny about this success.

In fact, however, the image of the ghostly resurrected revenant from the past has already appeared early in the preface when James speaks of his memories of Italy as 'haunting presences' (*AP*, vi). And the figure of the ghost was already present in the story itself. Juliana Bordereau, the old woman in the story who corresponds to Jane Clairmont in the 'real life' historical events, seems, to the unnamed narrator who has designs on her papers, 'too strange, too literally resurgent' (*AP*, 23). '[A]s she sat there before me', he says, 'my heart beat as fast as if the miracle of resurrection had taken place for my benefit. Her presence seemed somehow to contain and express his own, and I felt nearer to him at that first moment of seeing her than I ever had been before or ever have been since' (*AP*, 23). The resurrection of Juliana Bordereau is, in a manner of speaking, the resurrection of Jeffrey Aspern himself, James's fictional equivalent of Byron. Juliana's 'literal' resurgence generates Aspern's figurative resurrection. At various crucial moments in the story, the narrator imagines himself confronting Aspern face to face, even talking with him and hearing his voice:

That spirit [of Venice] kept me perpetual company and seemed to look out at me from the revived immortal face – in which all his genius shone – of the great poet who was my prompter. I had invoked him and he had come;

he hovered before me half the time; it was as if his bright ghost had returned to earth to assure me he regarded the affair as his own no less than as mine and that we should see it fraternally and fondly to a conclusion. It was as if he had said, 'Poor dear, be easy with her; she has some natural prejudices; only give her time. Strange as it may appear to you she was very attractive in 1820.' (42–3)

What the narrator says here employs the language that is ordinarily used to describe the invocation of a spirit. The rhetorical name for this is prosopopoeia, the ascription of a name, a voice, or a face to the absent, inanimate, or dead. To ascribe or inscribe a name or a voice is performatively to call into being, to invoke, to resurrect, to utter a new version of Jesus's 'Lazarus, come forth!' All historical story-telling depends on the efficacy of such performative prosopopoeias. From the dead words on the page these figures raise the illusions of the various personae, including the narrator. In that sense all historical stories are ghost stories.

One function of James's ghost stories proper, it might be argued, is to bring out into the open this basic aspect of all historical narration. 'I had invoked him and he had come.' The one who raises a ghost must then take responsibility for his or her act. That responsibility is most accurately figured in some demand the resurrected ghost makes on the one to whom he appears, as the ghost of Hamlet's father demands that Hamlet revenge his murder, or as the narrator of 'The Aspern Papers' incurs a responsibility, by way of Aspern's ghost, for Juliana and Tina. The narrator wants knowledge. He does not get the knowledge he wants, but he does get responsibility. Is it possible that our situation as readers may parallel that of the narrator? We have been taught to read literary works, for example 'The Aspern Papers', in order to understand them. Reading may, rather, put an unforeseen burden of obligation on our shoulders. The story demands not that we know but that we do.

IV

The narrator's failure to know is paralleled by the way the story by no means fulfills the retrospective promise of the Preface to give the reader knowledge of history, of 'a palpable, visitable past'. 'The Aspern Papers' is, rather, a story of the impossibility of knowing and possessing the historical past through narrative.

Why is this? Why is it that 'The Aspern Papers' is a narrative of the failure of narrative to reach and possess history, even that charmingly close period of the early nineteenth century the Preface promises the story will visit? The story is a brilliant putting in question of just that set of hermeneutical assumptions about the relation between narrative and history I began by describing as taken for granted, for the most part, in our tradition. Those assumptions are just the ones assumed in James's Preface. By 'hermeneutical' I mean the presupposition that the truth about a set of historical events, like the truth about a document or set of documents, for example a work of literature like 'The Aspern Papers', is inside the evidence and can, by proper procedures, be penetrated, reached, decoded, revealed, unveiled, and triumphantly brought out into the open where all may see it and where it may be told as a coherent narrative. Joseph Conrad expresses this assumption when he has the primary narrator in *Heart of Darkness* say that 'The yarns of seamen have a direct simplicity, the whole meaning of which lies within the shell of a cracked nut.'[4]

The narrator of 'The Aspern Papers', as any reader of the story knows, is a literary scholar who specializes in the work of an American poet of the early nineteenth century, Jeffrey Aspern. The narrator's basic professional assumption is that biographical facts will explain Aspern's poetry. He immensely admires the poetry, but James does not allow him the slightest insight into the possibility that the poetry might be worth reading for its own sake or that it might have any meaning that would exceed its biographical references. The narrator assumes that the more he knows about Aspern's life the more he will have established solid grounds for decoding the poetry. In explaining this, the narrator uses a religious metaphor that recurs in the story, and provides another version of the hermeneutical structure. In one place, the narrator says Juliana represented 'esoteric knowledge' about Aspern's life (*AP*, 44). Earlier he asserts, 'One doesn't defend one's god: one's god is in himself a defence' (*AP*, 5). This desire to get at the hidden facts of Aspern's life outweighs any compunction he might have about lying to Juliana and forcing his way into her intimacy, even though he says at one point, when he is trying to worm information out of Juliana's niece Tina: 'I felt almost as base as the reporter of a newspaper who forces his way into a house of mourning' (*AP*, 82).

Later on, in a crucial discussion with Juliana, the narrator tells her he is 'a critic . . . an historian' and writes about 'those who are dead and gone and can't . . . speak for themselves' (*AP,* 89). The interchange that follows identifies just what form the narrator's interpretative assumptions take. The narrator assumes that getting the full biographical facts about Jeffrey Aspern, and then narrating them as a full history of his life, will serve as a solid ground or *logos* by which to measure his works. He defends himself to Juliana by asking: 'What becomes of the work I just mentioned, that of the great philosophers and poets? It's all vain words if there's nothing to measure it by' (*AP,* 90). Juliana pours scorn on this idea by saying it is like applying a measuring tape to someone in order to make him a suit. 'You talk as if you were a tailor', she says (*AP,* 90). The truth, for Juliana, is inaccessible by the narrator's kind of search for historical truth.

The working-out of the story dramatizes why Juliana is right and the narrator wrong. Juliana is so appalled when she catches the narrator in the act of trying to break into her 'secretary' to steal the papers, that she dies of the shock (*AP,* 117). The narrator has, in a manner of speaking, killed her. Juliana's middle-aged niece, Tina, is right when she suspects that the narrator would have been capable of 'violating [her] tomb' (*AP,* 134). Tina has functioned throughout as an intermediary and go-between. She gives the narrator indirect access to Juliana, just as Juliana will give him indirect access, he hopes, to Aspern. After Juliana's death, Tina offers to give him the papers if he will marry her: 'What in the name of the preposterous did she mean if she didn't mean to offer me her hand? That was the price – that was the price!' (*AP,* 136). The narrator refuses to marry her, and leaves. Tina then burns all the papers, telling him when he returns, in her inadvertently comic literalism: 'It took a long time – there were so many' (*AP,* 143). The narrator says 'a real darkness for a moment descended on my eyes' (*AP,* 143). He is left with the portrait of Aspern and with his chagrin: 'it hangs above my writing-table. When I look at it I can scarcely bear my loss – I mean of the precious papers' (*AP,* 143).

What does this denouement mean? As many critics have noted, the unnamed teller of this story is unreliable not because he deliberately lies, but because, though he is intelligent, he fails more or less completely to understand what has happened to him. The 'real darkness' that descends on him when he nearly faints is the correlative of the figurative blindness that has afflicted him all along. That other blindness keeps him permanently in the dark about the meaning (if that is the right word) of his experience. When he identifies his unbearable loss as being of the precious papers, he almost recognizes, in the pause indicated by the dash, that he has brought on himself another worse and unrecognized loss. It is worse, in part, because it is unrecognized. 'The Aspern Papers' parallels in this another celebrated story by James, 'The Beast in the Jungle', though in that tale the narrator may get insight at the end of the story, when it is too late.

The narrator of 'The Aspern Papers' has assumed that his only responsibility is to the historical biographical truth about Aspern. Any means, even a theft that is presented as a figurative sexual assault, even as a kind of necrophilia, 'violating a tomb', are justified in the name of finding out that truth. The narrator's responsibility to this kind of truth is underwritten by the entire institutional apparatus of literary history as a discursive practice in our culture. It is not an accident that *The New York Times Book Review*, for example, today routinely reviews literary biographies, good or bad, while passing by even distinguished critical readings of the same authors. This notion of literary history is institutionalized also in university study of literature. The search for literary historical truth is one version of the university's commitment to a selfless search for the bringing to light of knowledge. The motto of Yale University is 'Lux et Veritas'. The motto of Harvard is 'Veritas'. The motto of the University of California is 'Let There Be Light'. The university assumes that everything has its reason, its underlying explanatory 'Grund'. Our primary and exclusive responsibility is to bring that truth to light. The commitment to the search for a narratable historical truth is only a version of a more inclusive commitment to truth-seeking in our culture. The university is one of this commitment's main institutional guardians.

What the narrator does not see, and what his narration allows the reader to glimpse indirectly, to 'read between the lines', as one says, is that historical events are not open to this kind of knowledge and therefore cannot be narrated. All that can be narrated is the failure to see, know, possess, or uncover the actual events of the historical past. The paradigmatic example of an historical event in the story is the presumed affair between Juliana Bordereau and Jeffrey Aspern. Such an event, the story implies, cannot be known from the outside. It is not something that could ever have been known through research and then told in a narration. It can only be 'known', without being known, in an event that repeats it, that bears witness to it by doing something like it again.

Why can an historical event like the presumed love-making of Juliana and Aspern not be known? A true historical event, the story indicates, does not belong to the order of cognition. It belongs to the order of performative acts, speech acts or acts employing other kinds of signs in a performative way. Such an event makes something happen. It leaves traces on the world that might be known, for example the Aspern papers if they were published and read, but in itself it cannot be known. Even if the narrator had taken possession of the papers and read them, he would not have known what he wanted to know.

Two kinds of knowledge may be distinguished. One is the kind obtained from historical research or from seeing something with one's own eyes. That kind can be narrated. The other kind is that blind bodily material kind that cannot be narrated. We can only witness to it, in another speech act. This kind is expressed in the biblical formula: 'Adam knew his wife and she conceived.' The sex act is paradigmatic of this other kind of knowledge. All speech acts, for example promises, are of the same order, as is the unknowable event of my own death. The connection among these three forms of non-narratable historical events is indicated in the way the three crucial events in Hyacinth Robinson's life, in James's great political novel, *The Princess Casamassima*, are not directly narrated. They are blanks in the text. These events are Hyacinth's act of promising the revolutionaries that he will commit a terrorist act, Hyacinth's experience of sleeping with the Princess, and Hyacinth's suicide.

In 'The Aspern Papers', the narrator can only 'know' what he wants to know by a present performative act that repeats the earlier one. That 'knowledge' will not be the sort of clear retransmissible cognition that we usually mean when we think of historical knowledge. It will be the sort of knowledge that Adam had of his wife, an unknowing knowing. Such an event is unavailable to clear knowing in the same way as the performative side of speech acts cannot be known, or as the materiality of any inscription is not phenomenal, since it is instantly seen as a sign, or as the rhetorical dimension of language as it interferes with clear grammatical and logical meaning makes that language unreadable.

To repeat what Aspern did by marrying Tina, as the story makes clear, would put the narrator in an impossible double bind. It would be impossible, at least from the point of view of his goal of revealing history through narration. In order to get possession of the papers, the narrator must marry Tina. That this would repeat what Jeffrey Aspern did is made clear earlier in the story when the narrator says of Aspern: 'Half the women of his time, to speak liberally, had flung themselves at his head, and while the fury raged – the more that it was very catching – accidents, some of them grave, had not failed to occur. [Nevertheless,] he had been kinder and more considerate than in his place – if I could imagine myself in any such box – I should have found the trick of' (*AP*, 7). The narrator, as he says, 'had not the tradition of personal conquest' (*AP*, 22), that is, he has not been successful with women. In spite of that, he finds himself, in a manner of speaking, in Jeffrey Aspern's place before the story is done. Tina 'throws herself at his head', and he does suffer a 'grave accident' with her. The difference is that Aspern did apparently sleep with at least some of the women who threw themselves at him. The grave accidents that occurred were, so the narrator hints, a result of that. The narrator, however, refuses Tina, even though for a moment his 'literary concupiscence', as James called it in the first edition of 1888 (*CT*, VI, 380), leads him to think he might marry her: ' "Why not, after all–why not?" It seemed to me I *could* pay the price' (*AP*, 142). His delay in deciding about that costs him the papers, since, by the time he is ready to marry Tina, to 'pay the price', she has already burned them.

On the other hand, if he had married her he would have become, as Tina says, 'a relation'. 'Then', she says, 'it would be the same for you as for me. Anything that's mine would be yours, and you could do what you like. I shouldn't be able to prevent you – and you'd have no responsibility' (*AP*, 133). If, on the one hand, he would have no responsibility of the sort he would have incurred if he had stolen the papers, rapt them away, on the other hand, he would have the infinite responsibility Juliana incurred towards Jeffrey Aspern by becoming his mistress (if she did, in fact, do that, which can never be known), that is, the responsibility to keep their liaison secret. Married to Tina, the narrator would have had the absolute responsibility of a husband to keep his wife's family secrets. He cannot have the papers if he remains an outsider, so cannot publish them. He can have them if he becomes an insider, but then he cannot publish them because he will have incurred a family responsibility that will far outweigh his responsibility as a literary historian.[5] The knowledge he would have as Tina's husband would repeat the knowledge Jeffrey Aspern had, but it is not the kind of knowledge that can or should be narrated in a cognizable historical text. Such an event can only be repeated in another performative act. An example is the way Aspern's presumed affair with Juliana appears to be repeated in the poetry that Jeffrey Aspern wrote about her. The reader is not given one single word of that poetry. All we know is that the narrator wants to go straight through it to reach the biographical facts that will explain and 'measure' it. That poetry is both intimately connected to the historical events that 'generated' it, and at the same time disconnected from them by an uncrossable breach, a chasm as uncrossable as that between the 'sources' of James's story and the story itself. To understand 'The Aspern Papers', or to find out if it is intelligible, you have no recourse but to read it. Reading it, as I shall argue, may be another kind of performative repetition. The narrator's story in 'The Aspern Papers' is a parody of this kind of repetition. It repeats as a narrative of non-knowledge the non-event of the narrator's refusal to marry Tina. The narrator does indeed witness to the destruction of 'The Aspern Papers' as a truth-telling historical narrative as well as to the destruction of the Aspern papers.

V

The line of analysis I have been following would seem to put the canny reader in a position of superiority to the unperceptive narrator. The narrator cannot read the data with which he is confronted, but at every point the reader can second-guess him. He or she can do this thanks to the abundant clues James has strewn throughout the story for the reader's enlightenment. But is this really the case? For one thing, for the perceptive reader, the reader in depth, this assumption would appear to reaffirm, just that hermeneutic model of penetration within or behind the data to reach a hidden meaning that has been thoroughly discredited in the story itself. It has been discredited as the mistaken paradigm that not only prevents the narrator from achieving real knowledge, but also makes him responsible for despicable acts toward Juliana and Tina, not to mention his desecration of the grave, so to speak, of Jeffrey Aspern.

The answer to this apparent contradiction is that what the reader learns is not a definite knowledge, but at most a kind of bodily understanding of why he or she cannot, in principle, objectively and impersonally know, but can only do, perform, act. The new act in question would be an interventionist reading possibly repeating James's story in another mode, but certainly not giving definitive knowledge of the meaning of James's tale. Or better, the reader does not even understand that, since it cannot be understood in the ordinary sense of that term. Reading, it may be, is a mode of doing, not a mode of knowing. I say 'possibly' because there is no way, in principle, to know whether a given reading works in that way. If it does work that way, it belongs not to the order of truth and knowledge, but to the order of non-cognizable speech acts. If it were a speech act, it would be a new historical event repeating the previous one of James's writing the tale, just as by marrying Tina the narrator of 'The Aspern Papers' would have repeated Jeffrey Aspern's liaison with Juliana Bordereau, if that liaison did in fact exist. The story keeps that eternally secret, just as I cannot, in principle, have knowledge of the efficacy of speech acts I perform, since they are a doing, not a knowing.

VI

Let me try to explain this further, in conclusion, by a brief discussion of four views of history that parallel to some degree the relation between narrative and historical events I have identified in James's 'The Aspern Papers'. The idea that history may be unknowable and non-narratable is difficult to grasp, understand, or accept, but four authors may help to approach apprehension of it. In 'Vom Nutzen und Nachtheil der Historie für das Leben', Friedrich Nietzsche distinguishes between two relations to history. On the one hand, there is the relation to history of those who write academic history, for example that institutionalized literary history the narrator of 'The Aspern Papers' wants to practice. On the other hand, there is a paradoxical negative relation to the historical past, the act of deliberately forgetting it. The past must be forgotten in order to make a space for present action. To turn history into the object of scientific knowledge is to neutralize it and to neutralize ourselves too, to make us all like university professors in the humanities (Nietzsche's main polemical target in this essay), learned men whose learning has no effect on the world. The paradox, as Nietzsche recognizes, is that we are what history has made us. To expunge our memory of the historical past in order to act freely in the present would be to expunge ourselves also. The past must be forgotten as objective narratable knowledge in order not so much to be remembered as to be repeated in vigorous inaugural present action that gives birth to the future. 'We need history, certainly', Nietzsche says, 'but we need it for reasons different from those for which the idler in the garden of knowledge [der verwöhnte Müssiggänger im Garten des Wissens] needs it . . . We need it, that is to say, for the sake of life and action [zum Leben und zur That], not so as to turn comfortably away from life and action.'[6]

In one way or another, both Jacques Derrida and Paul de Man hold that historical events cannot be known in the way monumental historians claim to know and narrate it. For them, the performative, therefore the non-phenomenal and non-knowable, aspect of literature, philosophy, and criticism, of language and other signs generally, makes history. This distinction between cognitive statements and performative speech acts has been the basis of my reading here, though it must be remembered that the separation can never be made absolute. There is always a cognitive side to performatives, and vice versa, even though these two sides of language can never be reconciled. The performative side of language is not something that can be known, even though there is an imperative need to know it in order to find out what we have done with words and to take responsibility for that doing. This impossibility of knowing speech acts is part of what Derrida meant in recent seminars when he said 'the gift, if there is such a thing', 'the secret, if there is such a thing', 'witnessing, if there is such a thing'. Since the gift, the secret, and witnessing are kinds of speech acts or sign acts, they are not the objects of a possible verifiable cognition. They must remain a matter of 'if'.

De Man's way of putting this was to say that the performative force of language, its power to make something happen in history and society, is linked to its materiality, that is, to a non-referential non-cognitive side of language. In the lecture on 'Kant and Schiller', given at Cornell University a few months before his death, de Man discusses the sequence in Kant's *Third Critique* from a 'cognitive discourse as trope' to 'the materiality of the inscribed signifier'. He argues that only the latter is historical, a historical event. The regressive misreading of Kant initiated by Schiller is not historical, not a series of historical events. There is in Kant, said de Man:

a movement, from cognition, from acts of knowledge, from states of cognition, to something which is no longer a cognition but which is to some extent an *occurrence*, which has the materiality of something that actually happens, that actually occurs . . . that does something to the world as such . . . There is history from the moment that words such as 'power' and 'battle' and so on emerge on the scene; at that moment things *happen*, there is *occurrence*, there is *event*. History [has to do with] the emergence of a language of power out of the language of cognition.

He means by 'language of power' not just language that names aspects of power, but language that has power, language that does what it names, as 'I pronounce you man and wife', spoken in the right circumstances, brings it about that the couple is married. This conception of the materiality of inscription is worked out by de Man in 'Shelley Disfigured', in 'Aesthetic Formalization: Kleist's *Über das Marionettentheater*', and in 'Hypogram and Inscription', as well as in the essays on Kant and Hegel.[7]

De Man, like Derrida or Nietzsche, argues for a potential performative, history-making power in language, including the language of literature, philosophy, and even 'practical criticism'. This potential power may or may not be actualized or effective in a given case. It would be a foolhardy person who would claim that what he or she writes is a historical event. It is, in any case, not of the order of cognition. To put this in de Manian terms, the 'linguistics of literariness' includes the performative dimension of literary language. Understanding it will help account for the occurrence of ideological aberrations, but knowing those aberrations will not change them. Only the performative, material, 'word–thing' side of language will do that. A rhetorical reading, registered in the most responsible critical terms, may actively liberate a past text for present uses. This new act is not engineered by a previously existing self-conscious 'I', the sovereign reader in full control of his or her knowledge of a text. The reading is constitutive of the 'I' that enunciates it.

Walter Benjamin describes in somewhat consonant terms, in the seventeenth of the 'Theses on the Philosophy of History', the way a 'historical materialist' sees 'a revolutionary chance in the fight for the oppressed past' when he finds a way to 'blast [herauszusprengen] a specific era out of the homogeneous course of history – blasting a specific life out of the era or a specific work out of the lifework'.[8] 'Herauszusprengen' names here a speech act that has effects on the future, not a historical cognition that tells something true about the past. A historical event (as all these authors, including James in 'The Aspern Papers', posit) cannot be known through narration. It can only be performatively repeated, since it was a speech act in the first place. For that repetition the one who repeats must take responsibility. The doer must take responsibility, that is, for what he or she does not know but can only perhaps succeed in reinscribing. He reinscribes it in a new, singular, unheard-of way, with incalculable effects on the future.

NOTES

1 I have discussed this passage in 'Narrative and History', *English Literary History*, 41 (1974), 455–73.
2 Thus in the revision of the story for the New York Edition of 1909. The first version (of 1888) has: 'When I look at it my chagrin at the loss of the letters becomes almost intolerable' (*CT*, VI, 382). James made a number of changes in this story for the New York Edition, for example changing the name of Juliana Bordereau's niece (if she is a niece) from Miss Tita to Miss Tina. In general, where there are changes they seem to me usually to add important nuances. I have therefore cited the revised version. The changes act as a kind of reading of the story after the fact by its author, like the famous Prefaces themselves. The Preface to *The Golden Bowl* discusses the way rereading is re-vision and revision.
3 See, for example, the Preface to *The Portrait of a Lady*, where James speaks of 'the anxiety of my provision for the reader's amusement' (*PL*, I, xvi).
4 Joseph Conrad, *Heart of Darkness and The Secret Sharer* (New York: Signet, 1950), 68. Paul de Man works out the implications of this inside/outside figure for a hermeneutical way of reading in 'Semiology and Rhetoric', in *Allegories of Reading* (New Haven: Yale University Press, 1979), 3–19. An admirable paper by Naomi Silver on 'The Aspern Papers' called my attention to the relevance of this paradigm for reading this story.
5 One critic has read the story as a disguised representation of James's feelings about his book on Nathaniel Hawthorne for the English Men of Letters series. That book is, in large part, biographical. James had tried unsuccessfully to persuade Hawthorne's son Julian (perhaps obliquely referred to in the name 'Juliana' in 'The Aspern Papers') to give him access to Hawthorne's private papers. Julian later published his father's intimate papers himself and was widely criticized for this as a 'publishing scoundrel' (*AP*, 118), to borrow the words Juliana Bordereau hisses at the narrator in the climax of the story. See Gary Scharnhorst, 'James, "The Aspern Papers", and the Ethics of Literary Biography', *Modern Fiction Studies*, 36 (1990), 211–17.

6 Friedrich Nietzsche, 'On the uses and disadvantages of history for life', in *Untimely Meditations*, trans. R. J. Hollingdale (Cambridge University Press, 1983), 59; original in *Sämtliche Werke*, Kritische Studienausgabe, ed. Giorgio Colli and Mazzino Montinari (Berlin: Walter de Gruyter, 1988), vol. I, 243.
7 Paul de Man, 'Shelley Disfigured', in *The Rhetoric of Romanticism* (New York: Columbia University Press, 1984), 93–123; 'Aesthetic Formalization: Kleist's Über das Marionettentheater', in *The Rhetoric of Romanticism*, 263–90; 'Hypogram and Inscription: Michael Riffaterre's Poetics of Reading', in *The Resistance to Theory* (Minneapolis: University of Minnesota Press, 1986), 27–53; 'Phenomenality and Materiality in Kant', in *Aesthetic Ideology*, ed. Andrzej Warminski (Minneapolis: University of Minnesota Press, 1996), 70–90; 'Sign and Symbol in Hegel's Aesthetics', in *Aesthetic Ideology*, 91–104. The citations from 'Kant and Schiller' are from *Aesthetic Ideology*, 134, 132.
8 Walter Benjamin, *Illuminations*, trans. Harry Zohn (New York: Harcourt, 1968), 265; original in *Illuminationen: Ausgewählte Schriften* (Frankfurt-on-Main: Suhrkamp, 1961), 278.

Index

Adams, Henry 82, 91n
Aeneas 76–8, 82, 84, 89–90n
aesthetics 16–19, 25, 29–34, 62–3, 73, 138, 143, 160, 168–70, 172, 196
Agnew, Jean Christophe 35n
Allen, Elizabeth 35n
anality 133–4
Anderson, James William 103, 108n
Anesko, Michael 35n, 163n
Aristotle 193
Armstrong, Paul B. 37n, 53–6, 60n, 155, 164n
Arnold, Matthew 81–2, 88
art, as power 8, 10, 20, 33–4, 39n; as social activity 16, 18–19, 33
Auchard, John 163n

Baier, Annette 171–2, 184, 189n, 191n
Baldwin, James 166–7
Balzac, Honoré de 64–7
Banta, Martha 42, 59n
Barth, Fredrik 191n
Bartlett, Neil 144n
Bell, Ian F. A. 184, 191n
Benjamin, Walter 208, 210n
Ben-Joseph, Eli 190n
Bercovitch, Sacvan 36n
Bersani, Leo 143, 145n, 147n, 192n
Besant, Walter 55
Bhabha, Homi 191n
biography, James's 1–7, 99–107, 120–1, 179–80
Blackmur, R. B. 36n, 154, 164n
Blair, Sara 169–70, 189–90n
Boelhower, William 188, 192n
Booth, Wayne C. 196
Boren, Linda S. 35n
Borus, Daniel 35n
Bristow, Joseph 145–6n
Brodhead, Richard 37n, 38n
Brooks, Van Wyck 148
Buelens, Gert 12, 190n
Burr, Anna Robeson 90n
Butler, Judith 142, 144, 146–7n

Byron, George Gordon, Lord 197–8

camp 11, 142–3
Caramello, Charles 162n
Cargill, Oscar 59n
Chénetier, Marc 38n
Cheyette, Bryan 190n
Clairmont, Jane 153, 197–8
class 16, 19, 23, 35n, 37n, 176, 183–4
classical literature 76
Cleopatra 82, 86
closet, eroticism of 131–3, 135; *see also* homoeroticism and -sexuality
Coburn, Alvin 152
Cohen, Ed 146n
Colli, Giorgio 210n
comedy 41–2, 45, 57
Conrad, Joseph 80, 109, 124n, 200, 209n
consciousness 49, 56, 66, 71, 73, 78, 170, 173–4, 179–82; and knowledge 6, 14, 25, 27, 32, 42, 48, 54, 58, 89, 98, 111, 116–8, 123; artistic 40, 106–7; loss of 105–7, 187
Craft, Christopher 144n
Crews, Frederick C. 37n
Crimp, Douglas 145n
critical theory 19, 22, 29, 36n
criticism, liberal 8, 17–20, 33–4, 36–7n; literary 9, 12, 16–34, 148, 151–62; radical 8, 19–22, 33–4, 35n; revisionist 16, 34, 35n, 151–8; James's self-criticism 69
Crowley, J. Donald 59n
cultural materialism 19, 73
culture 19–20, 74, 181, 183

Daugherty, Sarah 9
De Coppet, Louis 103
democracy 170, 172, 181–4, 187–8, 191–2n
Derrida, Jacques 60n, 207–8, 210n
determinism 8, 48
Dido 76–8, 82, 85, 88, 90n
domestic novel 26–7, 31, 37n
domination 25, 64

211

Donadio, Stephen 63–4, 74n
double narrative 109–25
double, the 132–7
drama 23, 28, 45, 63
Dreiser, Theodore 17–8
Dryden, John 90n
Du Bois, W. E. B. 167, 169, 183, 189n
Dumas, Alexandre 63

Edel, Leon 2–3, 6, 13–14n, 90n, 100, 103, 108n, 120, 123–4, 150, 152–3, 163–4n
Eeckhout, Bart 188n
Eliot, George 64–5, 76, 80, 84
Eliot, T. S. 76–9, 90–1n
Emerson, Ralph Waldo 49, 52, 80
empire: *see* Roman Empire
enacting history, defined 7–8
enacting, symbolical 5, 12
eroticism: *see* sexuality; *see also* closet; homoeroticism and -sexuality
ethics 1–13, *passim*, 17–18, 26–31, 34, 40, 52–8, 63, 72–4, 93–107, 109–25, 145, 155–62, 167–8, 171–88, 194–209; and explanation 53–5; and morals 13n; *see also* responsibility

fallibility 161–2
Felman, Shoshana 4–6, 14n
femininity 62–3, 69, 74, 84, 109–24, *passim*, 131, 136, 152, 160, 171, 181
feminism 16, 35n, 63, 69, 73–4, 168, 171
Fielding, Henry 193
Firbank, Ronald 143
Fischer, Sandra K. 68, 74n
Fitzgerald, Robert 90n
Flaubert, Gustave 62–5
Fluck, Winfried 8, 189n
fluctuation, moral 52–8
Fogelman, Bruce 89–90n
forgetting: *see* memory
formalism 18, 30, 33, 61–74, *passim*, 148
Forster, E. M. 146n
Foucault, Michel 22, 29, 113
Fox, Richard Wightman 35n
Freedman, Jonathan 34–6n, 190n
freedom 8, 9, 20, 28, 48–9, 56, 61–74, *passim*, 93, 157
Freud, Sigmund 42, 132, 134, 136, 138, 141–2, 145n, 198
Fullerton, Morton 1–3, 6, 13–15n
functionalism, 54–5

Gardner, Isabella Stewart 80
gender 8, 19, 23, 63, 74, 145, 167; *see also* femininity; masculinity
germ, narrative 8–9, 23, 40–60, 62, 153

Gidley, Mick 192n
Gilligan, Carol 171
Godden, Richard 35n
Goldberg, S. L. 71–2, 74n
Goncourt, Edmond and Jules de 64
Graef, Ortwin de 188n
Griffin, Susan M. 35n, 54, 60n, 189n
guardian figure 26–8, 98

Habegger, Alfred 10, 35n, 107–8n, 124n, 163–4n
Hadella, Paul 74n
Haralson, Eric 191n
Harpham, Geoffrey Galt 71, 74n
Haviland, Beverly 162n
Hawthorne, Julian 209n
Hawthorne, Nathaniel 80, 86, 92n, 209n
Heath, Stephen 131, 145n
Hegel, Georg Wilhelm Friedrich 200, 210n
Hestetun, Øyunn 188n
hermeneutical method 2, 6–7, 10, 57, 200, 205, 209
heterosexuality 120, 129–44, *passim*; see also Sexuality
Heyns, Michiel 10
history 1–13, *passim*, 23–8, 30–34, 41, 43, 56–7, 73–4, 80, 87–9, 99–107, 111, 116, 118–19, 126, 129–30, 136–8, 142–4, 149–62, 179–84, 193–209; defined 7–8; *see also* memory; politics; Roman Empire
Hocks, Richard A. 8, 59–60n
Hoffman, Charles and Tess 107n
Holland, Laurence B. 125n, 191n
Hollingdale, R. J. 210n
Holly, Carol 163–4n
Homer 90n
homoeroticism and -sexuality 3–5, 10–11, 113, 120–1, 126–44, 165n, 181, 186
Honig, Bonnie 170, 181, 183, 189n, 191n
Horne, Philip 90n, 163n
Howe, Irving 36n
Howells, William Dean 9, 23–6, 38n, 40–1, 43–4, 48–50, 90n
Hugo, Victor 62
Hume, David 171
Hunt, William Morris 101
Husserl, Edmund 60n

Ickringill, Steve 39n
Ickstadt, Heinz 38n
identity, authorial 12, 48, 74, 151–3, 157; cultural 12, 157; ethical 31, 155–62; loss of 187; personal 11–12, 126, 137, 154, 157, 188; sexual 11, 120, 126–44
imperialism: *see* Roman Empire

Index

indeterminism 49
insight: *see* consciousness
integrity 56, 58, 181
irony 10, 17, 41, 56–7, 69, 85, 97–9, 101, 109–24, *passim*, 126, 130, 140, 181, 191n, 195–6

Jacobson, Marcia 34n
James, Alice 99, 107n, 163n
James, Francis Burr 99
James, Garth Wilkinson ('Wilkie') 103, 180
James, Henry, works by: 'The Altar of the Dead' 11, 84, 138–44; *The Ambassadors* 8–9, 40–58, 78–80, 83–8, 121, 148, 191n, 195; *The American* 27, 58, 155 *The American Scene* 11–12, 75, 80, 88, 100, 149–53, 157–9, 166–88; 'The Aspern Papers' 12, 84, 86, 110, 121–2, 153, 155, 193–209; *Autobiography* 10–11, 99–107, 149–50, 152–3, 157–8, 163–4n; *The Awkward Age* 100, 110, 121, 150, 162n, 195; 'The Beast in the Jungle' 10–11, 84, 109–24, 202; 'The Bench of Desolation' 123, 127; *The Bostonians* 24, 28, 69; 'A Bundle of Letters' 59n; *Complete Notebooks* 41–5, 59n, 61, 68, 71, 75, 80, 98, 127, 150; *Daisy Miller* 121–2, 157, 162n; *English Hours* 175; 'Fordham Castle' 127; *The Golden Bowl* 9, 21, 27–8, 30, 32–3, 37n, 39n, 58, 66, 69–74, 80, 83–4, 93, 122, 126, 148–9, 152, 156–8, 189n, 194–5, 209n; 'The Great Good Place' 43; *Guy Domville* 100; *The Ivory Tower* 149; 'The Jolly Corner' 11, 131–7, 142, 145–6n, 149–50; 'Julia Bride' 127; *Letters* 1–3, 7, 13n, 50, 60n, 81–2, 152, 161; literary criticism 55, 62–6, 73–4, 93, 121, 193; 'Mora Montravers' 11, 126–30, 137; New York Edition 9, 11, 47, 51–2, 61–2, 66, 69, 72–3, 86, 100, 110, 126, 130, 138, 143, 149–55, 157–62, 163–5n, 194, 196, 199–200, 209n; *The Other House* 100; 'The Papers' 127, 146n; *The Portrait of a Lady* 9, 27, 31, 47, 61, 66–70, 74n, 75, 93, 174, 195, 209n; Prefaces: *see* New York Edition; *The Princess Casamassima* 14, 15n, 24, 62, 80, 156, 164n, 203; *Roderick Hudson* 7, 63, 76, 81–3, 91n, 150, 157, 159; 'A Round of Visits' 127; *The Sacred Fount* 84; *The Sense of the Past* 84, 149–50; *The Spoils of Poynton* 58, 122; 'The Story in It' 109–10; 'The Story of a Year' 84; *The Tragic Muse* 150, 157; *The Turn of the Screw* 4–6, 8, 14n, 28, 58, 100, 162n, 198; *Washington Square* 121; *Watch and Ward* 26–7, 31; *What Maisie Knew* 10, 93–107; *William Wetmore Story and His Friends* 79, 84, 88–9, 92n, 100, 149; *The Wings of the Dove* 6, 27, 30, 45, 58, 78–9, 83, 110, 121, 148, 155–6; *Within the Rim* 149
James, Henry ('Harry') 160–1, 163n
James, Henry, sen. 101–3, 108n, 157, 180
James, John Barber 99
James, John Vanderburgh 99
James, Mary 101, 103
James, Robertson ('Bob') 103, 180
James, William 49–50, 52–7, 60n, 101–3, 157, 161, 163n, 171, 180, 183
Joyce, James 144n

Kant, Immanuel 171, 207–8, 210n
Kaplan, Fred 3–5, 13–15n, 108n, 120, 125n, 179–80, 191n
Keats, John 82–3
Kleist, Heinrich von 208, 210n
knowledge 4, 24–5, 29, 31–2, 38n, 93, 120, 193, 199–202; and ethics 53, 55; cognitive 4–13, 118–19, 203–10; performative 4–13, 19, 27, 31, 53, 118–19, 203–10
Koestenbaum, Wayne 145n
Kroes, Rob 38n
Krook, Dorothea 37n

language 5–6, 12, 19, 41–3, 46–7, 49, 73, 94, 130, 160, 171, 183–8, 194–5, 199, 203, 207–8; *see also* power
Lawson-Peebles, Robert 192n
Lears, T. Jackson 34n
Lentricchia, Frank 34n
Lesser, Wendy 38n
Lewis, R. W. B. 152, 164n
Leys, Ruth 146n
liberalism 8, 16–7, 19–20, 22, 36, 166, 168, 170, 173; *see also* criticism, liberal
Lincoln, Abraham 180
literature, function of 19–20, 22, 188
loss 138–44, 175, 201–2; *see also* consciousness, loss of; identity, loss of
love as power 21, 29, 37n, 113

Macmillan, Frederick 1–2, 13n
Man, Paul de 207–9, 210n
manipulation 0–9, 12, 23, 25–33, 37n, 38n, 79
manners 9, 12, 75–89, 183–4, 186, 188, 191
Marcuse, Herbert 36n
Marxism 16–17, 19
masculinity 16, 63, 65, 67, 73–4, 109–25, *passim*, 130–1, 133, 136, 144, 168, 171, 181
masochism: *see* sadomasochism
Matthiessen, F. O. 36n, 148–9, 162n
McCormack, Peggy 35n
McGann, Jerome 45, 59n
McWhirter, David 11–12, 162–5n, 191n

melancholy 45, 52, 56–7, 138–9, 142–3
melodrama 23, 25–6, 28–9, 31, 143–4; *see also* sentimentalism
memory 75, 83–4, 106, 112, 150–1, 198
Merleau-Ponty, Maurice 60n
metaphor 8, 43, 46–53, 62, 66, 73, 153, 160–1
Michaels, Walter Benn 20, 173–4, 190n
Miller, J. Hillis 5, 12–13, 81, 118
Millgate, Michael 151, 154, 160–1, 163–5n
Mills, Stephen 39n
Mitchell, Weir 90n
modernism 16, 24, 31, 65, 148
Molière 42
Montinari, Mazzino 210n
Moore, Marianne 157, 164n
moral guide, James as 2, 10, 73–4, 107, 195
morals: *see* ethics and morals
motif 8, 26, 49, 155
mourning 138, 143

narcissism 132, 135–6
new historicism 19, 29, 32, 35, 39, 148; *see also* cultural materialism
Nietzsche, Friedrich 63–4, 206–8, 210n
non-violence 12, 181–2, 188
Norton, Charles Eliot 80, 90n
novel as genre 18, 20, 31, 39, 61–6, 73, 109, 143
Nussbaum, Martha C. 62, 70–3, 74n, 164n

omission 61–2, 66, 73, 78, 88, 110, 113, 151; *see also* seeking in vain; silence

Parker, Hershel 163n
Parrington, V. L. 36n, 148
perception: *see* consciousness
Perosa, Sergio 39n
Perry, Thomas S. 103
phenomenology 57, 60
Pinker, J. B. 42, 163n
Plato 146n
Polanyi, Michael 55, 60n
politics 12, 17–21, 30, 34, 73, 138, 145, 166–88, 203; *see also* democracy; power
Pollak, Vivian R. 162n
Poole, Adrian 9, 191n
Porte, Joel 151–2, 163n
Porter, Carolyn 20, 34n
Posnock, Ross 34n, 36n, 149, 151–3, 157–8, 162–3n, 168–70, 189–90n
possession 4, 12, 22, 27–8, 68, 166–88, 199–200
postmodernism and poststructuralism 16, 19, 62, 73
power 1–13, *passim*, 19–20, 22, 32–4, 58, 79, 169, 187, 189n, 191n; and empowerment 9, 11; and sexuality 134; authorial 8, 10, 61–74, 89, 152; imaginative 28; in language 8, 20, 22, 208; material 174–5; narrative 112–24; of consciousness 53, 175; political 20, 76, 169, 184; relations 8, 21–3, 27–30, 109–24; will to 63; *see also* art; love
pragmatism 54–7, 169
Przybylowicz, Donna 146n
Purcell, Henry 82

queerness 4, 10, 93–107, 112–3, 136, 145–6n; *see also* homoeroticism and -sexuality

race and racism 12, 19, 35n, 152, 166–88
radicalism 8, 19–20, 22, 29–31, 33–4, 36n, 39n, 169–70
Rahv, Philip 36n
Rawls, John 171
realism 9, 17, 23–4, 26, 29, 31, 38n, 63–4, 68, 144, 167, 172–3
relations, sexual 8, 113, 126; social 8, 21, 23, 25, 29–33, 37n, 126, 142, 177; *see also* power relations
renunciation 66, 122, 195; *see also* loss; seeking in vain
representation, artistic 8; excessive 64
repressive tolerance 36–7n
responsibility 7–8, 11–12, 18, 73, 89, 93, 104, 157–9, 193–209
restraint, artistic 65
Reubell, Henrietta 15n
revision 59, 150–62, 209n
Ricoeur, Paul 11, 154–6, 158–60, 164–5n
Riffaterre, Michael 210n
Rivkin, Julie 164n
Roman Empire 9, 75–89
romanticism 9, 62–9, 76–7, 178–9, 181, 184–5, 187–8
Rosenbaum, S. P. 59n
Rowe, John Carlos 35n, 148, 162n
Rowe, Joyce A. 57, 60n

sadomasochism 130, 134–7, 186–7
Sainte-Beuve, Charles Augustin 77
sameness 154–6, 159
Sand, George 62–4
satire 69
Scharnhorst, Gary 209n
Schiller, Friedrich 207
Schloss, Dietmar 36n
Schmidgen, Wolfram 38n
Schor, Naomi 63, 74n
Scott, Joan W. 146n
Scott, Sir Walter 62–3

Index

Sears, John F. 163n
Sedgwick, Eve Kosofsky 10, 113–14, 118, 120–1, 124–5n, 129, 144–5n, 165n
seeking in vain 6, 14n
selfhood 11–12, 154–7, 160
Seltzer, Mark 20–2, 29–30, 34–5n, 37n, 39n, 189n
sentimentalism 63; *see also* melodrama
sexuality 5, 120, 129–44, 181, 186, 188, 195, 203; *see also* identity, sexual; homoeroticism and -sexuality; power; relations, sexual
Shakespeare, William 64, 75, 82, 86, 89n
Shelley, Mary 153
Shelley, Percy Bysshe 62, 197–8, 208, 210n
Showalter, Elaine 145n
silence 6, 8–9, 66, 71, 76, 78–9, 85, 122, 152
Silsbee, Edward 197
Silver, Naomi 209n
Smith, Henry Nash 34n
Smith, Janet Adam 74n
Sollors, Werner 191n
speech acts 10, 12, 203–9
Spiller, Robert 36n
Stafford, William T. 190n
stereotyping 166, 172
Stoddard 24
Stevens, Hugh 11, 107n, 124n
Stevenson, Robert Louis 81–2, 87, 91n, 131, 145n
Story, William Wetmore 83–4, 88–9, 92n
Sturges, Jonathan 9, 14n, 40–1, 44, 50
Symonds, J. A. 145–6n
Systemic effects 8, 11, 16, 19–20, 30

Tanner, Tony 175, 190n
Tchaikovsky, Peter 146n
Temple, Bob 99
Temple, Minny 108n, 152, 157, 163–4n
Tennyson, Alfred, Lord 79, 160
Thackeray, William M. 101, 105, 193
Tintner, Adeline 89–90n
tragedy 17, 41–2, 45, 56, 193

Trilling, Lionel 17–18, 20, 36n
Trollope, Anthony 193
Turgenev, Ivan 65–6, 73
Turner, J. M. W. 160
Twain, Mark 23–4

unity 40, 50, 61, 152–4

Vance, Norman 82, 90n
Vance, William 79, 90–1n
Veza, Laurette 91n
Virgil 76–8, 81–2, 90–1n
vulgarity 5, 12, 123, 127, 151, 173–9, 183–4, 186–7, 190n

Walton, Priscilla L. 35n
Wardley, Lynn 35n
Warminski, Andrzej 210n
Warren, Kenneth 35n, 163, 166–70, 172–4, 176, 182, 188–91n
Washington, Bryan 166–7, 188n, 190n
Weeks, Jeffrey 145n
Wells, H. G. 41
Wharton, Edith 1–3, 6, 14n, 59n
Whistler, James McNeill 40–1, 43, 59n
Whitman, Walt 100, 192n
Wiesenfarth, Joseph 74n
Williams, Merle A. 60n
Wilson, R. B. J. 39n
Woolf, Virginia 6, 8
Woolson, Constance Fenimore 83, 121
Wyckoff, Albert 99
Wilde, Oscar 130, 144–6n

xenophobia 152

Yeats, William Butler 152, 154, 164n
Yeazell, Ruth Bernard 34n
The Yellow Book 100

Zohn, Harry 210n
Zola, Emile 64